CW00819816

50 YEARS OF THE PFA AWARDS

By Harry Harris

Welcome

Welcome to this special commemorative book, which has been produced to mark the 50th edition of the PFA Awards. It is a celebration of the history of the awards and, most importantly, those players who have been honoured with the ultimate accolade – the recognition of their peers.

The PFA Awards have always been held in high esteem by players for the simple reason that they are voted for by their fellow PFA members. It's an accolade given by those who our winners compete against every week, those who can recognise from close personal experience the players who have truly made their mark.

What also makes the PFA Awards so prestigious is the company that players know they will be keeping, and this anniversary offers us an opportunity to look back and to remember our previous winners. Doing so reveals a list of legends of the game whose performances were recognised in the moment but, in time, have become even more greatly appreciated.

Every new winner at the PFA Awards joins a lineage of players who have been recognised for excelling across a whole season, often leading their teams to major titles and producing memorable moments of magic when they are most needed.

The PFA Awards have become a landmark feature of our football calendar and no retrospective of any individual season is ever complete without acknowledging those who took home that year's prize. Wherever they have come from, it's the one award those in the English game want to win and a personal honour that we know is still special to those who have received it.

In producing this book we've had the opportunity to revisit those special seasons with many of our former winners, and we've loved having the chance to hear their memories and stories.

The way we present our awards and celebrate our winners has changed over the years and this 50th edition marks another evolution. The value of the honour, however, always remains the same.

I hope you will enjoy reading this history of the PFA Awards as much as we have enjoyed producing it for you.

Maheta Molango
PFA CEO

Contents

Above | The first PFA Players' Player Norman Hunter, 1973/74

Left | PFA award winner John Barnes, 1987/88

Opposite | PFA Young Player of the Year David Beckham, 1996/97

SHA

6
6

Contents

Opposite | Lucy Bronze, PFA award winner, 2013/14

Above | Cristiano Ronaldo, double PFA award winner in 2006/07

Left | Women's Players' Player of the Year Ji So-yun of Chelsea, 2014/15

"The PFA is indelibly linked to English football and the legends who have lit up our game"

Introduction

The PFA Awards, a night when football comes together to celebrate and reward its very best, is in many ways the "shop window" of the Professional Footballers' Association.

The global profile of this yearly event, and the passionate debate it generates among fans around the world, has helped make the PFA a name and a "brand" that is indelibly linked to English football and the legends who have lit up our game.

But it is often behind the scenes, away from the stage and the spotlights, where the PFA does its work. So, what is the Professional Footballers' Association?

The PFA is the trade union for professional footballers in England. Like its awards, the PFA is run by players, for players. For well over 100 years the PFA has been central to every significant development in player rights in the English game. It exists solely to protect and promote the rights and conditions of those who play football.

And that's where the PFA has its roots. The PFA is the world's oldest professional sport trade union and was established, as the Players' Union, in 1907 to help players fight for better wages and freedom of transfer.

It was Billy Meredith, along with a small group of players who came to be known as "Outcasts FC", who stood firm through suspensions and a ban on players joining before the Players' Union was formally recognised by the FA.

That early victory set the course. Fast forward to 1961 and it was the PFA, led by Jimmy Hill, who successfully campaigned to end the maximum wage. This was a seismic change in our game and a major victory for player power, with the Football League abolishing the £20 per week wage cap and enabling players to earn their value.

Change continued apace. George Eastham, with the backing of the PFA, challenged the rules that prevented players from transferring without club consent, a case that helped build the foundations of the modern-day transfer system. Then, in 1981 and after decades of struggle, the PFA was successful in its campaign for a Players' Standard Contract, which is still in place today and which represents the most robust and secure contract in world football.

As the game modernised, the PFA has remained at the forefront, through the formation of the Let's Kick Racism Out of Football campaign, the fight for players to share in TV revenue (an endeavour that saw 99 per cent of balloted union members vote in favour of strike action) and the welcoming of members from the newly formed Women's Super League.

These landmark developments have led to the PFA's influence being felt far and wide, with the work of the union often setting a benchmark of best practice for colleagues around the world.

Today, the PFA is bigger than ever. The game and the needs of players have changed beyond all recognition, but their union continues to be who they turn to when they need trusted and independent help in their professional careers, advice on their rights, or support and representation.

It is away from the pitch, however, that the PFA's influence has deepened, whether that's in supporting a player in their personal life or helping them plan for the future. The PFA is there, providing wellbeing services, supporting work in the community, taking players through their coaching badges and equipping players for new roles in the game through courses at its new Business School.

The PFA also continues to be a campaigning force, both domestically and internationally. Its reputation has ensured that the PFA is at the heart of many international alliances between global unions and player associations – in football and beyond.

The need for player advocacy remains, with the PFA turning its attention to a new wave of issues that have emerged in the modern game, such as excessive player workloads, the use of player data and the fight for fair and equal conditions for players in the women's game.

Whatever the future brings, the PFA will be there for its members. For Football, For Life.

A winning mentality

THE PREMIER LEAGUE LEGEND ARSÈNE WENGER AND AWARD-WINNING FOOTBALL WRITER HARRY HARRIS SAT DOWN TO TALK PFA AWARD HIGHLIGHTS, AND THE PAST, PRESENT AND FUTURE OF THE GAME

Harry Harris: This is a special year for the PFA – the 50th anniversary of its awards. Why is the PFA so important in your opinion?

Arsène Wenger: Good question. When I was a player, I didn't have a union, so I know how crucial it is to protect the players, to move things forward and to help them get their piece of the cake, as well as the other main actors. Without the PFA, the players would not be represented. So in all aspects of player development, whether on the technical front or in general, the PFA has a vital role to play.

HH: And how about the PFA Awards?

AW: When you see the winner being interviewed, they always say that it's the most meaningful for them because it's voted for by their peers. I respect it a lot, because in England it's done well and is valued – the players take it very seriously. It rewards a player's quality and consistency, and it means a huge amount to them. I know that from years of personal experience – I could see it in their eyes.

HH: What are your abiding memories of the PFA Awards and its winners?

AW: Well, you're always happy when one of your players wins it! When they chose Dennis Bergkamp and Thierry Henry, even today when I speak to people, those two players are monsters in people's minds. The fact that they were rewarded was very satisfying for me because, first of all, they deserved it, and secondly, people still bring them up to this day. They always remind me about Thierry and Dennis. I'm really glad that Robin van Persie won it, as well. We had other players who could have won it, but sometimes you're unlucky and someone else from another club beats you to it. Overall, I'd say that, looking back, the players are good judges – they didn't forget many great players. Maybe the offensive players get more credit than the defensive ones, even in the eyes of the players.

HH: What do you think it takes to actually win the Player's Player award?

AW: First of all, you need to be consistent. I'd say that in the first year you break into the Premier League, players generally don't vote for you. Also, when you play against someone, you have to get into their mind. You need to be really special to do that. When the players go out onto the pitch, they have an opinion about the quality of the other players. If you have that consistency and that capacity to get into the mind of others with your quality then they'll be

Right | PFA award winners and Arsenal icons Dennis Bergkamp and Thierry Henry

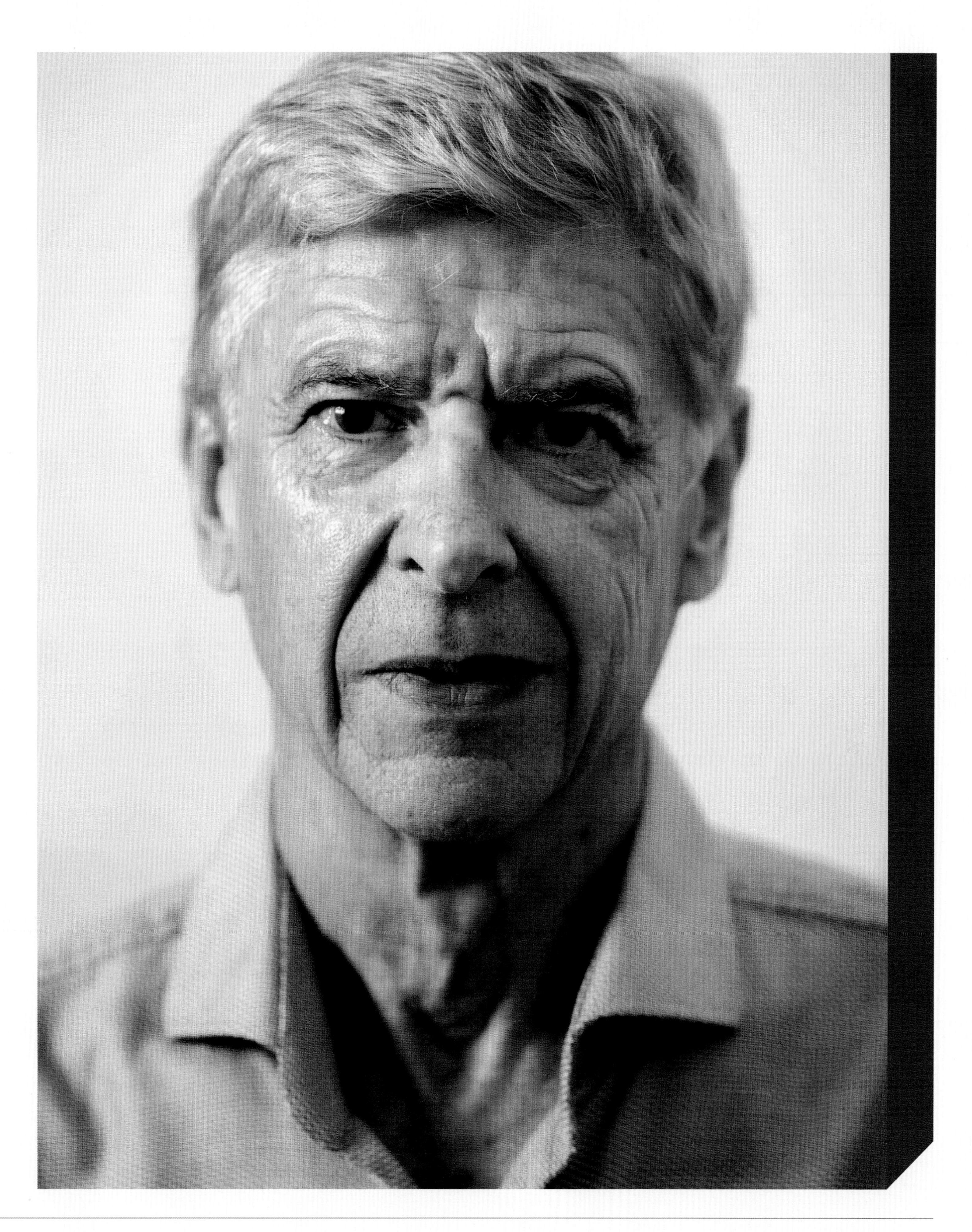

ETIHAD
AIRWAYS

FIFA

"I know how crucial it is to protect the players, to move things forward ... without the PFA, the players would not be represented"

impressed by what you do on the pitch – that is the highest reward you can get. And that's what happens with the PFA award – the player who says you're the best has experienced that on the football pitch when they played against you. That, for me, is what makes it the most important and certainly the most justified award.

HH: I totally agree that opposition players might want to see you play for a year or two before they vote for you, but I guess there's been an exception this season. It's been an incredible season for Manchester City, and one guy has really stood out.

AW: Yes, you're right, but times have changed. When I arrived in the English game, players who came from outside the country were a bit of an unknown. Now, when a player like Erling Haaland comes to England, everybody knows him already. So, maybe the modern player needs less time to convince their peers because they're already known.

HH: How highly do you rate Haaland in his first season?

AW: Even if you play in a pub team, it's difficult to score goals. So, when a guy scores that number of goals in the Premier League, it's absolutely exceptional. What I like about him, as well, is that he looks to me to be a team player. His focus is on football and he's passionate about the game and I like that very much. He knows where his priorities are – he's not concerned about how he looks or what people think of him.

HH: And he's only 23. We've had Cristiano Ronaldo and Lionel Messi competing against each other and achieving astronomical numbers for a generation. Do we now have the likes of Haaland and, say, Kylian Mbappé being capable of not just hitting those numbers, but surpassing them?

AW: Yes, that shows you that football is always moving forwards and that each generation comes to an end, as in other sports. You need new stars, and they'll certainly not be the only two – we'll have to see what the future holds.

HH: You mentioned the introduction and development of foreign players in this country. You were the first manager ever to play an entire team of overseas players – did you realise that at the time?

AW: When you're the manager of a football club, you don't look at the nationality of the players, you just pick the team who can win the next game. By coincidence, that was a moment when everybody was foreign. You want local players to play as well, but they were special circumstances and, when I look at England's results and its youth teams, I don't think it was detrimental to the development of the players.

HH: You're working at FIFA now as Chief of Global Football Development. There are some really important issues being discussed in football at the moment – VAR, the offside rule, the handball rule. How is FIFA addressing those subjects?

AW: Well, FIFA has three roles. Firstly, to be the guarantor of the rules of the game. Secondly, it's responsible for organising competitions. And the third, which I am responsible for, is its educational duty, something that FIFA takes really seriously. We've developed academies all over the world to help boys and girls play football. We analysed the game in more than 200 countries and in over 100 of them children have no opportunity to play and to develop. So that is where my main responsibilities lie. I also have a part to play in the rules of the game. There are some, like the offside rule as you mentioned, where I proposed a rule but then it has to be trialled and, at the end of the day, it's for the IFAB to decide if they accept it or not. My thinking is to make football more fluent and quicker, and to have less stoppage time.

HH: Hurrah to that Arsène. It seems to me that with the offside rule the intention was always to give the advantage to the attacking player – provided they were level, you would give the benefit of doubt to the attacker.

AW: I agree with you. VAR has taken away much of the uncertainty – before you'd get goals cancelled that were regular goals because it wasn't seen that the player was not offside – so one way we could give an advantage to the striker again is maybe to say that as long as any part of their body is in line with the defender, they're not offside.

HH: Is that being implemented?

AW: It's being experimented with, yes.

HH: What about the question of handball?

AW: Handball is difficult. Personally, I'd encourage people to be a bit more tolerant when a handball is accidental because it's so difficult to score a goal and to give a penalty because somebody hit the ball one yard or two yards into the arm of a player, I'd say people have difficulty accepting that. But no one has found the magical rule yet.

HH: We don't want to see defenders trying to defend with their hands behind their back.

AW: Yes, that's why I preach for more tolerance. When I see a player with their hands behind their back, I think, "That's not football". It's so hard to stop a forward player if you have your hands behind your back because you don't have good balance. It comes back to common sense with the rules.

HH: That's a fair point. Thanks so much for sharing your thoughts on the awards and the game Arsène, it's been a real pleasure.

AW: Thank you very much Harry.

Opposite, clockwise from top | A relaxed Wenger at the Emirates, 2016; the former manager in his new role at FIFA; Manchester City goal machine Erling Haaland

Chapter One

1973|74 – 1982|83

Fifty years of the PFA Awards and, despite the many transformations that the game has undergone in that time, one crucial feature remains unchanged – the prestige that goes with being voted "best in class" by your peers.

Launched in the 1973/74 season and championed by then PFA Chair Derek Dougan, the black-tie event not only honours English football's finest but also, during those early years, provided the chance to present "a more articulate, self-assured image" of the game and its players.

The first ten years of the PFA Awards were packed with personality and passion – two traits that the recipient of the inaugural Players' Player of the Year trophy, Leeds United legend Norman Hunter, had in abundance. Hunter won two First Division titles and one FA Cup in his 14-year senior career at Elland Road, and was a member of England's 1966 World Cup-winning squad. "He was a great player," said Peter Shilton, himself a winner of the PFA's top award in 1978. "He had a lot more than just being a tough man."

The first decade of award winners is notable for including both Shilton and, in 1976, Pat Jennings – the only goalkeepers to have been named Player of the Year in PFA Awards history. Honourable mentions also go to Andy Gray, who claimed both the Players' Player of the Year and the Young Player of the Year awards in 1977, and to Liam Brady, whose Players' Player win two years later made the Dublin-born playmaker the first non-UK footballer to receive the award.

Two Merit Award recipients of note for their contributions off the pitch were the PFA's Chief Executive, Cliff Lloyd, who was honoured in 1974 for 20 years of service. He would continue in the role until 1981, passing the mantle on to former PFA Chair Gordon Taylor. And George Eastham, who in 1976 was recognised for his pivotal role in improving players' freedom to move between clubs, following his successful 1963 legal action against the retain-and-transfer system.

Beyond the awards, the game boasted its own list of "firsts" during this period. Breaking with convention (and the Sunday Observances Act) in an effort to increase attendances, the first Sunday matches took place at the start of 1974. The use of goal difference as a tie-breaker was adopted by the Football League in 1976, and five years later it was decided to award three points for a win rather than two to encourage a more attacking style of play.

The decade also witnessed Britain's first £1 million transfer fee when Trevor Francis was sold by Birmingham City to Nottingham Forest for £1.18 million in February 1979. He proved his worth in no time, scoring the winning (and only) goal in the European Cup final between Forest and Malmö that May.

English teams starred in many a glorious European night from 1974–83. While Liverpool were the headline act, Brian Clough's Forest and Aston Villa, who lifted the European Cup in 1982, and Ipswich, who won the UEFA Cup in 1981, confirmed the top flight's bragging rights in continental circles. At domestic level, the lower divisions had their days in the sun as well, with Second Division Southampton and West Ham triumphing in the FA Cup in 1976 and 1980, respectively.

Since 1974, however, no individual accolade has outshone the PFA Awards – still the most prized of awards, voted for the players by the players.

crown
paints

1973|74

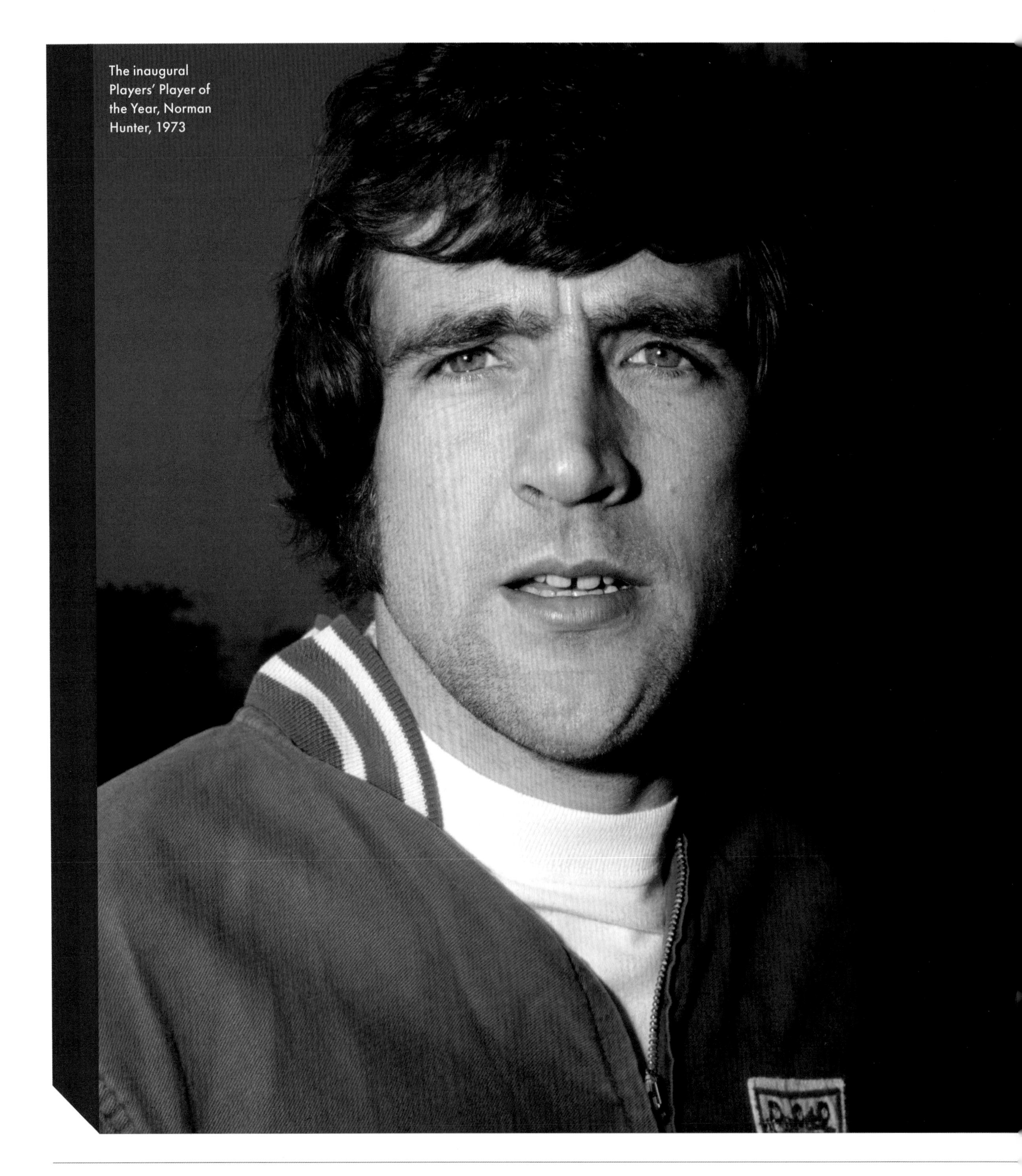
The inaugural Players' Player of the Year, Norman Hunter, 1973

PLAYERS' PLAYER OF THE YEAR

Norman Hunter

THE INAUGURAL PFA AWARD WINNER WAS THE DRIVING FORCE BEHIND LEEDS'S SECOND LEAGUE TITLE

Firsts matter in football. Some become sepia-tinged oddities, others break down barriers and a select few establish precedents. Norman Hunter winning the inaugural PFA Men's Players' Player of the Year award in 1973/74 unequivocally did the latter.

At the time, Hunter's "Bites Yer Legs" epithet had dominated his mythology since its appearance on a fan-made banner as Leeds United beat Arsenal in the 1972 FA Cup final. Yes, like Rocky Marciano, he found it hard to deny his strength – "you never intentionally went out to hurt anyone, but the will to win became so strong that you'd get wound up and the red mist would come down," he once recalled – but the consummate centre half was as comfortable on the ball as he was teak-tough in the tackle.

"If all I could do was tackle and supposedly kick people, all the players of the day would certainly not have voted for me," he later said. "You just don't get that award if you can't play."

Hunter's fellow professionals ignored the uncompromising caricature and voted the 30-year-old their first Player of the Year in recognition of an ever-present defensive leviathan who did more than any other Leeds player to ensure the First Division bridesmaids were finally English champions after three runners-up finishes in the previous four years. An accomplished reader of the game capable of both riot and recital in the same game, Hunter would rob opposition forwards then feed Billy Bremner and Johnny Giles's creativity with Peter Lorimer, Allan Clarke and top scorer Mick Jones to finish chances.

Marching on together, Leeds lost just four times – they started the season with a 20th-century record 29-game unbeaten run – scored only one goal fewer than top marksmen Ipswich Town, and that Hunter-led defence conceded the fewest to claim their first title since 1968/69 by five points. Manager Don Revie's paternalism towards his squad was legendary, but he reserved his most significant praise for the once-skinny centre back he'd first plucked from the youth team at 18 a decade earlier, bulked up with a diet of raw eggs and turned into a World Cup winner alongside England team mate Jack Charlton. "Wasn't Norman Hunter marvellous?" became a catchphrase, so often did Revie say it.

"Personally, it meant everything. It's the top award for any footballer, even for today's players," Hunter later said of making PFA history. "It was one of the best moments in my career, without a doubt, and from a personal point of view probably the best. It was the first one. Everybody was in there for it."

Hunter's sizeable sideburns and frilly shirt betray his era in his winner's photo, but the beaming pride etched over his face has been replicated ever since. The PFA will never forget its first.

YOUNG PLAYER OF THE YEAR

Kevin Beattie

Right | Beattie training for England, c. 1978

Ipswich Town's chief scout Ron Gray was awestruck. "Boss, we have got a colossus," he told Tractor Boys manager Sir Bobby Robson in early 1970 of the 16-year-old trialist the club had just signed. "He's got a neck like a bull. I've seen the finest thing I've ever seen in my life."

Four years later, Kevin Beattie was voted the PFA's inaugural Young Player of the Year, missing just 45 minutes of a 42-game season as Ipswich finished fourth to qualify for the UEFA Cup. Just 5ft 10in, Beattie's spring meant he could beat even the tallest opposing strikers in the air, while his strength and visceral acceleration earned comparisons to the great Duncan Edwards.

Cursed by persistent knee injuries, Beattie – Michael Caine's body double in *Escape to Victory* – was supported by the PFA after experiencing difficulty in his later life.

"He was the quickest defender I ever saw, with a left foot like a howitzer," said Robson. "Outside George Best, he must be the next best player this country has produced."

MERIT AWARD

Sir Bobby Charlton

Pulled from the 1958 Munich air disaster wreckage by his Manchester United teammate Harry Gregg, Sir Bobby Charlton sat in his hospital bed and resolved to be worthy of his providence. Fifteen years later, he left Manchester United as the leading appearance maker and goalscorer for club and country, with three First Division titles, the 1968 European Cup and the 1966 Ballon d'Or for his starring role in the Three Lions' sole World Cup triumph.

Related to Newcastle United icon Jackie Milburn on his mother's side, Charlton grew up in the Northumberland mining town of Ashington and never forgot the life down the pit he would have had without the ethereal skill that took him to Old Trafford as a 15-year-old. "Some people tell me that we professional players are soccer slaves," he once recalled. "Well, if this is slavery, give me a life sentence."

A determined self-improver, the attacking midfielder had "the lungs of a horse" according to 1966 World Cup final shadow Franz Beckenbauer, while also possessing a shot with either foot so hard it could "separate the leather casing from the bladder", said former England teammate Jimmy Greaves.

A year after his final United appearance, there could have been no finer recipient of the PFA Merit Award. "He was as near perfection as a man and player as it is possible to be," said mentor, manager and lifelong friend Sir Matt Busby.

"He's history in the flesh, is Bobby Charlton," added Greaves. "He's our greatest living football man." Saved by fate and one heroic goalkeeper.

"He was as near perfection as a man and player as it is possible to be"
Sir Matt Busby

Charlton on the ball during the World Cup final against West Germany, 1966

MERIT AWARD

Cliff Lloyd

Cliff Lloyd was a dependable full-back for Wrexham and Fulham whose best years as a player were robbed by the Second World War, but it was his natural diligence and dedication that made him the perfect PFA Secretary between 1953 and 1981 and revolutionised players' rights. Though more circumspect than Jimmy Hill, Lloyd and the effervescent PFA Chairman formed a formidable double act in winning a landmark court case to abolish the £20 maximum wage for footballers in 1961.

Two years later, Lloyd spent two hours in the High Court witness box as George Eastham challenged the Football League's retain-and-transfer policy that meant clubs kept players' registration even after their contracts had elapsed. The judge said Lloyd was "more in touch with the realities of professional football" and "the supply and interests of players than any other witness" in ruling the system was a restraint of trade.

A deserving winner, Lloyd was the inaugural recipient of the PFA Merit Award, presented by Sir Tom Finney. "Cliff Lloyd's contribution was a keystone in the success of the PFA," said Gordon Taylor, who would go on to replace Lloyd as chief executive in 1981.

Below | Lloyd (left) shakes hands with PFA Chairman Jimmy Hill, 1961

PLAYERS' PLAYER OF THE YEAR

Colin Todd

THE DERBY DEFENDER'S FIRST FULL CAMPAIGN AT THE CLUB SAW THE RAMS WIN THEIR SECOND TITLE IN FOUR YEARS

The dust was still settling at Derby County in the summer of 1974 after Brian Clough and Peter Taylor's controversial exits the previous October had sparked sit-in protests from an irate squad. That Clough's replacement was Dave Mackay, a former Derby player signed by Old Big 'Ead, only added to the Baseball Ground hornet's nest.

Colin Todd may have been instinctively pro-Clough, who had paid a British record fee for the defender in February 1971, but saw in Mackay a manager capable of taking an established defence-first formula and dusting it with glitter. A First Division winner under Clough in 1971/72, Todd united the players to lead Derby to a second title in four seasons.

"Clough's departure left a big hole and credit to Dave Mackay for coming into the team and settling matters down," the centre back later recalled. "Dave was more about scoring more goals than the opposition no matter how many they put past us."

Recent signings Bruce Rioch (who would score 15 from midfield), Franny Lee and Charlie George were proof of the new attacking philosophy, one Mackay knew was impossible without defensive linchpin Todd. Shorn of injured ball-winning partner Roy McFarland for much of the season, Todd took his calm, composed and almost supernatural talent for reading the game to new levels alongside former understudy Peter Daniel.

It was, however, a slow start. The Rams were 10th at Christmas, but a 1975 title-winning surge of just one defeat in their final 12 games – featuring six clean sheets from a flawless Todd – wrestled the title from Ipswich Town after the Tractor Boys failed to beat Manchester City in their penultimate game. Derby's players were in Bailey's nightclub at the time, celebrations for their Player of the Year ceremony going up a notch. They'd only gone top for the first time with three games of the season left to play.

"It was one of the most entertaining teams I have ever played in," recalled Todd, who went on to receive the Players' Player of the Year award from prime minister Harold Wilson. He remains the only Derby recipient. "The PFA award was the pinnacle of my career."

Todd receives the Players' Player of the Year award, 1975

YOUNG PLAYER OF THE YEAR

Mervyn Day

Mervyn Day looked to the manner born from the moment he definitively broke into the West Ham United first team in October 1973, his athletic performance in his ninth start – a 1–0 defeat to Liverpool – earning a standing ovation from the Kop. Hammers boss Ron Greenwood, who had signed Day as a 15-year-old, declared the club had found their number one "for the next ten years".

In his first full season, Day seemed determined to fulfil his mentor's prophecy, even if Greenwood's assistant John Lyall had taken the reins. Tall, agile and a commanding penalty box presence, the 19-year-old played every minute of the Irons' 1974/75 season, keeping 17 clean sheets as the club lifted the FA Cup, beating Fulham 2–0 in the final.

"As a kid, I had no fear, I took to playing in the first team really well," recalled Day, the FA Cup final's youngest goalkeeper. "At West Ham the keeper always had lots to do as we were an entertaining team."

He remains the only goalkeeper in 50 years of the PFA Awards to win the Young Player of the Year award.

Above | Day playing for West Ham against Tottenham Hotspur at White Hart Lane, 1974

Above | Law training at Old Trafford, 1963

MERIT AWARD

Denis Law

The first time he saw Denis Law, Huddersfield Town manager Andy Beattie thought the 15-year-old trialist had won a competition, recalling: "Never did I see a less likely football prospect."

That kid would go on to win two First Division titles, an FA Cup and a European Cup in 11 years at Manchester United, become the only Scot to win the Ballon d'Or, the club's third-highest goalscorer and break the British transfer record three times. Law had wit, grit and tenacity by the bucketload, plus a shirt-untucked swagger to ensure that modesty was never one of his handicaps. His 46 goals in 1963/64 remain a United record.

An inspirational figure at Huddersfield, Torino, Manchester City and beyond – future PFA Players' Player of the Year winner Dennis Bergkamp was named in his honour – Sir Alex Ferguson's teenage idol became the second member of United's Holy Trinity to win the PFA Merit Award in as many seasons after Sir Bobby Charlton, having retired 12 months earlier.

PLAYERS' PLAYER OF THE YEAR

Pat Jennings

THE ULSTERMAN WITH THE GIANT HANDS BECAME THE FIRST GOALKEEPER TO WIN THE PFA PLAYERS' PLAYER OF THE YEAR AWARD

Above | Jennings at a Spurs training session, 1976

PFA: This is a big year for the PFA Awards; where does winning Players' Player of the Year in 1976 rank for you?
Pat Jennings: On a personal basis, it doesn't get any higher than to be chosen by your fellow professionals as footballer of the year. I mean, looking back, when you think that I was the first goalkeeper to win it, and there were only two goalkeepers that won it, that tells you how big an award it is.
PFA: As time has passed and you've seen the number of world-class goalkeepers who haven't won the award, has that changed how much you appreciate winning it?
PJ: Yeah, without a doubt. In my time – Joe Corrigan, Phil Parkes, the great Ray Clemence – you look at what they have won, especially Ray at club level. That just shows you how difficult it is.
PFA: Was there a standout moment that you recall from your award-winning season?
PJ: Funnily enough, not that year. Going back, at the end of '75 we needed to beat the great Leeds to stay in the First Division. That was how desperate we were at that last match, having to beat Leeds who were playing in the European Cup Final the next week.
PFA: And in '76?
PJ: We finished ninth, which wasn't bad considering how poorly we'd done the year before. Looking back, I was Spurs Player of the Year from '71, '72, right up to '75, '76, so I must have been doing something right. And in 1973, I'm going back, I won the Football Writers' Footballer of the Year – I'm the only goalkeeper to have done that [won the PFA and FWA awards]. So that's something I'm very proud of.
PFA: You got the record for over a thousand games, but your total is a few more than that, right?
PJ: Yeah, in 1983 I became the first to play 1,000 first-class games. I played for another three years and finished up playing against Brazil in the World Cup finals on my 41st birthday. So, over those...
PFA: They've lost count?
PJ: How do you measure the games? You go abroad, there's pre-season, end of season, you play against the top teams in the world and they don't count as appearances. But I think I was up to or over 1,100 games.
PFA: As a keeper, how did you prepare for your matches? You were known for being athletic and for having great reactions.
PJ: Believe it or not, in the early days we never had a goalkeeping coach. I joined Watford at 17 and there was no goalkeeping coach. Then I moved to Tottenham in 1964. I was there for 13 years and had no goalkeeping coach. You were basically just learning through your mistakes. It was only when I joined Arsenal that I had Bob Wilson – it was just great to have somebody that you wanted to have a couple of hours a week with, simply doing the basics – handling and that.

YOUNG PLAYER OF THE YEAR

Peter Barnes

Peter Barnes' first full Manchester City season was real Boy's Own stuff. At 18, he made 27 First Division starts for the club he supported, and was central to the Cityzens' League Cup triumph. Soon he would be a full England international.

"He is very quick and well balanced," said Don Revie after watching the youngster shine for the Three Lions U18s. "This boy is brave enough to take anybody on."

A Sir Stanley Matthews throwback, Barnes's natural ability with either foot, imagination and express pace were the perfect complement to Dennis Tueart on the opposite flank. The pair scored both goals to beat Newcastle United 2–1 in the League Cup final – Barnes's well-controlled back-post volley following a goal and assist in the semi-final defeat of Middlesbrough.

More silverware came, courtesy of the PFA Young Player of the Year award, presented by World Cup-winning goalkeeper Gordon Banks.

"I was so nervous going up on stage I didn't know what to say, I got my words mixed up and froze," Barnes later recalled. "I just remember saying, 'thank you' and quickly went down the steps and back to my table."

Above | Barnes (left) lifts the 1976 League Cup with Dave Watson (centre) and Dennis Tueart (right)

MERIT AWARD

George Eastham

Right | Arsenal and England forward Eastham at the High Court, London, 1963

George Eastham could have let sleeping dogs lie in October 1960. Instead, he fought a point of principle to bring an end to football's archaic retain-and-transfer system whereby clubs kept a player's registration even when they were out of contract.

Nearly 18 months after his deal had ended, the Newcastle United midfielder had finally been granted a move to Arsenal, but only after having to go on strike and work in a cork factory in Surrey to make ends meet. He could have quietly continued his career but, with the PFA's help, continued his fight against his former club in the High Court.

"People in business or teaching were able to hand in their notice and move on," said Eastham. "We weren't. That was wrong."

It took another three years, but in July 1963, judge Mr Justice Wilberforce ruled in Eastham's favour that the existing 70-year-old system represented an unfair restraint on trade. It was a game-changing moment, even for a 26-year-old future World Cup winner.

A more worthy 1976 Merit Award winner there could not have been.

PLAYERS' PLAYER OF THE YEAR

Andy Gray

THE FIRST PLAYER TO WIN BOTH PFA AWARDS DELIVERED AN OUTSTANDING GOALSCORING DISPLAY IN 1976/77

Andy Gray's body was an outrageous instrument of his intentions. The youngest of four football-mad brothers raised in Drumchapel, Glasgow, Gray took after his hero Denis Law in deciding that a slight frame was no barrier when paired with matchless bravery and perpetual motion. The Scottish striker would frequently put his head where others feared to put their feet.

"I was fairly light, but I could spring and my timing was good," Gray, who joined Aston Villa from Dundee United in October 1975, later recalled. "I just had an ability to pick up the flight of the ball fairly early and get myself there in front of people."

Gray exploded in his first full season at Villa Park, thanks initially to a half-time boot change against Ipswich Town in early September. Having signed a deal with Gola – "they were rubbish and I was absolutely rubbish" – the 20-year-old switched to his trusty Adidas pair and promptly struck a second-half hat-trick in a free-flowing 5–2 win. A December brace in Villa's 5–1 defeat of defending champions, and soon-to-be European Cup winners, Liverpool was so good, the entire ground applauded Gray off the Villa Park pitch.

"Andy was a dream to play with," said strike partner Brian Little, with whom the Scot developed a telepathic understanding. "If you put the ball somewhere in front between him and the goal, 90 per cent of the time he'd get on the end of it. He was infectious, a dressing-room motivator who hated losing."

Gray, Little and midfielder John Deehan scored 51 of Villa's 76 league goals as Ron Saunders's side finished fourth to qualify for the UEFA Cup and beat Everton to the League Cup after a second replay. Gray's 25 goals earned him a share of the First Division Golden Boot with Malcolm Macdonald after a final-day hat-trick against West Bromwich Albion.

The first person to win the Players' Player and Young Player of the Year awards in the same season, Gray missed the ceremony after boss Saunders wanted his star striker to rest ahead of the upcoming first League Cup final replay.

Gray with his two PFA trophies, 1977

YOUNG PLAYER OF THE YEAR

Andy Gray

"When I got told that I'd won both I thought 'Wow, how can I, this wee kid from Drumchapel, be voted the best player in the country?' To think that only Cristiano Ronaldo and Gareth Bale have done it since ... to be in that little trio of players is very special"

Above | Gray shoots during a First Division match against Queens Park Rangers at Loftus Road, 1976

MERIT AWARD

Jack Taylor

From his imposing frame to a thousand-yard stare that could turn its target to stone, Jack Taylor was never the sort of referee whose best work went unnoticed. A demonstrative disciplinarian, Taylor proved just that in the biggest game of his career, the 1974 World Cup final.

With less than a minute played, Taylor gave the first penalty in final history as West Germany's Uli Hoeneß felled Dutch great Johan Cruyff. The hosts were apoplectic. "Taylor, you're an Englishman," spat captain Franz Beckenbauer. The official, however, knew he was right.

"The first penalty wasn't difficult to call. It was a 100 per cent correct decision," Taylor later recalled. Twenty-four minutes later, he gave another, this time for the Germans, though he always railed against suggestions he "evened things up".

The master butcher from Wolverhampton took charge of more than 1,000 games over 33 years, including the 1966 FA Cup final and 1971 European Cup final between Ajax and Panathinaikos at Wembley. He retired in 1977 and was duly honoured with the PFA Merit Award following a career that demanded respect.

Above | Taylor issues a yellow card during a Euro 1972 qualifier between Northern Ireland and Spain at Boothferry Park

PLAYERS' PLAYER OF THE YEAR

Peter Shilton

ONE OF ONLY TWO GOALKEEPERS TO BE NAMED PFA PLAYERS' PLAYER OF THE YEAR, THE NOTTINGHAM FOREST MAN ENJOYED A TITLE-WINNING DEBUT SEASON

Above | Shilton gets everything behind the ball for Forest in a match against Coventry City at Highfield Road, 1978

Opposite |The PFA Award-winner reading the game, 1978

Brian Clough couldn't hide his delight when he surveyed the Second Division fixture list in the summer of 1977. Not only were his recently promoted Nottingham Forest no longer playing in the second tier of English football, but also Stoke City would play Third Division champions Mansfield Town at Field Mill on the opening day.

Clough had resolved to replace goalkeeper John Middleton and his assistant Peter Taylor said only Stoke's Peter Shilton would do. "I had been obsessed with him since he was 19 and already a fixture in Leicester City's first team," said Taylor, a former goalkeeper himself whose Christmases were about to come all at once.

Yet Clough worried someone of the England keeper's pedigree – aged 27 with nearly 400 league appearances already to his name – wouldn't come to humble Forest. Instead, reasoning that to see Shilton at a dilapidated Field Mill was "like seeing Richard Burton in *Coronation Street*", Clough waited until after Stoke's opening-day fixture to approach Britain's most expensive goalkeeper.

Shilton didn't take much convincing. Nor did Clough, who came to view Shilton's presence as "the equivalent to ten points a season". Middleton conceded six goals in Forest's first five games of their top-flight return before an unceremonious mid-September swap deal for Derby County midfielder, and Clough disciple, Archie Gemmill.

Ruthless it may have been, but boy, did it work. In the remaining 37 league games, Shilton shipped just 18 goals, to silence Forest directors who bristled at paying a not insubstantial £270,000 for a relegated keeper. Themselves favourites for the drop, Forest didn't just stay up, they won their first (and only) First Division title, going unbeaten at home. This was no race, it was a procession. Everyone expected them to falter – they never came close.

"Shilton won us the title, he was the difference," Clough said. In the Tricky Trees' last 18 games, Shilton kept a superhuman 13 clean sheets. "The defenders felt safer, and the forwards thought if we could nick a goal, there was more than an evens chance that the opposition wouldn't score at the other end."

In a season of countless athletic prodigies – Shilton seemed to consider goals as personal affronts – the point-blank save from a Mike Ferguson header in the 0–0 draw with Coventry City that confirmed the title with four games to go stood out. "I was only four yards out," said Ferguson. "I was sure it was a goal."

Miraculous doesn't do it justice, yet Shilton was unmoved. "We just sat down and had half a glass of champagne each," he recalled, "as though it was another day's work."

As he beat teammate Gemmill to the Players' Player of the Year award – no gloveman has won it since – Shilton had Clough as his personal cheerleader.

"The opposition might get through our midfield," said his manager. "Very occasionally they might get beyond Larry Lloyd and Kenny Burns. But when they'd done all that, they'd look up and see a bloody gorilla standing there with shoulders like Mr Universe and they'd wonder where the goal had gone."

"Shilton won us the title, he was the difference"
Brian Clough

YOUNG PLAYER OF THE YEAR

Tony Woodcock

A conversation in the City Ground car park in early 1977 changed Tony Woodcock's career. Brian Clough had just spent an entire reserve team game chastising the out-of-position winger – "that's rubbish, Woodcock, get up the line!" – when the player told the Nottingham Forest manager that such "motivation" had the opposite effect.

Employing carrot over stick from that moment on, Clough was soon won over. Nineteen goals in all competitions as Forest swept to a 1977/78 league and League Cup double helped, but the centre forward's pace and tireless work ethic in his preferred position did the heavy lifting.

A magnificent display at Manchester United truly announced the Busby Babes-obsessed 22-year-old's brilliance. "If you want to do it anywhere, this is the place to do it," midfielder Ian Bowyer told the youngster before the game. Ninety minutes later, Woodcock scored twice and forced Brian Greenhoff into an own goal in a 4–0 demolition that confirmed Clough's better-than-the-sum-of-its-parts side's title credentials, going 42 games unbeaten.

"Woodcock could turn any defender grey," said Clough of the outstanding PFA Young Player of the Year winner – "rubbish" no longer.

Woodcock on the ball in Nottingham Forest's 2–0 defeat of Birmingham City at St Andrew's, 1977

MERIT AWARD

Bill Shankly

Right | Shankly, 1969

In December 1959, Liverpool had been stalled in the Second Division for five years, Anfield was in a sorry state and the Melwood training ground was little more than a ploughed field with a cricket pavilion.

Bill Shankly didn't so much transform the club as build a new one in his own indomitable image. When Shankly retired in 1974, the febrile, by then all-red half of Merseyside had won three First Divisions, two FA Cups and a UEFA Cup and adopted an inspirational new anthem courtesy of a *Carousel*-loving local band.

Bob Paisley went on to retain the European Cup soon after Shankly received the 1978 PFA Merit Award. But even Paisley, the great tactician to his Boot Room predecessor's natural orator, knew he'd only done so by standing on a giant's shoulders.

"I'd like to be remembered basically as an honest man in a game that is sometimes short on honesty," Shankly later said. "That I've put more into the game than I've taken out."

Liverpool would be nothing without their patriarch, who died in 1981. Nor would football.

PLAYERS' PLAYER OF THE YEAR

Liam Brady

THE MASTERFUL WINGER'S FINAL ACT BEFORE LEAVING FOR JUVENTUS WAS TO WIN PLAYER OF THE YEAR, THE FIRST FROM OUTSIDE THE UK TO DO SO

Effortlessness is a tricky trait to pull off in football, the line between unfazed cool and a lack of application can be notoriously blurred. Such was Liam Brady's singular genius, his socks-around-the-ankles insouciance and shock of curly hair only added to his magnetism.

Picked up by Arsenal at 15, the Dublin playmaker's innate talent was immediately obvious. "This boy Brady," recalled Bill Darby, the Gunners' legendary scout who found him, "he's got a left foot that practically talks."

Nicknamed Chippy by Darby because of his love of fried foodstuffs, Brady evolved into Arsenal's leading man inside two years. His spontaneous ingenuity made the word "virtuoso" unavoidable.

"Liam was a dream to play alongside, because he could deliver a perfect through ball," said Arsenal striker Malcolm Macdonald, the principal beneficiary of Brady's brilliance. "Right foot, left foot, and with that brilliant skill he had of making the ball backspin on impact."

As 1978/79 began, the 22-year-old with a figure skater's balance was determined to end his trophy drought. Brady's opening day brace against Leeds United featured a spectacular swerving effort he repeated in December's 5–0 massacre at White Hart Lane against bitter rivals Tottenham Hotspur just to prove it was no fluke.

Second on Valentine's Day, Arsenal's league form fell away as they took four replays to beat Sheffield Wednesday in the FA Cup third round, but the Gunners nevertheless reached the final against Manchester United. Brady's gliding run and cross set up Frank Stapleton for a 2–0 first-half lead, which Arsenal still held with five minutes to go, only for the Red Devils to score twice in a minute. Chippy wouldn't be denied, speeding between three defenders to start the move for Alan Sunderland's winner on the final whistle. The so-called "Five-Minute Final" was Brady's masterpiece.

Above | Brady in full flow against Chelsea's Tommy Langley, 1979

"The 1979 FA Cup final has to be the highlight," the Irish number seven later recalled. "It was probably the best six or seven minutes of a cup final ever."

Days after picking up the Players' Player of the Year award for his 13 league goals and cup heroics – the first non-UK winner – Brady announced that he would join Juventus 12 months later. It precipitated a decade's decline at Arsenal, a slew of replacement midfielders damned for lacking Brady's unique brilliance.

1978|79

MERIT AWARD

Sir Tom Finney

Vincent van Gogh sold one painting in his lifetime. Sir Tom Finney's only piece of silverware was one Second Division title. Both have legacies that outstrip their mortal toil to render shiny trinkets irrelevant. His statue outside Deepdale proves it.

Finney scored 187 goals in 433 games for childhood club Preston North End after making his Second World War-delayed debut aged 24. Not even when Italian prince and Palermo chairman Raimondo Lanza di Trabia tried to tempt him to the club in 1952 with a £10,000 signing-on fee, sports car and Mediterranean villa, did Finney leave the Lilywhites. At the time, he earned £14 a week and supplemented his income by running a plumbing business.

A skilful left-footed forward who could play in any attacking position, Finney redefined what an English footballer could do in scoring a then record 30 goals in 76 internationals, and was a deserving winner of the 1979 PFA Merit Award.

"Tom Finney would have been great in any team, in any match and in any age," said Preston mentor Bill Shankly, "even if he had been wearing an overcoat."

Above | Finney pictured before England's match against Uruguay during their tour of South America, 1953

YOUNG PLAYER OF THE YEAR

Cyrille Regis

Cyrille Regis was a part-time electrician when West Bromwich Albion chief scout Ronnie Allen first saw the striker's spark at non-league Hayes in spring 1977. Baggies directors were unconvinced that £5,000 represented good value for money, but relented when club-record goalscorer Allen said he'd put up his own money. Two years later, Regis was voted the best young player in the country.

A powerful centre forward with a graceful touch and penchant for the spectacular, Regis scored 17 goals in all competitions in 1978/79 as the Baggies reached the UEFA Cup quarter-finals. A 13-game unbeaten First Division run that began in October with braces against Leeds United and a 7–1 drubbing of Coventry City had Regis as the emblematic focal point.

His complete centre forward display in the Baggies' 5–3 December win at Manchester United was the apogee. The 20-year-old's sublime backheel set up Len Cantello, a flicked header did the same for Laurie Cunningham, before Regis himself bludgeoned the Baggies' brilliant fifth, following a fluid team move that typified West Brom's attacking abandon.

Top in January 1979, West Brom's entertainers would eventually finish third, but Regis was the standout Young Player of the Year candidate, the award presented to him by England captain Kevin Keegan.

"Every one of his goals would win goal of the month," Baggies boss Ron Atkinson once said of Regis's propensity to score bangers over tap-ins. Nevertheless, 112 goals in 297 Baggies appearances between 1977 and 1984 was some return. Seldom has £5,000 been better spent.

Regis shields the ball from Arsenal centre half David O'Leary during a First Division match at The Hawthorns, 1979

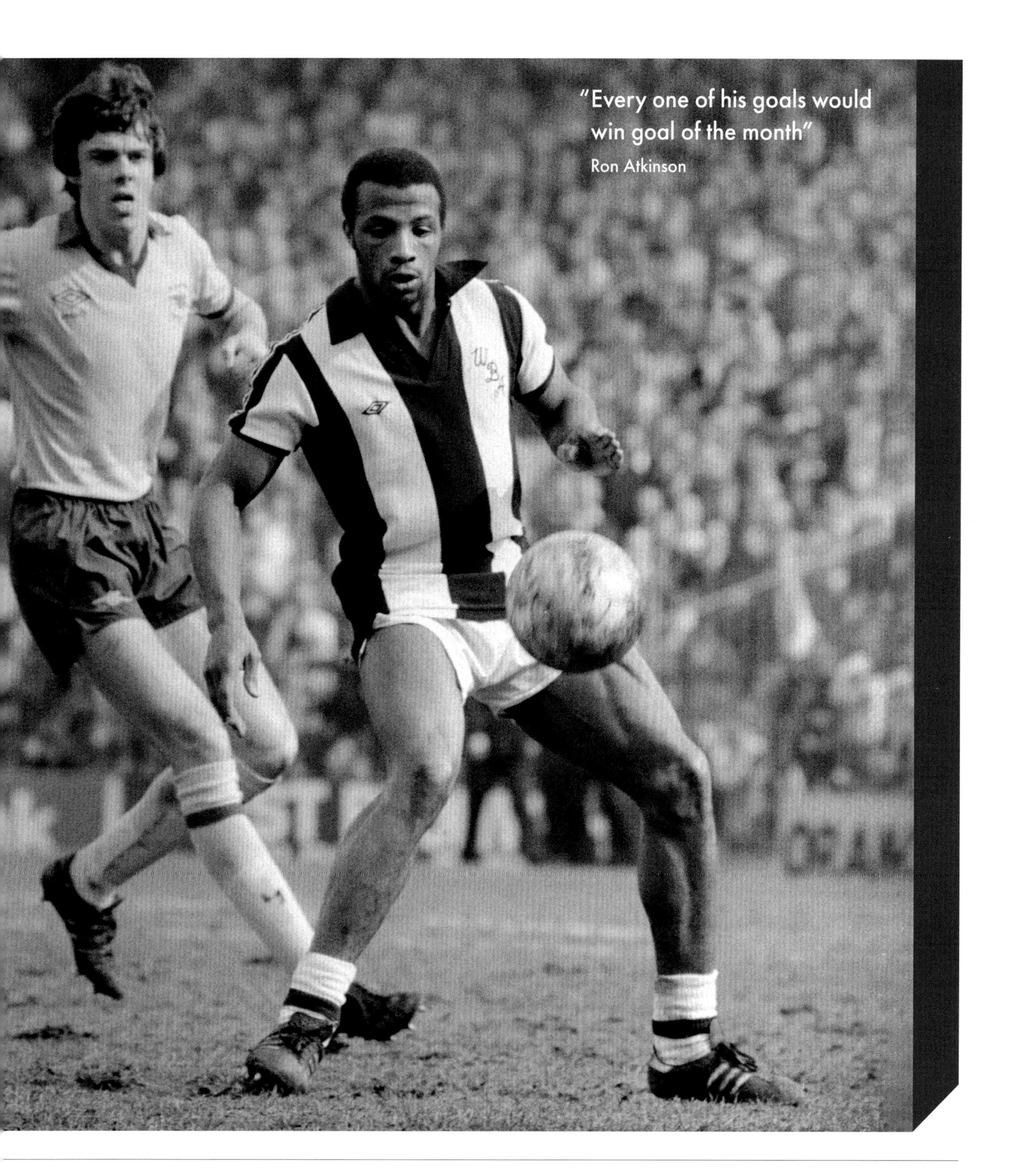

"Every one of his goals would win goal of the month"
Ron Atkinson

PLAYERS' PLAYER OF THE YEAR

Terry McDermott

THE 1979/80 SEASON WAS THE LIVERPOOL STALWART'S FINEST HOUR, AS THE CLUB RETAINED THE LEAGUE TITLE

Terry McDermott realised his lifelong ambition in November 1974 when the boyhood Red signed for Liverpool from Newcastle United. Anything he achieved from that moment on, he decided, would be a bonus. In 1980, he did something no one else ever had.

After struggling in his first two seasons, McDermott would be freed from any defensive shackles, evolving into one of the country's finest goalscoring midfielders with a passing range and work rate to match. In 1979/80, the Kirkby lad had scored 11 First Division goals by mid-February to become the leading candidate for the Players' Player of the Year award.

"I'm sure Terry had two pairs of lungs," said teammate Kenny Dalglish. "He was a creature of instinct and intelligence, a killer mix. If I even hinted at darting into a particular area, Terry read my mind. The ball was waiting for me, almost smiling at me. Only the very best can do that."

Dalglish, McDermott and top scorer David Johnson were flown down to the PFA ceremony in March, but only after the eventual winner took some persuading.

"I said the only reason I'd go was if I'd *won* it," McDermott told PFA secretary Cliff Lloyd. "I think you'd better come then," came Lloyd's winking reply. The Liverpool trio returned to Merseyside the same evening.

Still the insatiable McDermott wasn't done. In April's FA Cup quarter-final, billed as "McDermott vs Glenn Hoddle" for the Football Writers' Association individual prize, the moustachioed midfielder flicked up a clearance to volley into the far corner for his second Goal of the Season in four years. Though Liverpool fell in the semi-final to Arsenal, the Reds retained their league title and McDermott sealed his personal double to become the first to win the PFA and FWA awards in the same season.

"I remember saying at the time that I couldn't understand why a ragbag like me should be the first one to do it," the larger-than-life three-time European Cup winner said. "And that's still my opinion."

McDermott chases the ball in Liverpool's 3–1 Charity Shield win over Arsenal, 1979

YOUNG PLAYER OF THE YEAR

Glenn Hoddle

So deep was Glenn Hoddle's reservoir of flicks, feints and pirouettes, he could make opposition defenders look like they had sludge for veins. Nor did the prodigiously gifted Tottenham Hotspur midfielder's tricks only work on limited journeymen.

"Glenn once sold me a dummy so good that I nearly lost my cartilages," Liverpool's Kenny Dalglish once said.

In an otherwise forgettable Spurs season, their leonine playmaker produced a career-best 22 goals in 49 1979/80 appearances in all competitions, their quality every bit as eye-catching as their quantity. In December, a month after scoring one and creating another on his England debut against Bulgaria, the 22-year-old delivered the goal that went a long way to ensuring his Young Player of the Year award. Following a deft one-two with Ossie Ardiles, Hoddle span to his right and struck the purest of mid-air scissor volleys that flew into the far corner against Manchester United.

"My all-time favourite has always been that United goal," the two-time FA Cup winner later recalled. "I don't mean this in a big-headed way, because I wasn't a great goalscorer, but I scored great goals."

A diamond, who lit up English football.

Above | Hoddle during Tottenham Hotspur's First Division match against Coventry City at Highfield Road, 1979

Above | Busby with Manchester United and England's first European Cup, 1968

MERIT AWARD

Sir Matt Busby

Sir Matt Busby never gave up on his dream to make Manchester United England's first European champions, not even when it robbed him of perhaps his finest side. Eight members of the Busby Babes perished on the freezing runway just outside Munich in February 1958 but the former pit-boy from Bellshill, Scotland, carried them in his heart for evermore. Just over a decade after being read the Last Rites himself (twice), he achieved immortality.

In 25 years as United's manager from 1945, the former Liverpool and Manchester City wing half found his "paradise", specialising in bringing through youngsters from across the United Kingdom who thrived in representing the area, including the Holy Trinity of Sir Bobby Charlton, Denis Law and George Best.

"It is our duty," he once said, "to provide a little spark, a little colour, for the men and women who come to Old Trafford at the end of a working week."

He remained at Old Trafford as a director and received the 1980 PFA Merit Award for his decades-long service to the game, two years after his compatriot and fellow club revolutioniser, Bill Shankly.

PLAYERS' PLAYER OF THE YEAR

John Wark

THE DEFENSIVE MIDFIELDER MADE HIS MARK IN EVERY MATCH AS IPSWICH TOWN WON THE 1981 UEFA CUP

John Wark was a one-man cheat code in 1980/81, a defensive midfielder who scored an absurd 36 goals in all competitions as Ipswich Town chased what would have been a monumental treble. Described as "the best goalscoring midfielder of his generation" by Tractor Boys boss Sir Bobby Robson, the relentless 23-year-old had the team spirit to start revolutions.

By mid-March, Ipswich had lost just two of their first 32 league games to top the First Division, the Scot's 17 league goals in that period comprising bullet headers, volleys and calm finishes at the end of lung-bursting forays forward from a nominal starting position in front of centre backs Russell Osman and George Burley.

"It was just the system we had," Wark explained. "When we went forward it was as a team – and people could not handle us. We didn't just beat teams, we battered them."

Nowhere was that truer than in the UEFA Cup. Ipswich dispatched Aris Salonika 5–1 and Widzew Łódź 5–0 in the early rounds, but it was Wark's display in the quarter-final first leg at Saint-Étienne that confirmed his brilliance. Not only did the Scot mark Michel Platini out of the game, he also burst forward to score a towering 76th-minute header that sealed a 4–1 victory. Eleven days later, he received the PFA Players' Player of the Year award from former FIFA president Sir Stanley Rous, pipping teammates Frans Thijssen and Paul Mariner.

"My best mate Mariner stood on a chair and really applauded," Wark recalled. "It was a great feeling to have the team behind me like that."

Ultimately, however, Ipswich's 66-game season caught up with them. The Suffolk side lost seven of their last ten league games and an FA Cup semi-final defeat to Manchester City, but steeled themselves to win the UEFA Cup. In the final, Wark's European record-equalling 14th goal of the tournament ultimately delivered their only continental trophy, even as AZ Alkmaar staged a late comeback. He had scored in every round.

"It was my best ever season in football," he recalled. "It was an achievement that could have been up there with the Liverpools and Manchester Uniteds if we had won the treble." Clone John Wark and they'd have done it, too.

Top | Wark on Ipswich Town duty, 1980

MERIT AWARD

John Trollope

There are one-club men and then there is John Trollope's love affair with Swindon Town. Over the 21 seasons that followed Trollope's senior debut, aged 17, in a 1–1 draw with Halifax Town in August 1960, the only time the unassuming left back was ever out of the team for an extended period was for a broken arm in 1968 and because he retired in the summer of 1979. Just over a year later, the 1968/69 League Cup winner made history.

Against Carlisle United on 18 October 1980, the unretired 37-year-old made his 765th league appearance for Swindon to break former Portsmouth left half Jimmy Dickinson's Football League record of most appearances for a single club. Trollope appeared another five times to retire for good on a still-unsurpassed 770 league games.

"I've stayed loyal to the club, that's true," he later said after receiving the 1981 PFA Merit Award from Dickinson, the man whose record he had beaten. "But equally, they've been loyal to me. I couldn't have been treated better anywhere else."

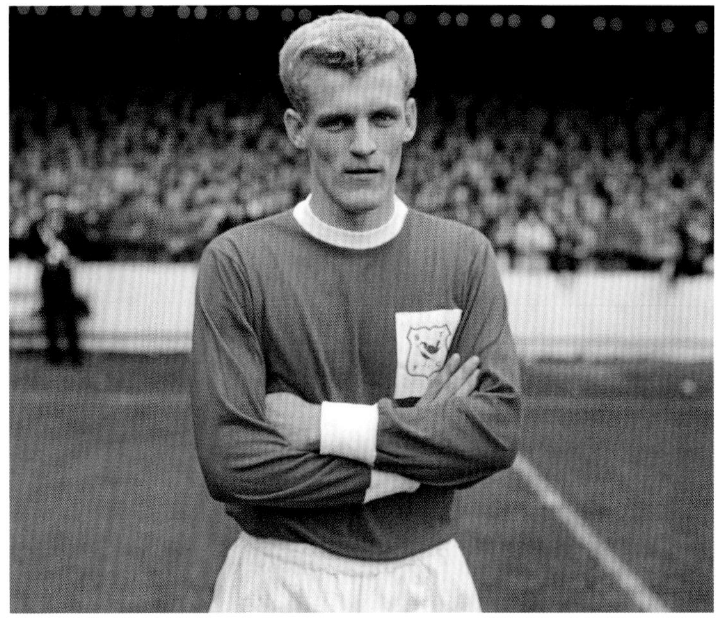

Above | Trollope in an outing for Swindon against Sunderland at the County Ground, 1963

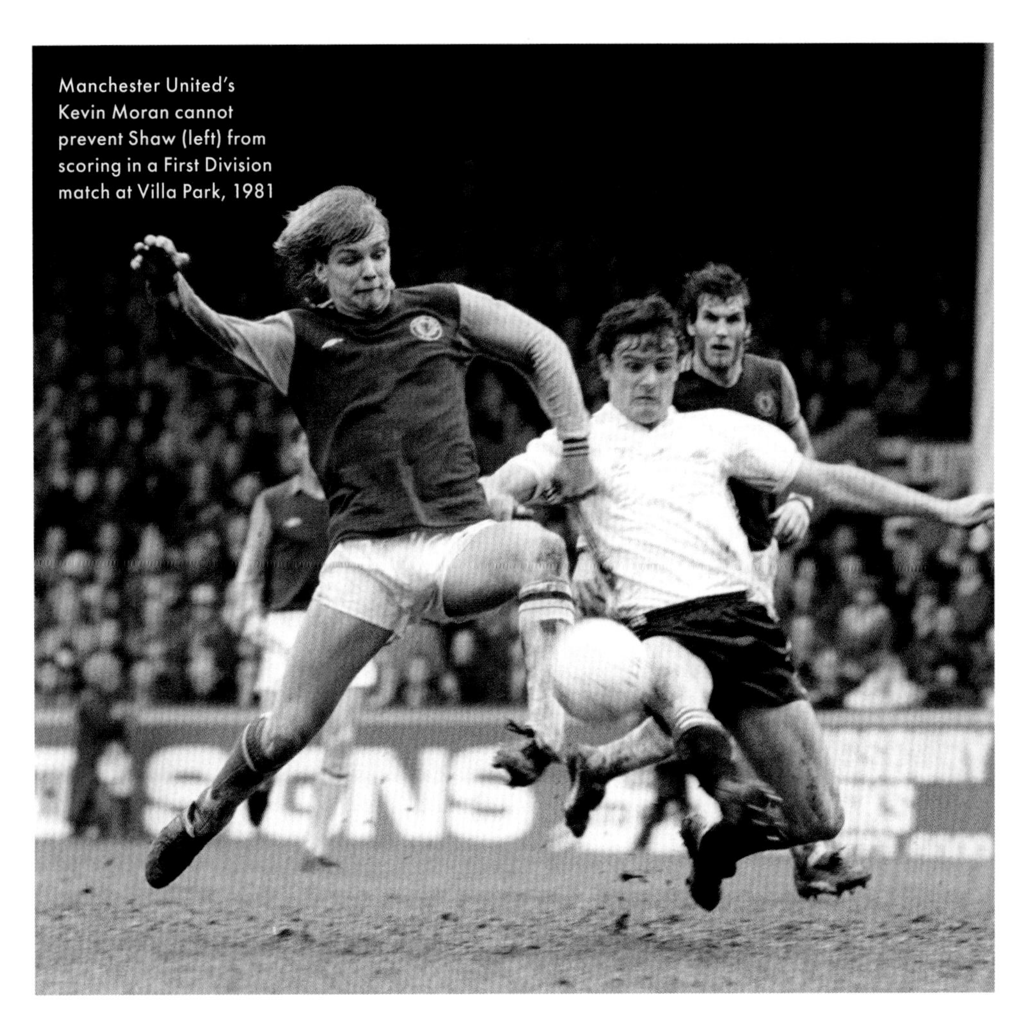

Manchester United's Kevin Moran cannot prevent Shaw (left) from scoring in a First Division match at Villa Park, 1981

YOUNG PLAYER OF THE YEAR

Gary Shaw

Aston Villa manager Ron Saunders famously used just 14 players in lifting the 1980/81 title – arguably the best of the lot was the side's sole Brummie, who only turned 20 halfway through the season.

Gary Shaw's 18 league goals trailed only leading marksman Peter Withe to end the Villans' 71-year wait for a top-flight title, his speed of thought as quick as his razor-sharp movement. Shaw scored important goals, too, his instinctive opener in Villa's penultimate fixture of the season – a 3–0 defeat of Middlesbrough – putting one claret-and-blue hand on the First Division.

Shaw's reputation extended beyond English football after winning the following season's European Cup. Barcelona's Diego Maradona asked for his shirt after the 1982 UEFA Super Cup final, but a serious knee injury in 1983 robbed Shaw of the pace that had so electrified his peers in voting him the PFA Young Player of the Year in 1981.

"Gary is a scoring machine," said Saunders of the striker born a ten-minute drive from Villa Park. "He used to stand with his pals on the Holte End ... now he's scoring goals and winning cheers from his mates."

PLAYERS' PLAYER OF THE YEAR

Kevin Keegan

IN THE 1981/82 SEASON, THE TWO-TIME BALLON D'OR WINNER MADE A TRIUMPHANT RETURN TO THE ENGLISH GAME

Lawrie McMenemy had a novel approach to persuading Kevin Keegan to decline the advances of Real Madrid and Juventus and instead sign for lowly Southampton in 1980. The Saints boss called Hamburg's turbo-thighed forward, who had just won his second successive Ballon d'Or, and asked him for a type of light fitting for his home.

"They're only made in Hamburg, Kevin," he pleaded. "Could you bring a few back for me on your next visit?" It didn't take long for McMenemy to wonder aloud what the 29-year-old was going to do when his contract ran out at the end of the season. He knew Keegan's wife Jean wanted to return to the UK and that former club Liverpool weren't interested, and by the end of the call McMenemy had pulled off the transfer coup of the century.

Somehow keeping the deal quiet, McMenemy called a press conference for 11 February 1980 at the Potters Heron hotel in Romsey to a bemused fourth estate. "I've got a surprise for you, lads," he said as the England captain walked in to announce a £400,000 move for that summer.

Was it ever, not least because the 1976/77 European Cup winner hadn't exactly been effusive in his praise of The Dell's tightly packed stands as a Liverpool player. "If you were going down the wing and [Saints full back] Denis Hollywood didn't get you, an old lady would reach over the wall with her umbrella and trip you up," he once declared.

Crucially, though, Southampton appealed to Keegan's self-made instincts. The perma-permed striker had reached the elite through pathological hard work and game intelligence, and had just taken also-rans Hamburg from obscurity to the Bundesliga title and a European Cup final. He wanted to do the same with Southampton.

"Kevin was Europe's player of the year and probably the best footballer in the world," recalled strike partner Mick Channon. "You don't often get characters like him at Southampton."

McMenemy's memorable footballing philosophy was "Four concert violinists and seven road sweepers" and in Keegan, Channon, the mercurial Charlie George and precocious young striker Steve Moran he had the former, with 1966 World Cup winner Alan Ball in charge of the artisans. McMenemy's lead soloist scored 11 goals in 27 First Division outings in 1980/81 as the Saints finished a then record sixth to qualify for the UEFA Cup – it was a decent return but a persistent hamstring injury limited Keegan's assorted physical gifts.

In 1981/82, the fully fit number seven went stratospheric. Keegan scored in Southampton's opening four league games and barely let up to have Hampshire dreaming of something big. Now in his 30s, his professionalism and determination instilled belief at the club.

"Kevin was in his prime," recalled strike partner Channon. "He'd score goals, make goals and dictate games. If his name was on the team sheet, you knew we were guaranteed another few thousand fans through the turnstiles."

Never was that better exemplified than the Saints' 3–2 victory against Manchester United at a pyretic Dell. Keegan laid on Moran's equaliser, then scored a typically deadly tap-in to help set up the victory, but it was the goal he didn't score that lives longest in the memory. Hanging like a hummingbird, Keegan's mid-air scissor volley was disallowed for what can be charitably described as a non-existent offside elsewhere in the move. Many Saints still regard it as the greatest goal that never was.

When Keegan struck the only goal of the game at Middlesbrough in January 1982, Southampton went top and stayed there for the next two months, spending longer at the summit than any other team. Throughout that period, Keegan begged McMenemy to sign Nottingham Forest's unsettled goalkeeper Peter Shilton to plug a leaky defence, but the manager demurred. That and a small squad cost them.

Eventually conceding 67 times, Southampton won just three of their final 14 games to fade to seventh despite Keegan, who missed just one league game all season, scoring 26 goals to win the First Division Golden Boot. The near-unanimous choice for the Players' Player of the Year award would be the extent of the silverware for Keegan, who joined Newcastle United that summer.

"I was the mongrel who made it to Crufts, and that was fine by me," the self-effacing Keegan once said. That mongrel didn't just make it to Crufts in 1981/82, he won Best In Show.

Left | Keegan with his First Division Golden Boot after a prolific season

Opposite | In action for Southampton, 1982

"Kevin was in his prime. He'd score goals, make goals and dictate games. If his name was on the team sheet, you knew we were guaranteed another few thousand fans through the turnstiles"

Mick Channon

YOUNG PLAYER OF THE YEAR

Steve Moran

Southampton manager Lawrie McMenemy was watching his son in Hampshire's junior Tyro League when a striker on an adjacent pitch caught his eye. At the interval, McMenemy told the youngster he'd give him a pair of boots if he scored a second-half hat-trick. Forty-five minutes later, Steve Moran had his new footwear and, once he'd finished his A-Levels at Prices School in nearby Fareham, he also had his first professional contract in the summer of 1979.

A rosy-cheeked, nippy striker who came to life in the penalty box, the 21-year-old scored 12 goals in 24 starts in all competitions in 1981/82 – including the winner to beat eventual champions Liverpool 1–0 at Anfield – as the Saints ensured a second consecutive season of UEFA Cup football at The Dell. "I'm always at my best sniffing around the penalty area and I like to feed off a target man," he once said.

Though the England U21 international's season ended in January with a back problem that would later cause his early retirement, Moran was a superb foil for Mick Channon and Kevin Keegan, matching the latter to pick up the PFA Young Player of the Year award.

Above | Moran at The Dell, 1981

MERIT AWARD

Joe Mercer

Joe Mercer the player won six major honours and the 1950 Football Writers' Association Player of the Year Award for Everton and Arsenal between 1932 and 1955, but it was in turning Manchester City into the country's most exciting team in the late 1960s that he is best remembered.

Mercer immediately recruited future City legends Colin Bell and Mike Summerbee to win promotion, later adding Tony Book, Franny Lee and Neil Young to win the 1967/68 First Division, the following season's FA Cup and a European Cup Winners'-and-League Cup double in 1970. "Joe was much more than just a manager to me," recalled Summerbee, "he was like a father figure."

Described by football writer Brian Glanville as a "beguiling interregnum", Uncle Joe's last job was a 36-day spell as England caretaker between the end of Sir Alf Ramsey's tenure in 1974 and the appointment of permanent successor Don Revie. His attack-minded philosophy yielded three wins, three draws and one defeat.

Eight years later, having become one of a select group of men to have captained and managed the Three Lions, Mercer received the 1982 PFA Merit Award in recognition of his titanic contribution to football.

Above | Mercer takes to the Wembley pitch before Manchester City's victory in the FA Cup final, 1969

PLAYERS' PLAYER OF THE YEAR

Kenny Dalglish

KENNY DALGLISH AND IAN RUSH REFLECT ON A MEMORABLE SEASON IN WHICH THE REDS DEFENDED THEIR FIRST DIVISION TITLE AND WON A THIRD SUCCESSIVE LEAGUE CUP

Above | King Kenny at the 1982 Charity Shield match, in which Liverpool defeated Spurs 1–0 by virtue of a lone Ian Rush strike

PFA: Kenny, Ian, you won the Players' Player award in consecutive years during a special era at Liverpool. What was it like in that team? You had so much success as a partnership and as a club…

Kenny Dalglish: They had success before we arrived, and we just followed on. Everything was set in place when we went there – the rules, how they worked, how they operated, what they did in training, how you were expected to prepare. But I think the most important thing about the success we had was obviously the quality, the people working at the club. And that wasn't just the manager or the players, that was everybody. Everybody chipped in, and to get an individual award was recognition for the work the people at Liverpool had done.

PFA: Ian, how did you find it going into that dressing room full of people who had achieved so much?

Ian Rush: He was a nightmare [indicates Kenny]. He used to take the mickey all the time, but that was Liverpool Football Club for you. When I signed, I'd only seen these guys on TV, so I just kept my mouth shut and got on with it.

"The most important thing about the success we had was the quality, the people working at the club. That wasn't just the manager or the players, that was everybody"

Kenny Dalglish

PFA: You two obviously had such a strong partnership. Kenny, how quickly did you realise that here was someone that you could really work with?
KD: We knew right away that we had somebody that was going to be special. I think it's just that you come in, you're welcome, you relax, you want to play well. He'd been well-received, and it just gets you into the swing of things.
PFA: The season you won the award Kenny, any standout moments?
KD: I think I got 21 goals.
IR: But he must have had about 98 assists or something!
PFA: And for you the following year Ian?
IR: When I won it, I think I scored 47 goals, so it was amazing. We also did the most important thing – the treble. Kenny had so many assists. I was pretty quick in them days, you know, so Kenny would put the ball into the space and I would just run into positions and a lot of times I ended up one-on-one.
PFA: That Liverpool team were a really together unit, but also had a bit of an edge. How did you build that mentality going into games?
KD: Listen, if you don't compete, somebody is going to have a kick at you. I remember an old Spurs player, Danny Blanchflower, a long, long time ago, he said, "It's best to equalise first." And I sort of changed it a wee bit, I said, "Probably best to retaliate first and then got on with it."
PFA: When you look back at that period, is there an achievement that you're most proud of?
KD: For me, one of the greatest moments for Liverpool Football Club was when old Bob [Paisley] was manager in his last season and we won the League Cup. Graeme Souness was the captain and said, "Bob, at Wembley, you go and pick up this trophy." For me, that was the most emotional one.
PFA: A special moment?
KD: Yes, for a special man. I mean, he only won six league championships in nine years and threw in a couple of European Cups. People ask me, "Who's your most successful manager?" I say, "Tell me somebody that beats that."

Below | Liverpool after their 2–1 extra time win against Manchester United in the 1983 Milk Cup final

YOUNG PLAYER OF THE YEAR

Ian Rush

Ian Rush initially struggled to live up to the pressure of being English football's most expensive teenager after joining Liverpool for £300,000 from Chester City in April 1980. "I didn't say a word for a year," the moustachioed number nine later recalled.

Thirty goals in 1981/82's title-winning season helped, but by November 1982 Rush had struck just four times in the First Division as the Reds went into the first Merseyside Derby of the season. Had the Welsh goalscoring well run dry? No chance. The cornerstone of a 5–0 win, Rush plundered four against ten-man Everton at Goodison Park to register the first derby hat-trick in the league since 1935.

It began a goalscoring deluge of 16 in Rush's next 13 league games, the 21-year-old going on to better his previous season's numbers with 31 in all competitions as the Reds retained their title with so much room to spare they didn't win any of their last seven games and still led the league by 11 points. They'd already won the League Cup and Charity Shield.

"He never missed!" said Mark Lawrenson of his PFA Young Player of the Year team-mate. He was only half-joking.

Above | Wreaking havoc against Manchester United, Rush jumps out of a Ray Wilkins challenge, with Remi Moses also in pursuit, Milk Cup Final, 1983

MERIT AWARD

Bob Paisley

In 1974, Bob Paisley only replaced Liverpool's retiring messiah Bill Shankly through a sense of duty and because no one else would take on the job. Nine years later, the former assistant stepped down as the club's most successful manager. He still is.

Nicknamed the Quiet Genius in his trademark battered cardigan and slippers, Paisley's tactical acuity and astute eye for the right player delivered 20 honours, including six league titles (to go with one as a player in 1946/47), a then-record three European Cups and three League Cups.

"It was like having your granddad in charge," Mark Lawrenson later said. "But he was a genius, and the master of the unfinished sentence."

Ensuring a 1983 PFA Awards clean sweep for Liverpool with the Merit Award, Paisley handed over to successor Joe Fagan at the end of the season. "This club has been my life," Paisley said. "I'd go out and sweep the street and be proud to do it for Liverpool FC if they asked me to." That quote now sits beneath an 8ft statue outside Anfield. If Shankly established the Liverpool roots, it was Paisley who nurtured them into the mightiest of oaks.

Above | Bob Paisley at Anfield, having taken over as Liverpool manager from Bill Shankly, 1974

Role model behaviour

PFA COMMUNITY LIAISON EXECUTIVE DAVE PALMER REFLECTS ON THE POSITIVE IMPACT THAT PLAYERS HAVE HAD ON A LOCAL AND NATIONAL LEVEL, AND THE NEED TO SUPPORT THE NEXT GENERATION'S EFFORTS TO ENGAGE AND ENTHUSE

Dave Palmer, PFA Community Liaison Executive

Marcus Rashford did more than just draw attention to food poverty in helping provide families with the basics during the pandemic and beyond. The Manchester United forward proved that footballers who engage with their community can implement lasting change and even affect government decision making.

"Marcus is a beacon for what players can achieve with their involvement in programmes where they have lived experience," says PFA Community Liaison Executive Dave Palmer. "He grew up around food poverty and has gone on to change government policy, such has been his unbelievable impact.

"Our key focus is making sure there's an appropriate network for our members to support community projects they're passionate about. They're the most influential people in society now, they make a huge difference with their involvement and impact on community work up and down the country. They inspire, enthuse, make a difference and raise awareness of important social issues through their profile."

Since the mid 1980s, the PFA has played a leading and instrumental role in engaging its members. Recently there were up to 40,000 visits per season before the pandemic struck, with players playing there part in helping to generate £865 million of social value to towns and cities local to Football League clubs and their Club Community Organisations (CCOs) alone. The PFA invests over £12 million a season in corporate social responsibility.

"Even during Covid many of our members supported the most isolated and vulnerable with fundraising, food drops, telephone calls, school programmes and volunteer work with local charities and the NHS," says Palmer.

"We've recently made our tenth visit to South Africa to help support local schools, charities and the Homeless World Cup. The highlight was taking out 16 Premier League scholars, who included Nathan Aké and Jordan Pickford when they were at Chelsea and Sunderland, in 2012 after the recent World Cup. They went into townships, coaching kids, seeing a different world, the hardship that exists out there. That was so impactful for many of them as young players with a number continuing the connections made on their return with personal fundraising.

"Seeing how our investment in CCOs has grown is huge. They provide the platform to get our members engaged – without them we wouldn't be able to get our players into the community. Some of those CCOs are now huge charities and involved in a wide range of social issues at a local level where players' input can make a big difference."

Celebrating that difference via the PFA Community Champion Awards at each club – Rashford himself is a former winner – is vital. Many are inspired to continue in community outreach long after retiring as players.

"It's vital they're recognised and their impact on society is highlighted for the extra distance they've gone," says Palmer. "The PFA chairman Omar Beckles recently won the EFL Player in the Community Award, which goes to show our own chairman is leading by example by giving back in corporate social responsibility."

Beckles is one of many players to have started their own foundation with PFA support.

"The most important thing is that the players set it up correctly, so, initially, we provide legal support for players and ensure applications to the Charity Commission are fit for purpose," says Palmer. "It's great to see more and more players looking at that as an option and extending beyond the work they do with their club to set up their own meaningful foundations."

Inspiring the next generation to engage with community activities is a key part of Palmer's work. One new initiative is full-time Community Link Officers (CLOs) who act as a go-between with the PFA and CCOs with a specific brief to involve young players and identify activities of interest, from school and hospital visits to volunteering and community coaching sessions.

"Young players are the future and it should be part of their personal development to support community work," says Palmer. Ex-pro Ben Parker is Leeds United's CLO. "Ben's a former player so he also acts as a mentor to the youngsters to help explain why social responsibility and their engagement in the community makes such a big difference, as well as helping co-ordinate the work that is being done.

"The players who are coming through now will have had appearances from past players when they were young," says Palmer. "They know from personal experience the impact those meetings had on them and think: 'It's important I now do that as a professional player myself'. It becomes cyclical. That's what makes our work so rewarding."

Opposite, clockwise from top | A mural of Marcus Rashford in Withington, Manchester; Leeds United's CLO Ben Parker during his playing days; PFA Chairman Omar Beckles receives the Player in the Community Award from EFL Chief Executive Trevor Birch, 2022

"Our key focus is making sure there's an appropriate network for our members to support community projects. They inspire, enthuse and raise awareness"

Dave Palmer

The first London borough of sport

MERTON'S TRAILBLAZING SCHEME AIMS TO BE A BLUEPRINT FOR OTHER COUNCILS TO BRING ABOUT SOCIO-ECONOMIC BENEFITS THROUGH INVESTMENT IN SPORT

www.merton.gov.uk

The Borough of Merton in southwest London boasts two of the most inspirational, influential and internationally renowned sporting institutions in the world – albeit ones that operate at two very different ends of the scale. On the one hand, there is the All England Lawn Tennis Championship at Wimbledon – with a Championships that is the epitome of elite excellence and a highlight of the international sporting calendar. On the other is AFC Wimbledon, a fan-owned, fan-created community club that returned to Merton in 2020 after decades in exile. Together, they represent a vision of what can be achieved through sport, inspiring Merton's ambition to become London's first Borough of Sport.

"This is about how we can embed sport within everything we do as a council," says Ross Garrod, Merton's Leader of the Council. "It stems from an appreciation of the power of sport to impact lives. That doesn't mean creating elite stars – although we have done so historically within the borough – it's about the wider socioeconomic benefits, the health benefits, wellbeing, employment and giving children a route away from antisocial or criminal activity."

Approved in 2023, the Borough of Sport programme has already seen almost £12 million invested to improve facilities and pitches, provide grants to local sports clubs and ensure free access to sporting activity such as swimming for every young person once a week. The less affluent and young and older age groups are the main focus of attention. "We want to get more people active, with a laser-like focus on under-16s and over 65s, giving them free access to weekly activities, and developing a sense of pride about the borough as well as their own health and wellbeing."

In addition, Merton is consulting with outside organisations to create safer and more welcoming facilities for women. The ambitious project will ultimately encompass a wide range of stakeholders, from the tennis club to local football clubs, parks and gyms, schools, adult education centres and even new housing developments.

Ross conceived of the Borough of Sport idea in conversation with a local resident, who talked about how fortunate Merton was to have such celebrated institutions within its boundaries. That made Ross contemplate the positive impact sport had played in his own life – participating in running races and playing football. He could see the benefits that come with sport – and how these might have long-term gains by creating a healthier, happier population and a reduced demand for health services. He would also like to encourage schools and colleges to incorporate sports programmes into their curriculums, in areas such as coaching and physiotherapy, allowing local residents to deliver much-needed skills into the sporting economy.

"As a borough we have a rich sporting heritage," says Ross. "We have the oldest and best-known tennis tournament, we have one of the oldest cricket pitches that has been in continuous use, and we have two football clubs – AFC Wimbledon and Tooting & Mitcham United FC – who are heavily involved in supporting their communities. We have invested in infrastructure and our grassroots sport is second to none. We want to bring this narrative, that heritage and those powerful stakeholders together for the benefit of our residents."

One inspiring project that already exists in the borough, and has done so for more than 50 years, is Morden Little League. This not-for-profit football programme offers free football for more than 630 boys and girls from the ages of seven to 14. This undertaking requires 100 volunteers every weekend to ensure the games can take place, and it operates on the principle that participation is not based on ability; every player is guaranteed at least half a game each week. The emphasis is on mass participation

"It stems from an appreciation of the power of sport to impact lives"

rather than elitism; enthusiasm and endeavour rather than ability. Players are encouraged to develop team spirit, self-discipline and sportsmanship. "It is the largest Little League in the UK, and they do fantastic work in the area," says Ross. "They have started organising Family Fundays and are now a huge part of the community. It's not just about football on a Saturday, it's about what else can you do. So they do things like recycling old kit for those who can't afford new equipment."

For older residents, Merton offers walking football organised by AFC Wimbledon, while the borough is looking to introduce pickleball – that is, tennis that is played on smaller courts for residents who no longer feel comfortable on a full-size court. "We want to unlock these activities for over-65s," says Ross. "We do chair yoga, chair archery – it means thinking a bit more about what is appropriate for those with different needs."

When it comes to funding, Merton has attempted to take a different approach from simply raising revenue through taxation. "That means thinking counterintuitively rather than as a traditional council," says Ross. "We are looking for grants and sponsorship as this is a joint endeavour, not just for the council and its residents but for the whole borough, including sporting institutions." Among the local partners and stakeholders that the council has sought to leverage support from is the Lawn Tennis Association, which is investing in Merton's extensive tennis court refurbishment programme. Merton's ambition is applauded by partners such as AFC Wimbledon and Tooting & Mitcham United FC, who already do good work, engaging the community around their grounds.

Ross believes that Merton's template could even inspire other councils around the country to adopt a similar approach. "When they see the success of Merton and the dividends it provides, I am sure others will want to emulate our work as a trailblazing council that has seized the opportunity and understood the strength and power of sport," he says.

"In five years, we will have built up our capability around sport and developed stronger relationships with grassroots and internationally known organisations. We will see more people actively participating in physical exercise and believe that people across the city will start seeing Merton as London's Borough of Sport."

A spiritual homecoming

THE STORY OF AFC WIMBLEDON'S RETURN TO THE LONDON BOROUGH OF MERTON IS TESTAMENT TO THE POSITIVE ROLE OF FOOTBALL IN THE COMMUNITY

www.afcwimbledon.co.uk

It felt like a miracle. On 3 November 2020, AFC Wimbledon played its first game at its new Plough Lane stadium in Merton, the culmination of an arduous campaign that had started in 2002, when the club was formed by fans on Wimbledon Common from the ashes of Wimbledon FC. The original club was formed in 1889 – again on Wimbledon Common – but moved 70 miles to Milton Keynes to become MK Dons in 2004, forcing fans in London to build a new club from scratch.

The battle to bring AFC Wimbledon back to the London Borough of Merton had many champions, among them Stephen Alambritis, a former Leader of the Council. His determination has helped pave the way for Merton to become a Borough of Sport. "This is a club that lost its ground, left London, reformed, returned to the league and then returned to Plough Lane," he says. "We have our iconic tennis club, but we also have one of the greatest stories in football in the form of AFC Wimbledon."

When Stephen became Leader of the Council in 2010, he had already met AFC Wimbledon's co-founder Ivor Heller and Chief Executive Erik Samuelson to discuss their ambition to bring AFC Wimbledon home. Wimbledon FC had played at Plough Lane until 1992, when the ground was sold and redeveloped, forcing it to share with Crystal Palace. Stephen was open to the idea of a return. He had grown up near Fulham ground Craven Cottage and saw the presence of a football club in the borough as a blessing, not a curse. His first act was to apologise for the role Merton had played in allowing Wimbledon FC to leave its old Plough Lane stadium in 1991, long before his own time on the council.

"As the new leader I wanted a new start, and an apology goes a long way," says Stephen. "We then began discussions about bringing AFC Wimbledon back and looked for sites. The greyhound stadium just off Plough Lane – a few yards from where the old ground was located – was nominated. We then had an all-party motion supporting AFC Wimbledon coming back to the borough."

Acquiring the land, attaining planning permission, raising funds and building the ground took time and energy. As a fan-owned club, AFC Wimbledon was staffed entirely by volunteers, so Stephen and the council acted as a liaison between AFC Wimbledon and other parties, including the co-developer – a housing company that built hundreds of homes around the stadium. He was always confident of the benefits of bringing AFC Wimbledon home, which became apparent during Covid, when a local action group was formed by fans to raise funds and provide food and support to communities in southwest London. "It's a wonderful part of the club and it's the sort of thing any council would welcome," says Stephen.

In agreement is Ross Garrod, who took over Stephen's role and is spearheading the project to make Merton a Borough of Sport. "They went from trials on Wimbledon Common to returning to Plough Lane in a state-of-the-art 9,000-seater stadium," he says. "They aren't just a football club – they have won the hearts of the community through the work they do as a club and as fans."

A good role player

MERTON-BASED TOOTING & MITCHAM UNITED SHOWS WHAT A NON-LEAGUE CLUB CAN DO, NOT ONLY IN DEVELOPING YOUNG PLAYERS BUT FOR THE WIDER COMMUNITY

www.tmunited.org

The potential progress from non-league to football's highest level is neatly encapsulated in the career of Michail Antonio, West Ham's all-time leading Premier League scorer. Antonio started his career at non-league Tooting & Mitcham United, which play in the London Borough of Merton. But not every player can enjoy a career progression like Antonio's, and at non-league clubs, football development is only one aspect of the support given to young people through sport.

Tooting & Mitcham is rooted in the community, using football to inspire young people at every level. As such, it is a model of what Merton hopes to achieve as the London Borough of Sport. "We are proud to call ourselves grassroots," says club owner and Chairman Steve Adkins. "We have had a lot of support from our local MP and council. We pick up these lads and show them a pathway. We offer education, particularly those who have been excluded, and 50 per cent are offered university places following education delivered on our site. Our one simple rule is, if they don't do their homework, they don't play. Everybody does their homework because they want to play football."

Tooting & Mitcham were founded in 1932 from a merger of two local clubs. They play in the Combined Counties League at the Imperial Fields stadium in Mitcham, which was used by the then Chelsea Ladies to host the first ever Women's Super League match in 2011. The club's success is tied to its ability to develop players, some of whom have been rejected by larger London academies. Players can develop at the right pace, while benefiting from the safeguarding and support of a close-knit community club. In recent years, four players from the club have progressed into the Championship, including Isaiah Jones at Middlesbrough.

If a player does not reach professional status, Tooting & Mitcham can still support them. All academy players learn a trade and cost of living support is available to players' families. Steve feels that non-league football deserves more recognition for the role it plays both within football and as part of wider society. Summer football programmes provide free access to sports for local young people, and the club offers a safe environment for young people in a deprived part of London. This is only possible at a smaller club, where every individual matters.

"We are a very diverse organisation. Part of that is about football, but the other part is about community. When a player is rejected from an academy, it can be very difficult, but if you have good coaches who look after welfare rather than expectation, they can still progress. That is something that is allowed to happen in non-league which is why so many outstanding players have come from that route."

Although Tooting & Mitcham were relegated in 2023, Steve is full of optimism. The club is starting women's football and has planning permission to build affordable housing and two community buildings encompassing a new sports hall and an education block, with permission granted specifically because of these community benefits. Steve believes that the proven success of the club's pathway will produce more players of merit – well-rounded individuals who will thrive inside or outside the game. "We always feel that regardless of a boy's ambitions, we can provide a platform for them in life," he says. "Hopefully, we offer a possible way that others can follow."

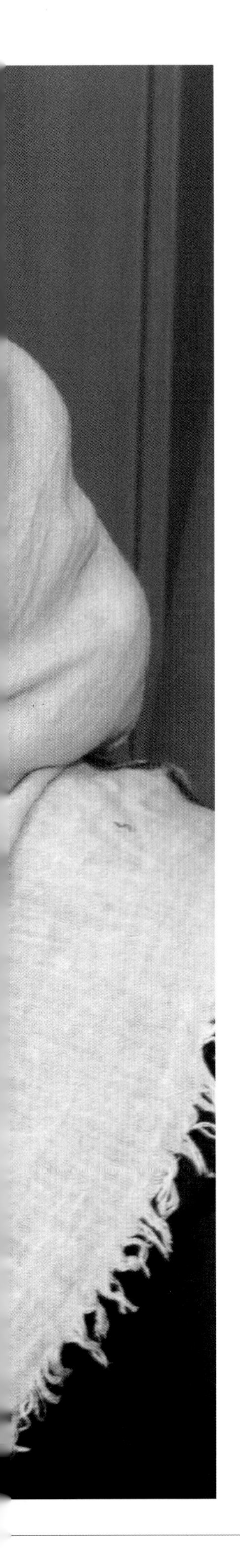

A beacon of hope

CHAIN OF HOPE ASSEMBLES FIRST-CLASS CARDIAC EXPERTISE TO PROVIDE LIFE-SAVING OPERATIONS ON CHILDREN WITH CONGENITAL HEART CONDITIONS AROUND THE WORLD

www.chainofhope.org

One child in every 100 is born with a congenital heart defect. In countries such as the UK these are usually detected and treated as a matter of course, but in many countries they go unrecognised. That means thousands of children needlessly die from treatable conditions, while others – such as footballer Fabrice Muamba – will not discover any problems until it is almost too late. Chain of Hope aims to rectify this global healthcare inequality. The charity utilises the skills of international heart surgeons to change the lives of children around the world, with support from patrons and ambassadors such as former Arsenal footballer Robert Pires and boxer Chris Eubank Jr.

"The work Chain of Hope does with children with heart disease is important. We try to reach beyond boundaries as a small charity with a big ambition," says Professor Victor Tsang, Consultant Cardiothoracic Surgeon at Great Ormond Street Hospital and Vice-Chair of the trustees. "These children would die or remain severely malnourished if we don't reach them."

Founded in 1996 by Sir Magdi Yacoub, Chain of Hope originally brought children to London for treatment via a network of volunteers – the "chain of hope" of its name. The concept evolved, with surgical teams travelling overseas to treat children. Today, the UK charity also transfers knowledge by developing specialist hospitals abroad, often with the support of local celebrities, such as Usain Bolt in Jamaica.

One of the charity's most popular initiatives is the star-studded annual gala. Attendees have included Fabrice Muamba, who survived cardiac arrest during a match in 2012, caused by a congenital condition. "We auction unique experiences such as the chance to fly to Jamaica to watch Usain Bolt train," says Director Emma Scanlan. "With the money, we have bought a portable cardiac scanner for the hospital there. People can help fund our missions – it can cost £50,000 to take a team overseas to treat ten to 15 children – or an operation or equipment."

Alongside a dedicated cardiac unit in Jamaica, Chain of Hope has established new cardiac hospitals, including one in Egypt that treats 3,000 patients a year, and others in countries such as Uganda, Mozambique and Ethiopia. Teams regularly travel to treat children overseas, including to Jordan, which is used as a hub to treat children from Syria, Yemen and Iraq.

"The evolution of the charity has been very rewarding," says Emma. "We started by bringing just a few children each year to the UK for treatment, but now we can treat several hundred children with complex conditions, thanks to the support of our patrons. We want to branch into the US and are always looking for more ambassadors. We want more spokespeople, high-profile personalities who can raise awareness on our behalf and help save more lives."

Ambassadorship is rewarding. "I am very happy to have supported Chain of Hope for many years as an ambassador," says Robert Pires. "What inspires me is the generosity of the doctors and nurses who give up their time to help these children. I feel fortunate to have access to healthcare, and when I hear the stories of the thousands of children being saved by Chain of Hope doctors, I am even more pleased to be involved and to lend my voice to help."

The benefits of the work, too, are clear. As Professor Tsang says, "I think I can say, on behalf of all the global volunteers of Chain of Hope, that it is immensely satisfying to undertake surgical missions to treat babies and children with congenital heart disease, help them to recover well and have the potential to live a happy life."

Caring for the young

THE SHARE FOUNDATION HELPS YOUNG PEOPLE ACCESS FUNDS THEY ARE ENTITLED TO, BUT MAY BE UNAWARE OF, UNDER GOVERNMENT FINANCIAL SUPPORT SCHEMES

www.sharefound.org | www.ctfambassadors.org.uk

Every child in the UK born between September 2002 and January 2011 received a Child Trust Fund, a scheme organised by the government. But not everyone knows about these funds, with nearly £2 billion unclaimed by around 900,000 young adults. The Share Foundation, a charity created to help children in care manage their financial futures, can help all young people aged 16 and over to locate and claim their Child Trust Funds.

The charity is seeking ambassadors to spread the message about the services it provides. "We are looking for people who are prepared to be an ambassador for young people, to tell them they have this money," says Anthony Walker, Director of Operations. "There are all these people turning 18 and we already have an estimate that there is nearly £2 billion in unclaimed Child Trust Funds owned by young adults. We want to raise awareness and the first step is knowing it's there, because if they don't know about it, they will never look for it."

The Share Foundation's mission has evolved since it was founded by businessman and philanthropist Gavin Oldham in 2005. He originally created the charity to put additional funds into the Child Trust Funds of children in care. When the scheme came to an end in 2011, The Share Foundation and other charities successfully lobbied the government to introduce a similar scheme for children in care. Under the new name of Junior ISAs, £34 million has since been deposited in such accounts over the past 12 years. These accounts are managed by The Share Foundation for the young person until they turn 18.

The first Child Trust Funds began to mature in September 2020 and The Share Foundation can locate funds for those turning 18 who cannot find their account. "With the original scheme, parents were sent a voucher for £250 to open an account. If they didn't use it, HMRC opened an account anyway and sent them the details," says Anthony. "But lots of those unsolicited brown envelopes would have ended up in the bin. Our estimate is that of all the accounts opened by HMRC after 12 months had elapsed, more than 80 per cent are unclaimed. We have set up a scheme (www.sharefound.org/talkctf) for young people aged 16 or over to find their account, and they can use this service to look for their Child Trust Fund. We also locate accounts that were moved to other providers. There is no charge for this service."

Another aspect of The Share Foundation's work is the financial education it provides to ensure 18-year-olds in care can make the best use of their matured funds. A six-stage programme of incentivised education has been developed; after each stage is completed, more money is deposited in their savings account, with the final stage fulfilled when the young person proves they are in education, training or employment. If they complete all six steps they "earn" an additional £1,500. Recently, the organisation received a donation allowing 700 young people to go through this programme.

The Share Foundation allows anyone to donate to a young person's Trust Fund. "Over ten years that has meant more than £13 million in additional contributions," says Anthony. "These can come from any source, and we are there to channel it and make sure the recipient knows where it is. We can say it's with this provider and this is how you get access to it. It's another example of how our work has evolved as we've learned what is needed. There is a decade of experience behind what we do."

A kick-start for carers

CARERS TRUST IS CHANGING THE LIVES OF UNPAID FAMILY CARERS, AND FOOTBALL HAS A PART TO PLAY

www.carers.org

Some of this country's greatest heroes are our seven million unpaid carers. Among this group is an extraordinary cohort – the one million unpaid carers who are under the age of 18. Support for all carers, including this exceptional group of young people, comes from Carers Trust, a UK-wide network of 126 local carer organisations that provides funding and support, raises awareness and influences policy, while delivering innovative, evidence-based programmes. "Caring is an issue that will affect all of us at some point in our lives – three in five of us will take on a caring role," says Andy McGowan, Policy and Practice Manager at Carers Trust. "We work to transform the lives of unpaid carers of all ages across the UK."

McGowan believes that with so many young carers unable to participate in football – either as players or spectators – the game has an opportunity to make a genuine difference to some of those individuals who need and deserve it the most. "There are likely to be young carers in any football youth team or playground where a ball is being kicked. There will be many other young carers who would love a chance to play or watch football but can't because of their caring responsibilities," he explains. "Through our national voice, we have made a real difference to them through the power of football and other sports."

Like the PFA, Carers Trust also celebrates a 50th anniversary in 2023. Inspired by an episode of the soap opera *Crossroads* that focused on a character in a caring role, Crossroads Care was founded in 1973, and was followed in 1991 by the establishment of The Princess Royal Trust for Carers, on the initiative of Her Royal Highness the Princess Royal, to ensure that all carers receive information, support and recognition of their individual needs. The Princess Royal remained President when these two charities merged in 2012 to form Carers Trust. Its mission is to ensure every carer has access to a high-quality local carer organisation, that no carer is pushed into poverty or is financially disadvantaged by their caring role, and that all carers, regardless of circumstances or age, are able to enjoy a fulfilling life alongside their caring relationship.

Football clubs are uniquely well placed to help make that ambition a reality. Like carers, they are indispensable

parts of their communities. Clubs could not survive without the communities that support them week in and week out, and communities would collapse if unpaid carers stopped looking after their sick and disabled relatives. Recognising this, some clubs already fundraise for carers and provide free match tickets, chances to train with youth players and become team mascots.

By 2025, Carers Trust pledges to have increased the number of unpaid carers who receive quality support through the organisation to 1.5 million, extended the local network to ensure 100 per cent coverage of all UK authorities, and delivered measurable benefits to unpaid carers and local carer organisations through its policy and campaign work. Football is already part of this journey, but the potential – and need – for further support is vast. "We would love to explore opportunities with sportspeople and sporting bodies for unpaid carers," says Andy. "This isn't just the right thing to do for carers; it also helps develop communities as a whole, and that can only be a good thing for the clubs rooted in those communities."

Chapter Two

1983|84 – 1992|93

The formation of the Premier League towards the end of the PFA Awards' second decade makes it among the most decisive in the awards' 50-year history. In 1990, Greg Dyke, Managing Director of London Weekend Television, put it to the "big five" English football clubs of Arsenal, Everton, Liverpool, Manchester United and Tottenham Hotspur that they were entitled to a larger share of the game's television rights money. They resigned, along with the First Division's other 17 teams, from the Football League at the end of the 1991/92 season, and the Premier League was founded.

Today's Premier League – the most-watched league in the world – has its genesis in the 1980s, when clubs could rise up the football pyramid only to fall back down with alarming alacrity. Declining gate receipts almost forced the likes of Wolverhampton Wanderers, Middlesbrough and Swansea City out of business and deteriorating stadiums and a ban from European competition in 1985 left the English game in a rut. Several players, including PFA award-winners Gary Lineker, Mark Hughes, Ian Rush and David Platt, headed to the continent to ply their trade.

The era's nadir, however, was the Hillsborough Disaster in 1989, which struck the day before the PFA's 16th awards ceremony. The event began with a statement from then Chief Executive Gordon Taylor: "What was to be our normal evening of celebration has been overshadowed by the horrific tragedy at Hillsborough yesterday. We did have a difficult decision with regard to whether the dinner would continue to take place. We decided it should, as it was the first opportunity to pay our respects to those who have suffered."

The return of English clubs to European competition in the 1990/91 season was trumpeted by victory for Manchester United in the European Cup Winners' Cup in 1991.

A tumultuous era for the England national team delivered two agonising World Cup exits. Diego Maradona's "hand of god" and subsequent wonder goal put paid to the Three Lions' 1986 tournament, and Italia '90 provided the contrasting emotions of Gazzamania and defeat on penalties against West Germany in the semi-finals.

The game itself was changing over this period. Play-offs were introduced for the 1986/87 term, ensuring a larger number of competitive matches, and even more drama, towards the end-of-season. In a drive to encourage free-flowing football, the back-pass rule was introduced in 1992, deterring time-wasting and unduly defensive play. And that same year, the European Cup became the Champions League.

For the PFA, this was a period of continued success. The players' union grew in membership, sustaining a 100 per cent take up among Premier League and Football League clubs. The PFA's importance was underlined in cases where the union intervened to protect players who were being released from their contracts by cash-strapped football clubs, securing redundancy packages and even lending money to clubs that found themselves in financial difficulties.

As for the PFA Awards winners, Welshmen Rush, Hughes and Ryan Giggs claimed a total of seven trophies, with Hughes winning two Players' Player of the Year awards and a Young Player of the Year award, Rush taking one of each, and Giggs being named the best youngster in the country for two years in a row. The 1986/87 Players' Player Clive Allen of Spurs set a post-war goalscoring record that was only broken in 2023, and two teams, the England 1966 World Cup-winning squad and Manchester United's European Cup champions of 1968, were acknowledged for their triumphant exploits.

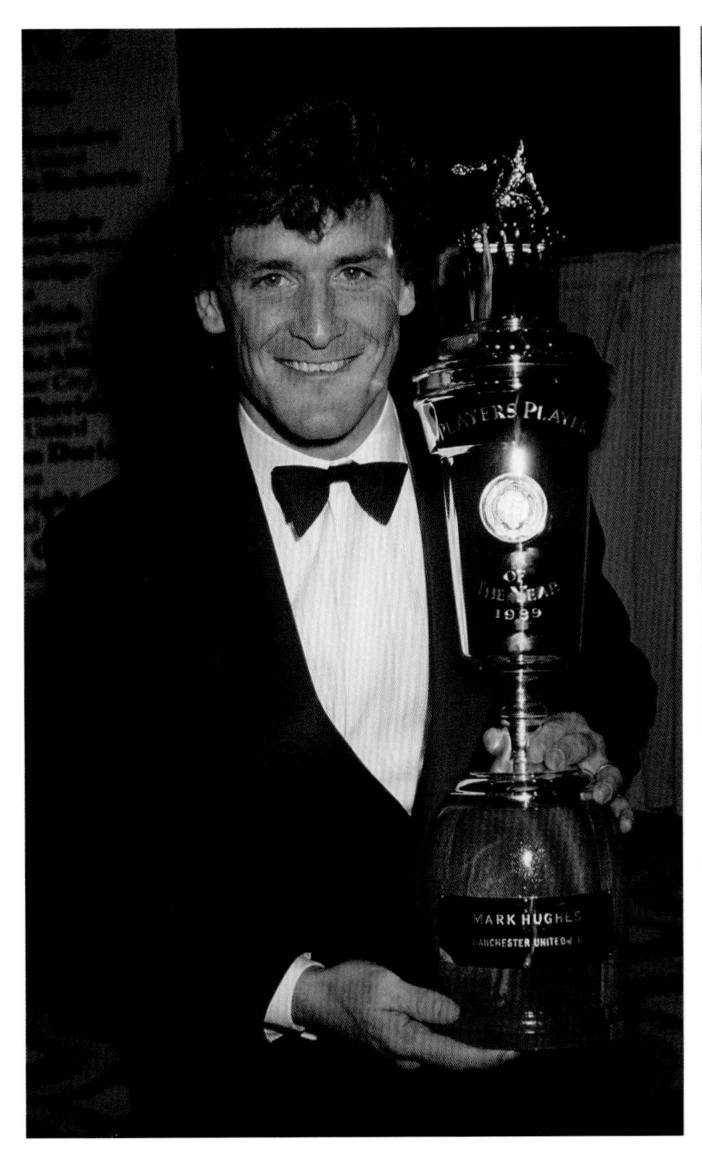
MARK HUGHES

mita
copiers

hummel

crown
paints

PLAYERS' PLAYER OF THE YEAR

Ian Rush

THE WELSH WONDER NETTED 47 GOALS IN LIVERPOOL'S MARCH TO A GLORIOUS TREBLE, OR WAS IT 50...

The Liverpool side that won the 1983/84 First Division, League Cup and European Cup treble was perhaps the ultimate distillation of the Boot Room's ability to forge a winning team. Nevertheless, for any club to dominate so completely, it needs a goalscorer, the matador to deliver the death blow. Ian Rush was that and more.

"People say I was born with a knack for scoring goals, but the truth is there's a secret to it," the Reds' forward once said. "Never be scared to miss."

In his most prolific season, Rush seldom did much of the latter, to cause a bout of the former. Beginning with three in his opening four league games, the Welshman's 47 goals in all competitions ran the gamut of poachers' tap-ins, impudent dinks and devastating blasts. His sheer weight of goals – five against Luton Town, four versus Coventry City and a hat-trick at Aston Villa – left opposition defenders feeling like they were trying to hold back an avalanche. He was only 23.

Quick off the mark and with a left-footed shot that rivalled a sniper's bullet for speed and accuracy, Rush scored ten more league goals than anyone else to finish on 32, eight as the Reds won a fourth League Cup in a row, two in the FA Cup and five in the European Cup. Socks around his ankles, he coolly slotted a spot-kick in the latter final against Roma for his last kick of a monumental season.

"I always maintain it was 50," Rush later laughed, "as I scored two for Wales, and in the penalty shootout against Roma!"

His magical 47 made him the first Briton to win the European Golden Shoe as the continent's top scorer, while also winning the Football Writers' Association's top individual honour and becoming the first Welsh winner of the PFA Players' Player of the Year award.

"The feeling? Pride," the club's all-time leading goalscorer later said of one of the most lethal seasons in British football history. "The stats are there. Look at that treble. We were a fantastic team, and that year, it all came together for us. It was the perfect mixture."

Rush holds the European Cup aloft after a nail-biting penalty shootout win over Roma at the Stadio Olimpico, 1984

YOUNG PLAYER OF THE YEAR

Paul Walsh

Seeing Luton striker Paul Walsh sweep to the PFA Young Player of the Year award in 1983/84 was like watching Hercules in full flight. Blessed with electric pace, a low centre of gravity to combine strength with his standout skill, and the flowing locks of a Disney hero, the 21-year-old former Charlton youth player scored 11 goals in 39 First Division games to earn a move to European champions Liverpool.

"Paul Walsh can play teams on his own some days," said Reds boss Bob Paisley. "He whizzes around the field like a cartoon character with the ball tied to his boot."

Walsh's lethal early-December hat-trick against Stoke, plus strike partner Brian Stein and Luton legend Ricky Hill, helped David Pleat's side to third by Boxing Day, although a subsequent run of just three wins in 24 games meant they survived by a mere three points. The Hatters hitman won his last two England caps that season.

Above | A fresh-faced Paul Walsh of Luton Town, 1983

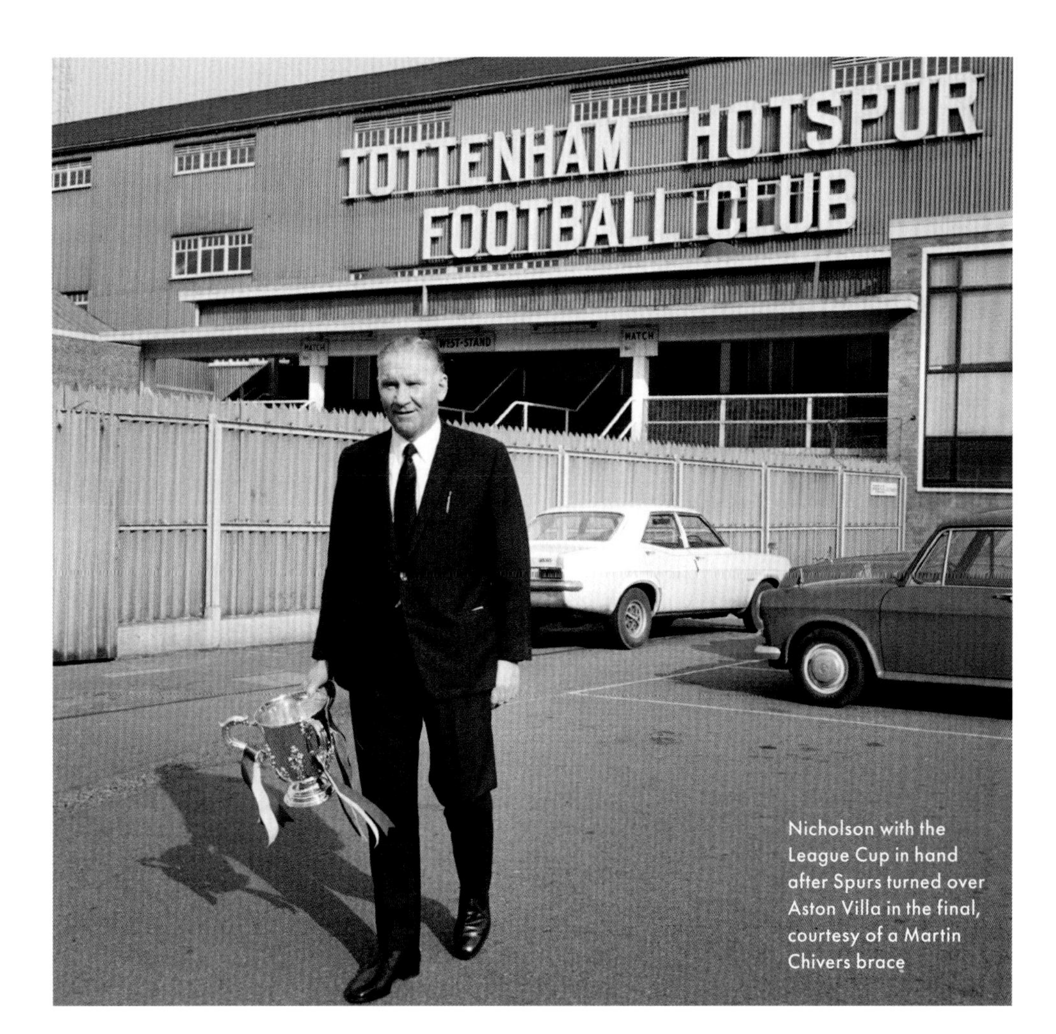

Nicholson with the League Cup in hand after Spurs turned over Aston Villa in the final, courtesy of a Martin Chivers brace

MERIT AWARD

Bill Nicholson

It wasn't enough for Bill Nicholson to win eight major honours – the 1960/61 double and 1971/72 UEFA Cup among them – in 16 years as Tottenham Hotspur manager. The inscrutable, occasionally gruff Yorkshireman was never satisfied unless silverware followed style.

"The rollicking we got if we didn't play good football," midfielder Alan Mullery recalled. "We once beat Burnley 4–0 and got a telling off."

A one-man club institution for seven decades as a player, coach, manager, consultant and finally president, Nicholson's genius lay in his judge of character, inventive coaching and blending of disparate talents into a cohesive unit. Danny Blanchflower, Dave Mackay and Cliff Jones remain bona fide Spurs greats, but it was Nicholson's alchemy and unrelenting quest for unachievable perfection that turned that team into the first double winners of the 20th century.

"Everything the club stands for emanated from Bill," said former Spurs captain and manager Glenn Hoddle in October 2004, following Nicholson's death. "He was Mr Tottenham Hotspur."

PLAYERS' PLAYER OF THE YEAR

Peter Reid

THE INDEFATIGABLE MIDFIELDER WAS AWARDED THE PFA'S MOST COVETED PRIZE IN 1985, AS EVERTON CLAIMED THEIR FIRST LEAGUE TITLE IN 15 YEARS

Above | Reid celebrates Everton's 2–0 victory over QPR at Goodison Park, which clinched the 1985 First Division title

Everton centre forward Graeme Sharp scored 30 goals in all competitions. Wingers Kevin Sheedy and Trevor Steven struck another 33 between them from midfield. Goalkeeper Neville Southall kept 31 clean sheets. Yet when it came to choosing their Player of the Year, PFA members had eyes for only one Toffee.

Peter Reid really was that good in 1984/85. Signed from second-tier Bolton Wanderers in December 1982 for a cut-price £60,000 amid concerns over his injury record, the defensive midfielder was the all-action conduit through which the Merseysiders' finest ever season flowed. It was no coincidence that the 28-year-old made a career-high 57 appearances as Everton won the First Division by 13 points, lifted the European Cup Winners' Cup and were the width of a post from beating Manchester United in the FA Cup final.

"He was a winner, a leader and a dream to play alongside," said Toffees skipper Kevin Ratcliffe. "He made everything look easy, he kept it simple and he made sure other players could play."

Tough and uncompromising with a superb passing range, the boyhood Liverpool fan excelled alongside Paul Bracewell as, in October, Everton won at Anfield for the first time in 14 years, then beat Manchester United 5–0 a week later. A first title in 15 years was on. "Everything clicked," Reid said.

From Boxing Day, the totemic Reid led Everton to 50 points from the next 54 available – conceding just nine times in the process – to win the title with five games to spare. Their 3–1 defeat of Bayern Munich in the Cup Winners' Cup semi-final second leg is widely considered the finest display in club history, while it was Reid who struck the woodwork – and was later fouled when clean through on goal by Kevin Moran – in the FA Cup final against United just three days after beating Rapid Vienna in the European showpiece.

"I'd like to thank all the lads who voted for me," said a typically modest Reid, who received the PFA trophy from Watford chairman Elton John. "This is the best award to have."

Above | Hughes was on the score sheet for Manchester United's 5–0 rout of Newcastle at Old Trafford in September 1984

YOUNG PLAYER OF THE YEAR

Mark Hughes

Manchester United manager Ron Atkinson's first impressions of Mark Hughes in the early 1980s weren't exactly gushing: "a bit dour, a bit deep, not terribly enthusiastic." Converted from a no-nonsense midfielder into a piston-pumping centre forward, Hughes soon won his manager over.

Such was Hughes's breakthrough 1984/85 form – featuring a stunning trademark volley for Wales against Spain – that summer signing Alan Brazil spent much of his time alternating with Frank Stapleton for a United starting spot up front, with Norman Whiteside pushed back into a deeper role. Still told to use the reserve team changing room at The Cliff training ground, Hughes nevertheless provided the cutting edge and back-to-goal determination his more senior colleagues seemed to lack.

The 21-year-old scored 24 goals in all competitions, including a first senior hat-trick in a 4–0 March defeat of Aston Villa, standing up to be counted as ten-man United beat Everton in the FA Cup final. Whiteside's solo winner was only possible thanks to Sparky's superb hold-up play and through ball.

"Winning the FA Cup was always one of the dreams you had growing up," recalled Hughes, who also picked up the Young Player of the Year award.

MERIT AWARD

Ron Greenwood

"Football is a simple game," Ron Greenwood said shortly after becoming England manager in 1977. "The hard part is making it look simple."

A coaching idealist, Greenwood wasn't the popular choice to replace UAE-bound Don Revie, but the son of a painter and decorator, and himself an apprentice Wembley signwriter was exactly the safe pair of hands the Three Lions needed. The former Chelsea defender's imaginative coaching acumen had shone in a 13-year spell as West Ham manager from 1961 that yielded the FA Cup in 1964 and European Cup Winners' Cup a year later.

"I wanted to see pleasure on the pitch and pleasure on the terraces," the arch-perfectionist once said. "Football is a battle of wits or nothing at all."

Three years after leaving the England job in the wake of Spain '82 to become a radio pundit, the 63-year-old received the PFA Merit Award. Credited with turning Hammers stars Bobby Moore, Sir Geoff Hurst and Martin Peters into England World Cup winners, few have done more for the game.

Above | England manager Greenwood, c. 1980

PLAYERS' PLAYER OF THE YEAR

Gary Lineker

EVERTON'S NEW BOY WAS AT THE PEAK OF HIS POWERS IN 1985/86, PICKING UP THE FIRST DIVISION AND WORLD CUP GOLDEN BOOTS IN THE SAME SEASON

PFA: What did winning Player of the Year mean to you?
Gary Lineker: It was incredible. It was my first and only season at Everton. I scored 30 goals in the league and another ten elsewhere. But it's your own teammates and the players you play against week in, week out, they're doing the voting. So it means an awful lot when it comes from them.
PFA: A lot of players can struggle going to a new club, but you had a standout season.
GL: I struggled at the start when I joined Everton because I took the place of Andy Gray and he was very popular there. I remember the first home game. We'd already lost at Leicester in my opening game, which was tough to take as it was my former club. They read the team out, and it was "Peter Reid!", the crowd cheers, "Trevor Steven!", the crowd cheers and "Gary Lineker!", "Boo!", and it was my own fans! Then I didn't score in the first three games or something and I was getting letters into the *Liverpool Echo* complaining. I scored six in the next three, I think, and ended up top scorer in the league.

I was playing in a great team, though, that's why. We had Trevor Steven on the right, Kevin Sheedy on the left, Paul Bracewell and Peter Reid in midfield, we were really strong at the back with Neville Southall in goal, and I played up front with Graeme Sharp mostly. It was a fabulous season, but it was tough that we didn't quite manage to win anything as a team. We lost in the FA Cup final and were pipped in the league by Liverpool, even though I felt we were the better side.
PFA: You scored 40 goals in 57 games that season. Did you feel you knew you were going to score going into games?
GL: I never felt like that, I just kept making the runs – that's how I scored goals. It's like mathematics for me, it's all about attacking areas, attacking space. I see [Erling] Haaland do it now, it's the same thing. Eventually the ball will go to you and you've got an easy strike. I never felt like I was a great player or anything – my game improved as I got older and my build-up play was fine – but I was all about the box, really. I never saw myself as a great footballer, but I knew how to score goals.
PFA: You then moved to Barcelona the following season.
GL: I was slightly bewildered that I was called in one day and Howard Kendall told me that they'd accepted an offer from Barcelona for me. It was kind of mixed emotions. Firstly, that they'd accepted an offer when I'd had such a good season. But secondly, I was so flattered that it was Barcelona and obviously that's where the superstars in world football always went to, Real Madrid and Barcelona. So, then I'm thinking, you know, this is amazing.
PFA: You had your fair share of success there, winning the Copa del Rey. Where does that rank for you?
GL: We won the Copa del Rey and the European Cup Winners' Cup, which was fabulous. I loved my time at Barcelona, the first two years were amazing.
PFA: Then you went to Spurs, where you won the FA Cup – your first trophy in English football. That must be up there in your list of achievements?
GL: It's right up there. To win the FA Cup, it's the trophy that you grew up with as a kid – certainly, if you're my age, that's the one. And obviously I look a bit like it! But yeah, it was amazing.
PFA: Do you ever get time to reflect on everything that you achieved in your playing career, now you're an established broadcaster?
GL: Yeah, I don't sit there thinking, "I've done this", but I feel incredibly fortunate in my life, genuinely. I always say that "I was born to be in the box not on the box", but I managed to learn the trade and to get through the early years, and now I'm doing something that I love, and that's talking about football. I can't play it anymore but it's the second-best job – playing is the best.

Below | Lineker wins an aerial battle with Manchester United's Paul McGrath in the 1985 Charity Shield

Opposite | The Everton man pictured before the Division One match against Aston Villa at Villa Park, 1985

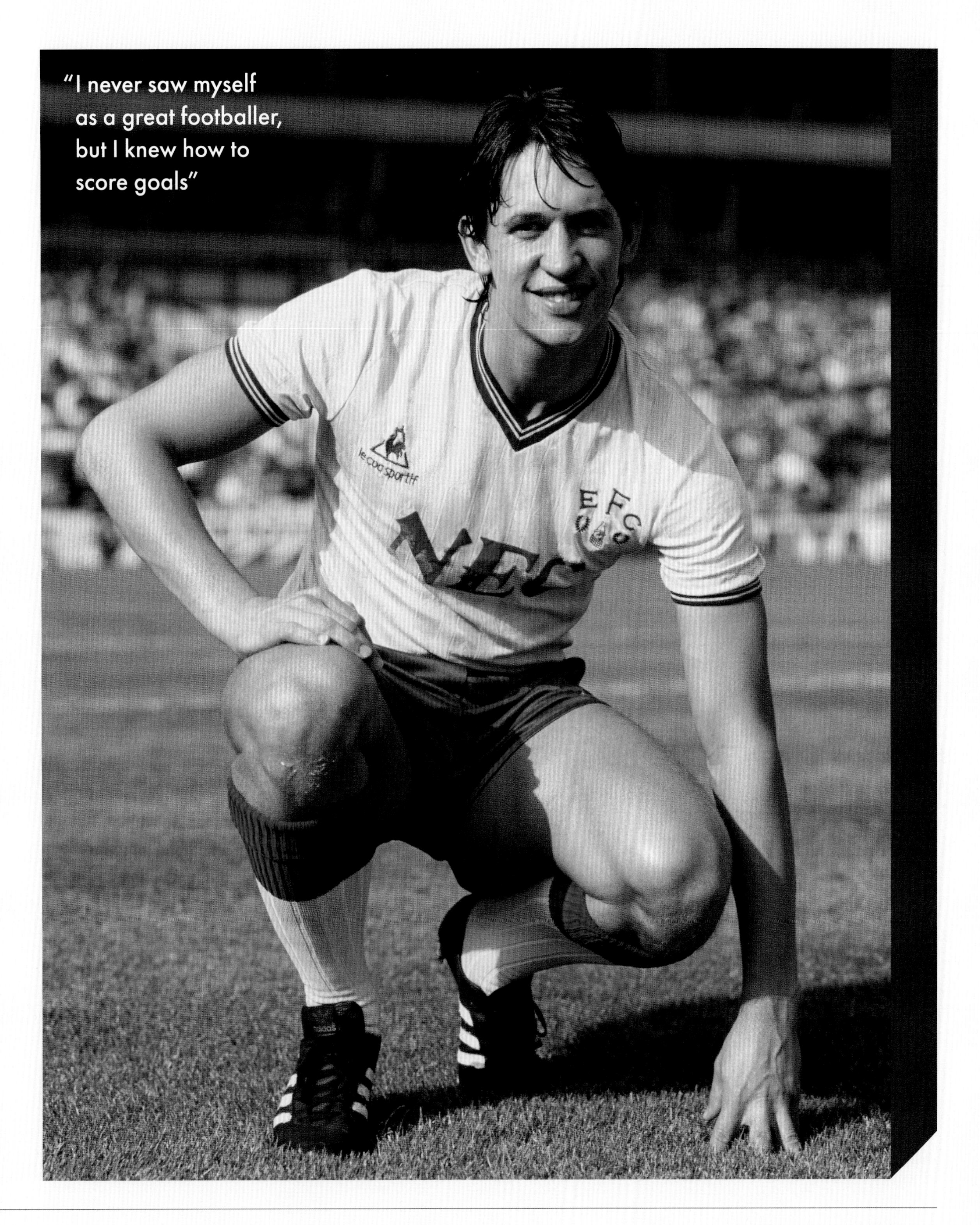

"I never saw myself as a great footballer, but I knew how to score goals"

YOUNG PLAYER OF THE YEAR

Tony Cottee

Tony Cottee was the local darling of West Ham's Boys of 86. Without the thunder-thighed PFA Young Player of the Year's 26 goals, a club-best third-placed First Division finish would have been impossible.

The Irons recovered from a slow start to post a record 18-game unbeaten run from late-August to Boxing Day that put them in the title mix. The diminutive Cottee and summer signing Frank McAvennie formed a deadly strike partnership, the duo scoring in all bar two of those fixtures, tallying 54 in all competitions by the end of the season.

"For probably the only time in my career," the Hammer of the Year later recalled, "I went into games truly believing that we'd win and I'd score."

Cottee's brace in a 4–0 defeat of Chelsea at Stamford Bridge was the highlight of 11 wins in 13 games from mid-March as the Irons took champions Liverpool to the final Saturday of the season. Still beloved in the East End.

Above | Cottee scored the opener in the Irons' 2–1 win against Tottenham at Upton Park in March 1986

MERIT AWARD

England World Cup squad 1966

Sir Geoff Hurst's final hat-trick. The "Russian" linesman. Dancing like Nobby Stiles. Pickles the dog. Bobby Moore cradling the Jules Rimet trophy, perched on his teammates' exultant shoulders.

English football's summer of love was just 20 years old when the PFA awarded the entire 1966 World Cup-winning squad its prestigious Merit Award, but so pervasive are that tournament's memories they have entered a shared consciousness. Crucially, the association chose to credit the collective for achieving immortality – it took FIFA until 2009 to give medals to all 22 players.

Manager Sir Alf Ramsey asked for two months' dedication at what his players came to call their "Stalag Lilleshall" training base. Jimmy Armfield, Ron Springett, Peter Bonetti, Gerry Byrne, Ron Flowers, Norman Hunter and George Eastham may not have played a minute but each set standards to help Ramsey's Wingless Wonders become the tournament's fittest team.

The squad bonded over nightly trips to the cinema and cricket practice. "It was circumspect cricket," recalled Sir Bobby Charlton, "there were no beamers and bouncers and very few heroics in the slips – but it was relaxing."

So relaxing that on the morning of 30 July 1966, Stiles went to mass as normal. Charlton and Ray Wilson went shopping. In the afternoon, they won the World Cup. They think it's all over? Never.

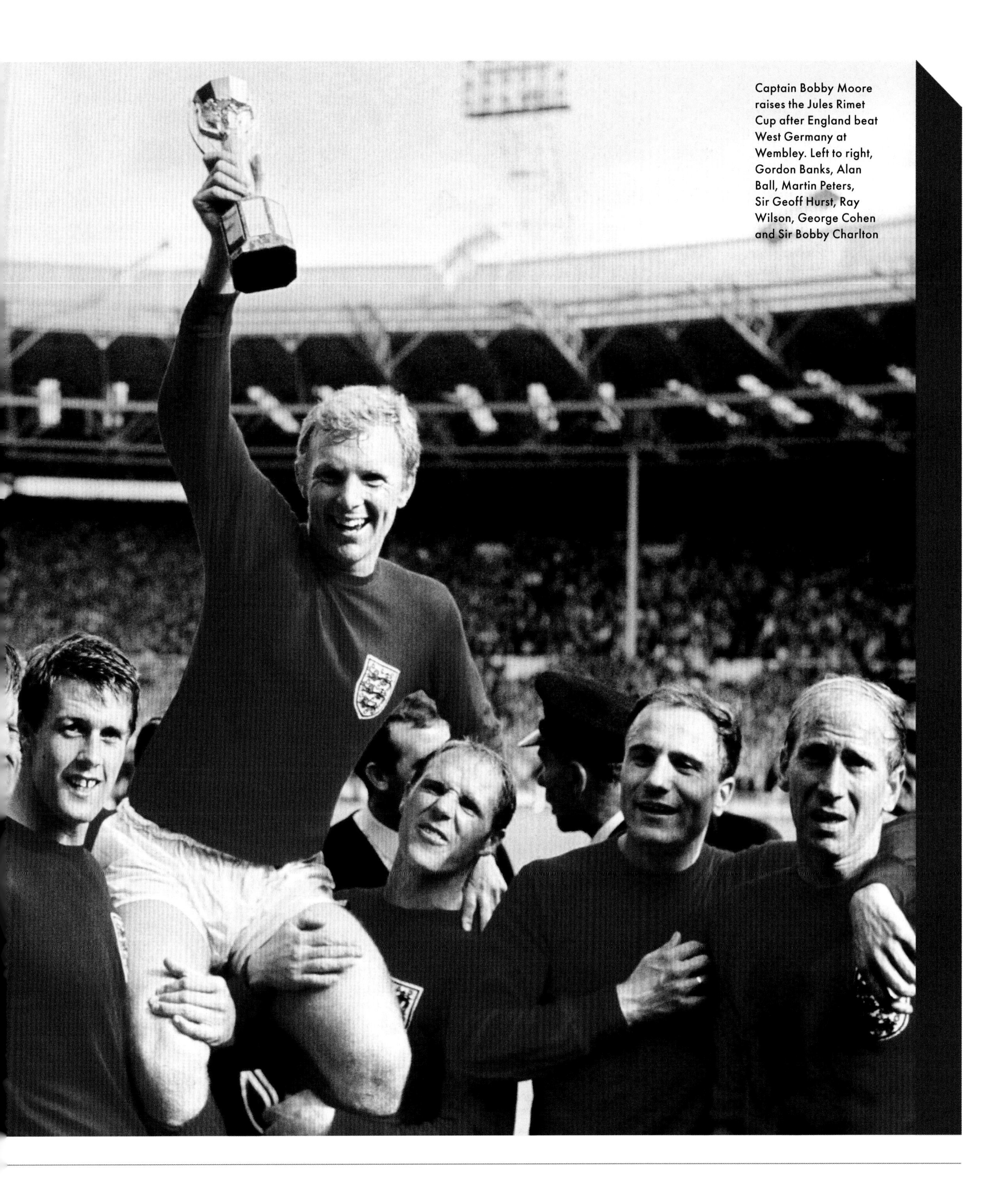

Captain Bobby Moore raises the Jules Rimet Cup after England beat West Germany at Wembley. Left to right, Gordon Banks, Alan Ball, Martin Peters, Sir Geoff Hurst, Ray Wilson, George Cohen and Sir Bobby Charlton

PLAYERS' PLAYER OF THE YEAR

Clive Allen

THE SPURS MARKSMAN SCORED AN INCREDIBLE 49 GOALS IN ALL COMPETITIONS DURING THE 1986/87 SEASON

"Clive Allen!" screamed commentator John Motson as the Tottenham Hotspur striker opened the scoring two minutes into the 1987 FA Cup final. "Would you believe it?"

Motty was incredulous not at Allen finding the net, but because the 25-year-old's near-post header was a 49th goal in all competitions of a lethal 1986/87 season. Only the great Dixie Dean, who plundered 65 in 1927/28 for Everton, had ever before struck more in one campaign.

Part of the Allen family dynasty – dad Les won the double for Spurs in 1960/61, younger brother Bradley played for QPR, and cousins Martin and Paul were West Ham regulars – the arch poacher began his career-best campaign with an opening day hat-trick in a 3–0 win at Aston Villa. He later fired 13 goals across November and December alone, and came alive in the box.

"I don't think anyone had cleaner feet when it comes to getting the ball round the goalkeeper," recalled manager David Pleat.

More impressive still, Allen was playing up front on his own. Villa wide man Steve Hodge's December arrival provided the final piece of Pleat's uber-creative five-man midfield with Glenn Hoddle, Ossie Ardiles, Chris Waddle and Allen's cousin Paul, as Spurs chased a domestic treble.

Though Allen's near-half-century made him the fifth man to win the PFA Player of the Year and Football Writers' Association award in the same season, they ended the campaign trophyless. Knocked out of the League Cup in a semi-final replay by North London rivals Arsenal – a competition in which Allen struck a record 12 – Spurs' league form dipped before losing the FA Cup final to Coventry 3–2, despite that early Allen opener. Nico Claesen and Chris Waddle were the only other Tottenham players to register double figures as a potential treble fell apart.

Allen's annus mirabilis featured three hat-tricks, nine braces and remains a modern goalscoring yardstick. "It is instinct more than anything," he later explained. "You can't teach people when and where to go in the penalty area."

Allen playing against Aston Villa on the opening day fixture, 1986

MERIT AWARD

Sir Stanley Matthews

Not even Stan Mortensen's FA Cup final hat-trick in Blackpool's 4–3 comeback win against Bolton – the only showpiece treble beneath Wembley's famous Twin Towers – could prevent 1953 becoming "the Matthews final".

Sir Stanley Matthews inspired the Tangerines from 3–1 down with 22 minutes left, the Wizard of the Dribble's jinking run and low cross for Bill Perry's injury-time winner one of the great FA Cup moments. Twice a beaten finalist, 38-year-old Matthews finally had his first winner's medal.

The maiden Ballon d'Or winner in 1956 as Blackpool nearly won an improbable First Division title, he was, said three-time World Cup winner Pelé, "the man who taught us the way football should be played". Thirty years on from becoming England's oldest international – aged 42 years and 104 days in May 1957 against Denmark – Matthews received the PFA Merit Award in recognition of a three-decade career on the pitch in which he was the first footballer to be knighted while still a player.

Above | Matthews makes his 600th league appearance at Bloomfield Road, 1959

YOUNG PLAYER OF THE YEAR

Tony Adams

Right | Adams on the ball at Highbury, 1986

Arsenal had won just one trophy in 16 seasons before a 19-year-old Tony Adams broke into the first team in 1986/87. Nine months later, he was lifting the League Cup at Wembley, the first of ten major honours that would follow before his 2002 retirement.

Coincidence? No chance. The gritty centre back featured in every one of the Gunners' 42 league games in 1986/87 as George Graham's increasingly parsimonious side conceded just 35 times to finish fourth in the First Division, their best return for six seasons. The come-from-behind League Cup final defeat of Liverpool also served notice of the number six's leadership and contagious will to win.

Adams made his senior England debut that February – former Three Lions captain Billy Wright presented him with his PFA Young Player of the Year award two months later – and would become Gunners captain within a year, aged just 21. Mr Arsenal was the physical embodiment of the club for much of the next decade and a half.

PLAYERS' PLAYER OF THE YEAR

John Barnes

IN HIS FIRST SEASON AT LIVERPOOL, THE SCINTILLATING WINGER WAS NAMED PLAYERS' PLAYER OF THE YEAR, REGISTERING 17 GOALS AND 18 ASSISTS IN ALL COMPETITIONS

PFA: You were the first black player to win Players' Player of the Year. What's your standout memory from that year?
John Barnes: My standout memory of that season – my first at Liverpool – was really just what a great team it was. We had six or seven in the team of the year, which is a great season for the team. As much as I may have been given the award, five or six of those players could have won it.
PFA: How did you find the transition to that team of superstars?
JB: It wasn't that difficult because Liverpool players didn't see themselves as superstars, the fans did. Peter Beardsley came as well, as the most expensive signing of that particular time, which helped me, and Ray Houghton came as well. So I wasn't the only new player.
PFA: You chipped in with 15 league goals that season, did you feel like you were having a really good year?
JB: Well, it's not so much from the scoring point of view because I was there to create chances for John Aldridge, which is what I did. The goals for me were a bonus. You know, the way I played was completely different to the way the wide players play now.
PFA: What motivated you, especially in the season when you won the PFA award?
JB: What motivated me was what motivated me ever since I was a young boy playing football in Jamaica – the way my dad brought me up in terms of maximising potential by your effort and your commitment and responsibility to the team and to yourself. Unfortunately, not so much with the schoolwork, but with the sport. So when I went to Watford, Graham Taylor espoused those virtues and values and coming to Liverpool it was the same thing about the effort, the effort that you put into training every day, which means that when you play on a Saturday, it all comes together. My motivation was to try to do as well as I could.
PFA: Is there a standout moment for you from that season?
JB: In fact, the standout moment for that season was the loss against Wimbledon in the cup final, because we just thought, "We're going to do the double". Not that we went into that game with any complacency whatsoever, Wimbledon were a good side.

When we played well and won matches, we never got carried away and made a song and dance of it. Ronnie Moran, as soon as the game's over, he's going "We've got another game next week". While you may think a standout moment is when I score a great goal or we won a great match or whatever, as soon as the game was finished it was, "That's gone, forget about that". So, there weren't any standout moments apart from the cup final.
PFA: Of all the great moments – winning the league, winning the trophy – the standout moment is the game you lost, that says a lot about your mindset.
JB: Well, that's a Liverpool mindset. I remember when we won the league that year, we came in and I expected a huge celebration, a huge party ... Ronnie Moran had the medals in a plastic bag, he put them on the table and all he said was, "Pre-season training, July 7th". If we'd then had the biggest party and wallowed in how great we are, we'd forget that the most important thing about success is the repetition. How do you keep that hunger for that repetition?

If all of a sudden, we think, "We're great, we're the league champions", that's an easy attitude to have when you've won, what about when you've lost? The next year we lost the league against Arsenal in the last game of the season. How devastated are we gonna be? Ronnie Moran came in, losers' medals on the table, all he said was "Pre-season training, July 7th." We didn't wallow in self-pity and despair or we'd never have raised ourselves to win the league like we did the following year. You do as well as you can, give 100 per cent, if you win, you win, if you lose, you lose. That was a big lesson I learnt in terms of how to really treat what success is.

Below | A familiar sight for the Anfield faithful, John Barnes gliding down the wing, 1988

Opposite | Barnes pictured with his Players' Player of the Year trophy, 1988

"When we played well and won matches, we never got carried away and made a song and dance of it"

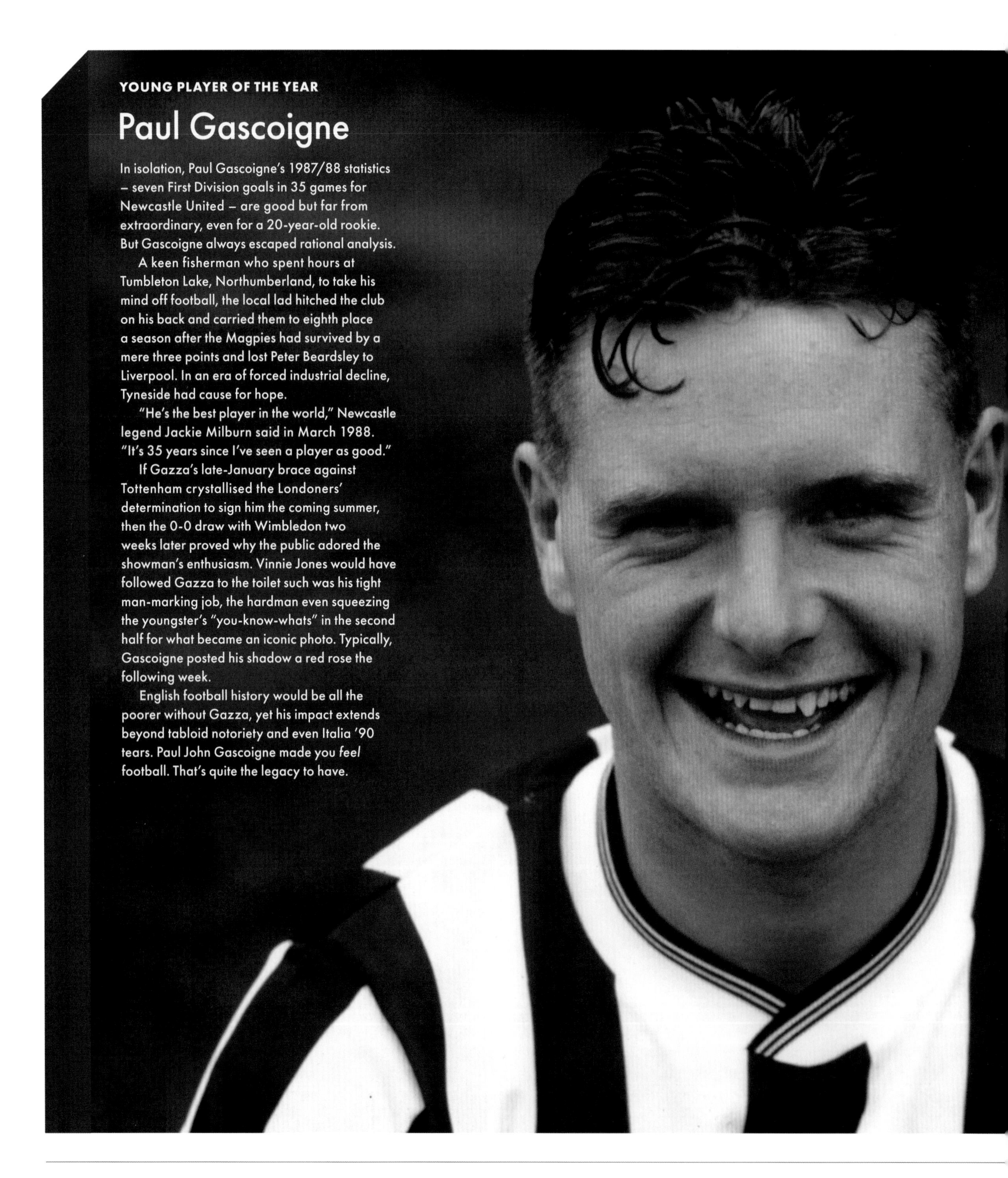

YOUNG PLAYER OF THE YEAR

Paul Gascoigne

In isolation, Paul Gascoigne's 1987/88 statistics – seven First Division goals in 35 games for Newcastle United – are good but far from extraordinary, even for a 20-year-old rookie. But Gascoigne always escaped rational analysis.

A keen fisherman who spent hours at Tumbleton Lake, Northumberland, to take his mind off football, the local lad hitched the club on his back and carried them to eighth place a season after the Magpies had survived by a mere three points and lost Peter Beardsley to Liverpool. In an era of forced industrial decline, Tyneside had cause for hope.

"He's the best player in the world," Newcastle legend Jackie Milburn said in March 1988. "It's 35 years since I've seen a player as good."

If Gazza's late-January brace against Tottenham crystallised the Londoners' determination to sign him the coming summer, then the 0-0 draw with Wimbledon two weeks later proved why the public adored the showman's enthusiasm. Vinnie Jones would have followed Gazza to the toilet such was his tight man-marking job, the hardman even squeezing the youngster's "you-know-whats" in the second half for what became an iconic photo. Typically, Gascoigne posted his shadow a red rose the following week.

English football history would be all the poorer without Gazza, yet his impact extends beyond tabloid notoriety and even Italia '90 tears. Paul John Gascoigne made you *feel* football. That's quite the legacy to have.

Gazza in pre-season training at Benwell, 1987

MERIT AWARD

Billy Bonds

If West Ham legend Sir Trevor Brooking calls you "the best signing in the club's history" then you've probably done alright. That a 41-year-old Billy Bonds made 24 Irons appearances in 1987/88 – his 21st and final season for the club – was testament to the talisman's longevity and willingness to bleed claret and blue, four years after reversing a brief first retirement to ease an injury crisis at the club.

Awarded an MBE in January 1988 and the PFA's Merit Award a few months after that, Bonds's 799th club outing in a 2–1 April defeat at Southampton set club appearance and age records that are yet to be beaten. A family man, ornithologist and voracious Thomas Hardy reader, Bonzo transformed into a warrior on the pitch.

"I honestly enjoyed winning a good, hard tackle just as much as supplying a precise pass or scoring a goal," the two-time FA Cup-winning captain once said. A true Irons icon.

Below | A 37-year-old Billy Bonds, West Ham captain, 1984

PLAYERS' PLAYER OF THE YEAR

Mark Hughes

MANCHESTER UNITED'S PRODIGAL SON ANNOUNCED HIS RETURN FROM SPELLS AT BARCELONA AND BAYERN MUNICH BY BECOMING THE CLUB'S TOP SCORER IN THE 1988/89 SEASON

PFA: Hi Mark. You're in a very exclusive club of players who have won the Players' Player award twice – in fact, you were the first to do it. Do you know the names of the others?
Mark Hughes: You're going to have to educate me.
PFA: Alan Shearer, Thierry Henry, Cristiano Ronaldo, Kevin De Bruyne and Mo Salah. Not a bad group to be in?
MH: Those names are quite distinguished in football, so yeah, I'll take my place among them!
PFA: When you look at everything you won – two Premier Leagues, four FA Cups, three league cups – where does winning the PFA award sit for you?
MH: It's a huge award. In football terms, being voted by your peers is really special. When I came back to United from my travels to Barcelona and Bayern Munich it was important that I made an impression. To win it when I first came back was important to me because it showed that people understood that maybe before I went I was a good player, but I came back a better player.
PFA: You came back to a quite different Manchester United and to Sir Alex Ferguson. How had it changed from your first spell with the club?
MH: Yeah, there was a change in discipline maybe. Certainly, from my memory prior to going abroad it was, at times, a little bit lax. But I think that was typical of football in that day and age. But yeah, certainly when I came back, there was a distinct difference in terms of levels and how you were expected to work and represent the club. I liked that because I'd been exposed to it in Munich, where they were quite disciplined, as you would imagine. They were quite ahead of the game in those days. A lot of the stuff that we take for granted now in terms of sports science, they were very much at the forefront of that, so I learnt a lot while I was away.
PFA: What changed for you to come back and have the impact you had?
MH: I don't think I approached the game any differently, it was just that I had probably grown up to a certain extent. I'd got married, had children at that point and I just had a different outlook on my professional work. Clearly that helped me to have a really good season. The team at that point was changing and it was the start of the Sir Alex era. At times we didn't play as well as we felt we should or as well as Sir Alex thought we should, but it was a process that we were all going through and to be at the start, that was really important.

Right | Hughes hits a trademark scissor kick, watched by Spurs's Paul Gascoigne and Terry Fenwick, 1988

Opposite | The Welshman at Old Trafford, 1988

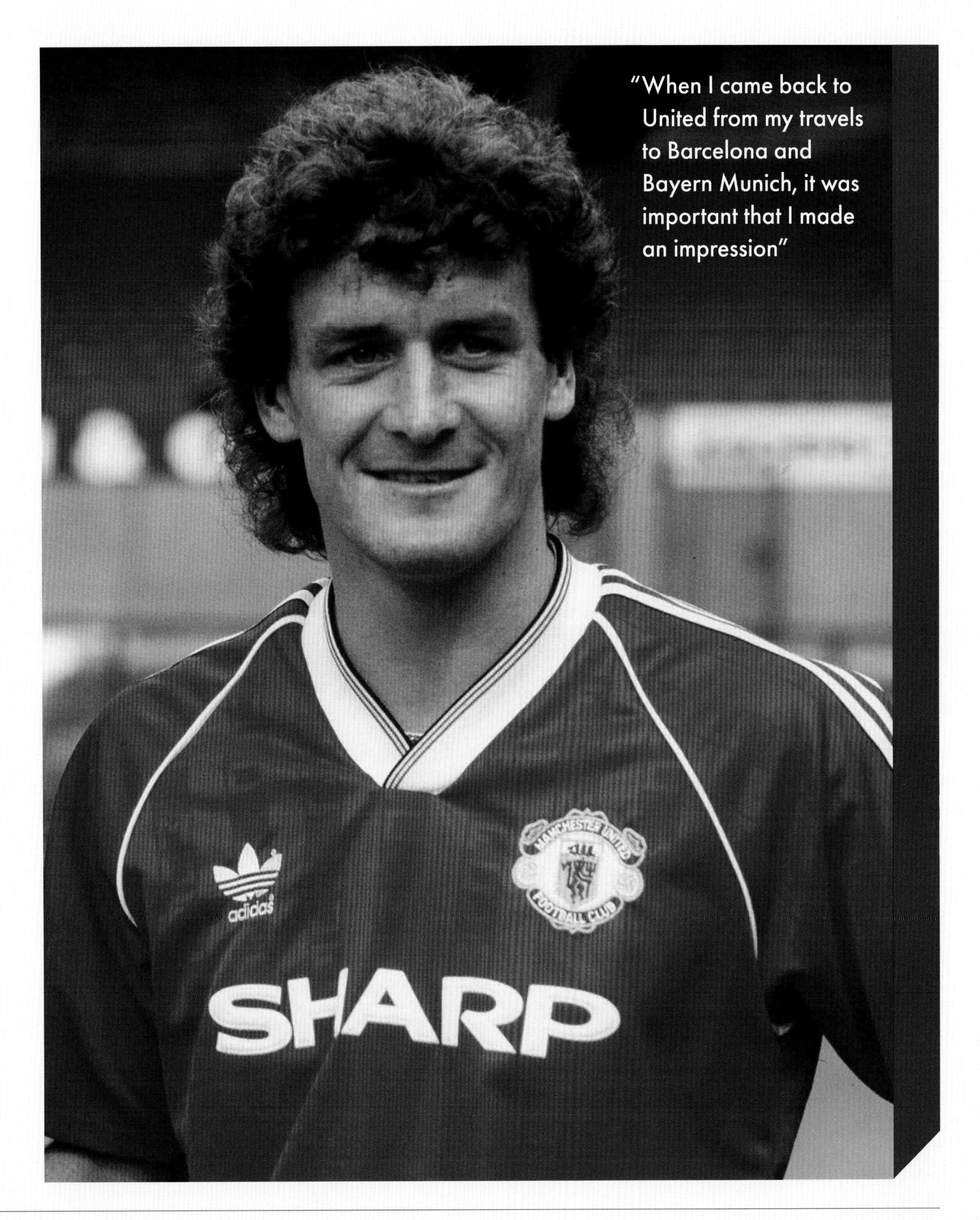

"When I came back to United from my travels to Barcelona and Bayern Munich, it was important that I made an impression"

1988|89

YOUNG PLAYER OF THE YEAR

Paul Merson

In a season defined by Anfield, Brian Moore's "and it's up for grabs now" commentary and Michael Thomas's 91st-minute title winner, Paul Merson enjoyed his breakthrough Arsenal campaign. The 20-year-old homegrown attacker's ten league goals and impish brilliance from either flank confirmed him as a fan favourite for the 16/1 championship outsiders.

Only 23-goal top scorer Alan Smith found the net more times than Merson and the pair's understanding shone throughout. A run of five goals in six games around the turn of the year, featuring a well-taken strike in the North London derby against Tottenham to mark the unveiling of a new Highbury clock, provided the ballast for *that* late 2–0 win at Liverpool to seal the best finish to an English league season ever. Sorry, Sergio.

Equally familiar as a pundit nowadays, the young Londoner provided the artistic flourish in George Graham's team of title winners.

Above | Merson celebrates the Gunners' 5–0 defeat of Norwich City, 1989

MERIT AWARD

Nat Lofthouse

The bravest footballer to lace up a pair of boots, Nat Lofthouse is so synonymous with Bolton Wanderers that the Trotters fan, player, captain, trainer, scout, caretaker manager, manager and president remains the only person to have a stand named in their honour at any of the club's three grounds.

Knocked out by an elbow in scoring the winner in England's 3-2 victory against Austria in May 1952, the Lion of Vienna bagged 30 goals in 33 internationals. "I never saw the ball enter the net," he later recalled, "but they tell me it was the goal of my life."

The fearless Lofthouse's aerial prowess delivered a record 285 goals for his only club, including two to clinch the 1958 FA Cup final, five years after he had scored in every round of the competition. Receiving the PFA Merit Award in 1988 to mark Lofthouse's 50th year in football was a fitting tribute to a Bolton icon – no other word does him justice.

Above | Lofthouse in his beloved Bolton shirt playing against Chelsea, 1955

PLAYERS' PLAYER OF THE YEAR

David Platt

THE MIDFIELD MAESTRO HAD THE SEASON OF HIS LIFE IN 1989/90, SCORING 24 GOALS AND ANNOUNCING HIMSELF TO THE WORLD AT ITALIA '90

There is a pre-destination to some footballers making it, while others have to sweat blood to force their way into the elite. For David Platt, the road to success was as much about hard work as it was raw talent.

Chest puffed out, the box-to-box midfielder's drive, determination and preternatural self-belief took him from amateur pitches as a teenager straight to Manchester United, before Ron Atkinson sold his protégé to Fourth Division Crewe Alexandra in February 1985. "When you get an England cap," Atkinson said, "remember what I told you. Just keep working hard. I've always liked you because you worked hard."

Platt *knew* he'd make it. He proved Atkinson right after just four-and-a-half years, making his England debut in November 1989 against Italy aged 23, his case inevitable. He had struck nine times in his first 15 league appearances of 1989/90 for Aston Villa, a superb brace in a 6–2 demolition of Everton channelling both his underrated aerial ability and quick feet in tight areas.

A 3–0 Boxing Day defeat of Manchester United featured another Platt masterclass. Before laying on the assist for Villa's third, the ex-Red Devil sat down goalkeeper Jim Leighton for his 12th of the season as Graham Taylor's pulverising side began a run of seven straight wins. Platt scored in five.

Top by late February, Villa won just five of their last 13 games to finish runners-up to Liverpool, but Platt ended the season with 19 league goals from midfield, the PFA Player of the Year award and a place in England's Italia '90 squad. His memorable 119th-minute last 16 volley against Belgium – allowing Paul Gascoigne's free-kick to drop over his shoulder – was testament to the industriousness that would later flourish with Bari, Juventus and Sampdoria during Serie A's 1990s pre-eminence.

"I worked hard on practising overhead kicks and volleys in training at Aston Villa," he said. "I had an eye for getting on the end of that sort of ball and the technical ability to finish those chances off."

David Platt cradles his PFA Players' Player of the Year award

1989|90

YOUNG PLAYER OF THE YEAR

Matthew Le Tissier

In the Catalan city of Terrassa, a 10-year-old fell in love in 1990.

"Our whole house was obsessed with Matthew Le Tissier," Barcelona midfielder Xavi later recalled. "He'd score these sickening, outrageous goals. Every. Single. Week. Incredible."

The four-time Champions League and World Cup winner wasn't alone in his adoration. In a youthful 1989/90 Southampton team that also included a young Rod Wallace and Alan Shearer, Le Tissier was the star. The 21-year-old scored 20 of the Saints' 71 league goals as Chris Nicholl's side finished seventh in the First Division. Only Gary Lineker and John Barnes struck more.

Le God always preferred quality over quantity. An anachronism even in the late 1980s, the Guernsey-born playmaker was, by his own admission, indolent and seldom defended but his velvet touch and innate virtuosity rendered such matters irrelevant.

A January 1990 hat-trick against Norwich, featuring a solo run and finish, then a delicious lob, was the PFA Young Player of the Year in microcosm. Captivating, daring and unique.

Above | Le Tissier with the Young Player of the Year award, 1990

MERIT AWARD

Peter Shilton

Nowhere in football is consistency a more valuable commodity than in goal, where 90 minutes' excellence can be undone by a single moment's hesitation. Peter Shilton's agility, shot stopping and reading of the game were always best-in-class, but it was the durable custodian's single-minded dedication to honing his craft that made him a record breaker.

"He's a perfectionist," said Ray Clemence, Shilton's great international rival and without whom his 125-cap England men's appearance record would be closer to a double century. "It's as simple as that."

Shilton's journey to overtaking Bobby Moore as the Three Lions' top appearance maker began by catching balls he'd throw against his father's grocer's shop in Leicester in the late 1950s. More than three decades later, following two European Cups, a First Division, nine successive appearances in the PFA Team of the Year from 1977/78 and the Hand of God, the 41-year-old Leicester City, Nottingham Forest and Derby County keeper was still putting in hours of graft as England reached the World Cup semi-finals to set up that Three Lions record. At that tournament, he registered his 10th World Cup clean sheet, also a record.

"I've always enjoyed competing," he said after receiving the 1990 PFA Merit Award in recognition of his services to football. "There's no point packing it up if you think you can still do your job."

Nor did he. Shilton continued playing until he appeared in his 1,005th, and final, Football League game in a 2–1 defeat for Leyton Orient against Wigan Athletic in January 1997. He'd earned his retirement, alright.

Shilton makes a crucial save against Tottenham for Nottingham Forest in 1978, almost 20 years before he retired

Hughes with his second Players' Player of the Year award, 1991

PLAYERS' PLAYER OF THE YEAR

Mark Hughes

"He's the most difficult forward in the division. There's not a lot you can do against him, and if he turns you've had it because he's so strong. He doesn't stop for 90 minutes and must be a dream to be in your team."

Tony Gale

Above | Sharpe battles Sheffield Wednesday's Roland Nilsson for the ball in the League Cup final, 1991

YOUNG PLAYER OF THE YEAR

Lee Sharpe

The first of Fergie's Fledglings to take flight, Lee Sharpe provided the inspiration as Manchester United beat Barcelona to lift the 1991 European Cup Winners' Cup, the 19-year-old winger rivalling even post-Italia '90 Paul Gascoigne as English football's most exciting youngster.

Signed from fourth-tier Torquay United in June 1988 aged 17, Sharpe's searing pace and dead-eyed delivery from the left wing in his third Old Trafford season delivered nine goals from 36 starts in all competitions. Three came in the 6–2 League Cup evisceration of Arsenal in November 1990 – one long-range curler, a towering header and a deadly one-on-one finish. Three days later, he scored the only goal at Everton, debuting a strutting celebration that became known as the Sharpey Shuffle. By March 1991, he was a full England international.

"I was flying that year," the PFA Young Player of the Year said. "When I scored that Arsenal hat-trick, it was like I'd achieved my life's ambition."

MERIT AWARD

Tommy Hutchison

Few are the footballers whose careers have spanned four decades. Tommy Hutchison's professional career began in the Scottish Second Division with Alloa Athletic in 1965 and ended more than a quarter of a century later – aged 43 years, five months and 19 days – with his final appearance for Swansea City in March 1991.

A moustachioed winger who came to be known as Mr Magic during an eight-year spell at Coventry City, the 17-cap Scot memorably scored at both ends in the 1981 FA Cup final, his cruel own goal cancelling out a superb first-half header for Manchester City against Tottenham Hotspur. City lost the replay.

A selfless teammate, Hutchison relished his role as the supply line for centre forwards. "Seeing goalscorers scoring goals is my greatest pleasure," he said during his final Swans season.

Hutchison received the PFA Merit Award in March 1991 to honour his status as the Football League's soon-to-be-retired oldest player. Three years later, he was still turning out for seventh-tier Merthyr Tydfil, aged 46.

Above | Hutchison celebrates scoring against Tottenham Hotspur in the FA Cup final, 1981

PLAYERS' PLAYER OF THE YEAR

Gary Pallister

THE CLUB STALWART PROVIDED A TOWERING PRESENCE AT THE BACK FOR MANCHESTER UNITED IN A SEASON OF HIGH POINTS FOR THE CENTRE HALF

At the age of 19, Gary Pallister had only ever played non-league football for tenth-tier Billingham Town, while working 16-hour shifts as a Teesside docker. Less than eight years later, the Manchester United defender's fellow professionals voted him the best player in the country.

A 24-year-old Pallister struggled initially at Old Trafford after a record £2.3 million transfer from boyhood club Middlesbrough but, given a specific weight-training programme to bulk up a lithe frame, he soon developed a borderline impregnable centre back partnership with Steve Bruce. Dolly and Daisy – Sir Alex Ferguson never let on which was which – were the cornerstones of an improving United.

"Pally is a defensive Goliath, has electric pace and can pass the ball," Fergie said. "What more can you ask from a centre half?"

In the 6ft 4in defender's finest individual season he missed just two league fixtures, as United went 12 league games unbeaten at the start of their campaign and swept to the League Cup, beating Brian Clough's Nottingham Forest 1–0 in the final with a Pallister masterclass. He also earned an England recall.

United led the league at Easter – Pallister becoming just the third defender to win the PFA Players' Player of the Year award – but three catastrophic defeats in six days in late-April resulted in Leeds United pipping the Red Devils at the post for their first title since 1974. A 2–0 defeat to Liverpool at Anfield extended United's own title wait to a 26th year.

"Everyone was devastated, we were better than Leeds," Pallister later recalled, "but we knew we were on course to win the title sooner rather than later."

A year later, as it turned out, Pallister scored a memorable free-kick against Blackburn with the title sewn up. United won four of the first five Premier League titles, but 1991/92's ultimate disappointment was their towering centre back's personal best.

"The utmost respect you can get is from your peers," Pallister said, as Sir Trevor Brooking presented his award. "It's the ultimate individual accolade for a footballer."

Pallister playing in United's 5–0 defeat of Luton Town, 1991

MERIT AWARD

Brian Clough

Where would the cult of the modern-day manager be without Brian Howard Clough? Well, football would be deficient to the tune of a certain José Mourinho for starters.

"I have huge respect for what he did," the Special One said in 2015. "I think if Brian Clough was around today, we would get on."

Beneath all the oft-quoted bombast, Clough's true genius lay in an innate ability to inspire. Would it work today? Possibly not, but Old Big 'Ead's stick, allied with assistant Peter Taylor's carrot, dragged provincial Derby County and Nottingham Forest to First Division titles, adding two European Cups and four League Cups with the latter.

Clough received the PFA Merit Award to mark the 20th anniversary of his Derby 1971/72 title win, retiring 12 months later. His legacy will forever endure as the ultimate builder of teams defined by the brilliance of their collective effort.

The best manager to never take charge of England? He was probably in the top one.

Above | Clough with the European Cup in 1980

A pacy young Giggs in an outing against Ipswich Town at Old Trafford, 1992

YOUNG PLAYER OF THE YEAR

Ryan Giggs

The mark of a generation-defining player is the aura of genius that surrounds them. According to teammate and fellow 1991/92 PFA award winner Gary Pallister, a 15-year-old Ryan Giggs was "special, a spindly little pipe cleaner of a footballer running amok" in a Manchester United youth team game.

Sir Alex Ferguson first laid eyes on the Welsh winger two years before that. "He just floated over the ground like a cocker spaniel chasing a piece of silver paper in the wind," the United boss recalled.

The teenage Giggs had the kind of build that made him elusive when standing still. The 18-year-old made 51 appearances in all competitions in a breakthrough season, also captaining United's youngsters to the 1992 FA Youth Cup final.

"A young Giggsy was like a ballet dancer," recalled the Class of '92's coach Eric Harrison. "I had never seen a young player like that and I had seen the Busby Babes."

Giggs was the overwhelming choice for the Young Player of the Year award and became the first person to retain the honour the following season.

PLAYERS' PLAYER OF THE YEAR

Paul McGrath

BACK FROM THE BRINK OF RETIREMENT, ONE OF IRELAND'S GREATEST FOOTBALLERS WAS A ROCK AT THE BACK FOR ASTON VILLA IN 1992/93

The deal was done. In 1989, Paul McGrath was to retire from football. PFA chief executive Gordon Taylor, Sir Alex Ferguson and Manchester United chairman Martin Edwards drew up terms: McGrath would get a pay-off and a testimonial, but his career was over, aged 29.

Four years later, the then Aston Villa centre back was the PFA Players' Player of the Year, receiving the award from Sir Bobby Charlton. How? When it came down to it, the McGrath fire still burned.

The athletic defender transformed from gentle giant into totemic leader on a football pitch. Born into a single-parent Irish family, McGrath spent much of his childhood shunted around various orphanages, using football as his release, before joining Manchester United in 1982, aged 22. Soon a first team regular for Ron Atkinson, he went on to win the 1984/85 FA Cup and pushed Gary Lineker close to the PFA Players' Player of the Year gong the following season.

Though Atkinson's replacement, Ferguson, appreciated the centre back's peerless elegance – "Paul was an exceptionally skilful and stylish defender whose abilities stood comparison with anyone in the game" – the Scot sought to break Old Trafford drinking cliques as McGrath's chronic knee pain caught up with him. The bravery and determination he continues to display in beating his addictions proves McGrath's character has always been his strongest trait.

"He saved me in a way," he later said of Ferguson. "When he let me go to Villa something welled up in me and I wanted to prove I could really play."

McGrath immediately struck up a close bond with Villa physio Jim Walker, who became "more than a friend, a hero" in prolonging the 83-cap Irishman's career by nearly a decade. McGrath didn't train with his teammates in seven years at Villa. "Jim created a regime where I just went in and did ten minutes on the bike each morning and that was about it," McGrath recalled. "Some days I would just have a bath. The games would look after my fitness."

Reunited with Atkinson, McGrath missed just eight minutes of the 1992/93 campaign, the finest of his career. "This is not possible," Atkinson's assistant Dave Sexton said after a November 1–0 win over former club Manchester United. "What McGrath is doing is just not possible with the amount of preparation that he's had."

Thanks to a magisterial McGrath, Villa conceded less than a goal a game – and just four in ten games from 13 February – to top the table with six games of the maiden Premier League season to go, but a late-season surge from United meant defeat to Oldham in their penultimate fixture ended the Villan title challenge. McGrath had the silver lining of the PFA award from his peers.

"Paul had had his problems but he was absolutely awesome that season," recalled Villa winger Tony Daley. "He was the best defender I ever played with. Incredible."

McGrath puts his body on the line for Aston Villa, 1991/92

"Paul was absolutely awesome that season. He was the best defender I ever played with"
Tony Daley

Manchester United, European Cup Winners 1968

MERIT AWARD

Manchester United European Cup squad

Twenty-five years on from becoming the first English team to win a continental crown, Manchester United's 1967/68 European Cup squad were justified winners of the PFA Merit Award.

The Munich air disaster was still fresh in the memory when United emerged onto a verdant Wembley pitch in May 1968. Manager Sir Matt Busby, defender Bill Foulkes and captain Sir Bobby Charlton had all survived the crash a decade earlier and the whole country was behind United to win Old Big Ears.

Though Charlton and the impish George Best scored three of United's goals in the 4–1 defeat of Benfica, with injured Holy Trinity member Denis Law absent, this was a squad effort. Brian Kidd struck on what was his 19th birthday, while unheralded left-winger John Aston's lung-bursting dynamism earned him man of the match.

"I laid plans for coping with Best and Charlton and the other stars," Eagles boss Otto Glória admitted at full time, "but nobody warned me about this boy Aston."

Above | Giggs shows off his second successive Young Player of the Year award, 1992

YOUNG PLAYER OF THE YEAR

Ryan Giggs

"When Ryan runs, he runs like the wind. You can't hear him he was that light on his feet. He has that natural body swerve, that way with a ball only the great players have got. He was always going to be a superstar. It comes from within – that fire in your belly that you still want to be the best. It's a very rare attribute"

Steve Bruce

Eusébio poses for a photograph in his Benfica home kit, 1970

MERIT AWARD

Eusébio

In October 1960, Benfica manager Béla Guttmann went into a Lisbon barber shop and happened upon an old friend. José Carlos Bauer waxed lyrical about an 18-year-old forward, who could already run the 100m in under 11 seconds, he'd recently seen playing in Portuguese East Africa (present-day Mozambique). A week later, Guttmann flew to watch the prodigy, who had a middleweight boxer's physique and a shot as fierce as a Sugar Ray Robinson hook.

Eusébio da Silva Ferreira was worth every second's effort. The Black Pearl scored a record 727 times in 715 Benfica appearances, winning 11 Primeira Ligas, the 1961/62 European Cup and the 1966 World Cup Golden Boot for Portugal. The prototype for the multi-functional centre forward, the 1965 Ballon d'Or winner could do everything.

A confirmed Anglophile, it was fitting that Eusébio received a PFA Merit Award alongside Manchester United's 1968 European Cup winners. In the last minute of normal time, the score locked at 1–1, he sportingly applauded Alex Stepney for the United keeper's save, despite the personal cost.

"I clapped because it was a great save," he later said. "To miss that chance, right at the end... We would have won the European Cup. Instead, it was one of the blackest days in my life as a footballer."

The three standing ovations Eusébio received in picking up the PFA award were testament to his universal legacy.

A healthy mindset

MENTAL HEALTH AWARENESS AND SUPPORT HAVE IMPROVED IMMEASURABLY IN THE SPORT OVER RECENT YEARS AND THE PFA IS AT THE FOREFRONT OF THAT CHANGE FOR THE BETTER, AS DIRECTOR OF PLAYER WELLBEING DR MICHAEL BENNETT EXPLAINS

Dr Michael Bennett, Director of Player Wellbeing

The year 2011 was a watershed moment in football's attitude towards player wellbeing. Gary Speed's untimely death that November put mental health awareness front and centre as football's biggest taboo had its sticking plaster definitively ripped off.

"Speed, who had had such a fantastic playing career and was managing his country, taking his own life made players question their own wellbeing," says Dr Michael Bennett, the PFA's Director of Player Wellbeing. "I'm a former professional footballer and have experienced the emotional rollercoaster of football. When I was playing in the '90s, I never felt there was any emotional support available in the way that there are first-class services for physical injuries. If you have a mental wellbeing issue you should be classed as 'injured' and treated the same way as a physical injury.

"The PFA is independent. We're not part of the football club. Players may not be comfortable talking at their clubs, with staff associated with their employers, but we're private and confidential, non-judgemental and empathetic."

A winger for Charlton Athletic, Brentford and Wimbledon, among others, Bennett qualified as a psychotherapist in 2004. He set up the PFA's wellbeing department in 2011, four years after joining the players' union's education division, and his whole department's lived experiences have played a crucial role in breaking down the stigma that surrounds footballers talking about mental wellbeing.

"Counselling meant 'problems' and players didn't want to associate with that. The whole subject was taboo," he says. "Once you get in front of players, with the catalyst being Clarke Carlisle, Leon McKenzie, Chris Kirkland, Stephen Caulker and more talking about their mental health issues and experiences, and players hear those stories it makes them understand more about what mental wellbeing looks like and how it impacts them."

As many as 600 players a season access the service, with more than 7,000 therapy sessions delivered. Crucial to the uptick has been the introduction of PFA mental wellbeing workshops taken to every Premier League, EFL and WSL club, U23 squads and academies since 2017 to outline what Bennett calls "industry hazards". These could be a long-term injury, a new manager or social media abuse, any of which could provoke a deterioration in a player's mental wellbeing. Post-session surveys help identify any players who need to access the service.

"Players can recognise 'oh, that's me'," says Bennett. "We show them the service's process: they can call, email, WhatsApp or contact us on social media. We listen, have a triage session, then pair the player with one of the 270 therapists nationwide that we access through our partnership with Sporting Chance.

By getting in front of the players and giving them this first-hand information, we've seen the number of members accessing the service increase year on year.

"The more workshops we run, the more members come forward. We currently do one workshop a season but we want to be present on a more regular basis so players know the face of their PFA wellbeing representative and feel more comfortable about engaging with the issues they may be facing. The personal touch always works, so we want to grow the department to be more region-specific. In the last two years, it's been clubs contacting us to arrange the workshops, with most Premier League clubs wanting their first team to undertake them, too."

The department also provides the Survivor Support Advocate service, which offers mental wellbeing support for those who have experienced sexual, racist or any sort of abuse, and has partnered with Sporting Chance since 2000 to provide residential care for players experiencing addiction issues. Working with players, clubs, club staff and governing bodies nationwide, the PFA also hosted the annual 'INJURED' conference from 2017 to 2019 to ensure collaboration.

"We've been at the forefront of the wellbeing agenda for some time now and it is other organisations or stakeholders who are trying to implement what we have in place for our members. We offer a gold standard," says Bennett. "We're at the cutting edge – proactive rather than reactive. We reach out to experts in the mental health field, away from the football bubble, to find out what best practice should look like.

"From a wellbeing perspective, we can't do things under the radar. Members need to know how to access our services, it's part of their membership and once you're a member you have that support for life. You might not need to use the services now, or in six months', two years' or ten years' time, but you need to know they exist.

"I get more pleasure from the work I do now than I ever did when playing football. I had a decent football career, but to be able help an individual who's going through a difficult situation and feels they're alone and you help bring them through it is amazing."

Opposite, clockwise from top | Tributes to former Leeds United player Gary Speed adorn the front of Elland Road; Steven Caulker and Chris Kirkland, who have both helped alter perceptions of mental wellbeing in the game

"We're at the cutting edge. We reach out to experts in the mental health field, away from the football bubble, to find out what best practice should look like"

Dr Michael Bennett

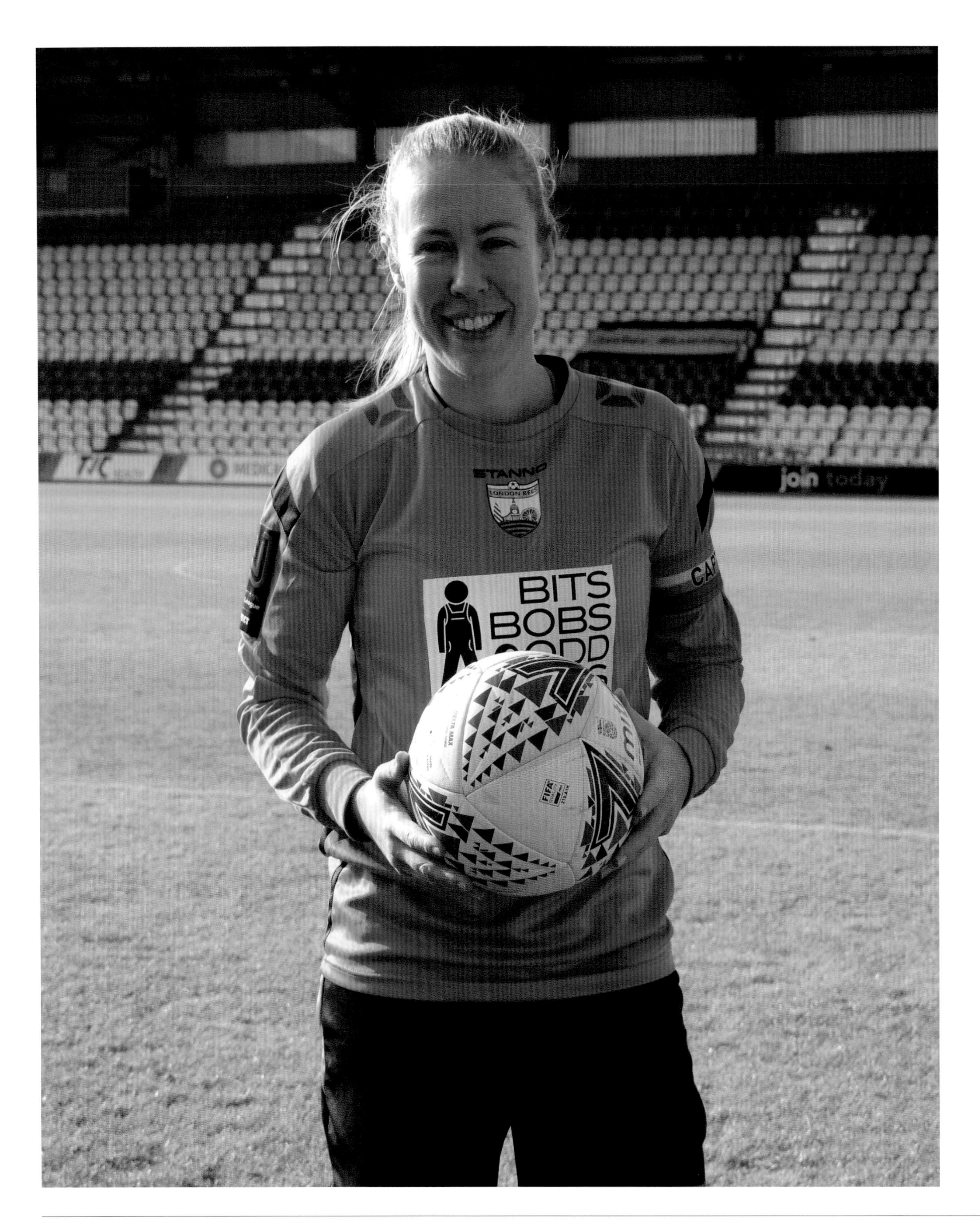
STANNO
LONDON BEES
BITS
BOBS
join today

A meeting of minds

THE NATIONAL BRAIN APPEAL AIMS TO IMPROVE OUTCOMES FOR PEOPLE WITH NEUROLOGICAL CONDITIONS, AND ITS WORK IS PROVING A LIFE-SAVER

www.nationalbrainappeal.org

When former Crystal Palace footballer Ashleigh Goddard (opposite) was knocked out during a match in 2019, a routine scan at the National Hospital for Neurology and Neurosurgery revealed she had an arteriovenous malformation (AVM) and an aneurysm. During life-saving treatment, she suffered a stroke. This could have meant the end of her football career, but Ashleigh was able to resume playing following rehabilitation, even organising a charity match for The National Brain Appeal, the National Hospital's dedicated charity, raising £8,000.

"My neurosurgeon explained that an aneurysm is a bulge in a blood vessel caused by a weakness in the blood vessel wall and that it was highly likely to burst at some point," says Ashleigh. "She said it could be fatal or cause life-changing disability. I feel so lucky that the chain of events following my head injury led doctors to discover this. One of the senior nurses said to me that being young, and if I put effort into rehabilitation, I would be more likely to recover. I wanted to get back to playing football and I celebrated every little win when it came to getting my movement back. The more progress I saw, the harder I worked."

Ashleigh, now captain of the London Bees, is one of several high-profile footballers to have suffered brain-related injuries, putting them among the one in six of the population affected by neurological conditions such as strokes, multiple sclerosis, brain cancer, epilepsy, Parkinson's disease and dementia. The National Brain Appeal is the only charity dedicated to supporting projects for people with all types of neurological conditions, investing in research, innovative treatments and world class facilities at the National Hospital for Neurology and Neurosurgery, and the UCL Institute of Neurology, known collectively as Queen Square.

"We fund what the NHS cannot," says the charity's CEO, Theresa Dauncey (above right). "That means bringing new initiatives to the fore and enabling things that might not otherwise have happened or take a long time to happen. It might be a piece of equipment or a big capital project. We also have an Innovation Fund and a Small Acorns fund for smaller projects. We get interesting ideas through that and have funded more than 140 of those smaller initiatives."

The National Brain Appeal is currently funding two major capital projects: a patient research hub, stem cell facility and two MRI scanners at the new UCL Neuroscience Centre, and a Rare Dementia Support

Centre, part of the UCL Queen Square Institute of Neurology. It has pledged to raise £7 million for each of these over the next few years. The charity raises around £4 million a year but plans to increase this to £15 million to ensure that Queen Square continues to be a world leader in treating neurological conditions. Essential support for the charity has come from within the football community, including from Junior Agogo, the Nottingham Forest footballer who suffered a stroke at 35, before passing away in 2019, aged 40, and comedian David Baddiel, whose father experienced a rare form of dementia.

"One in six people have a neurological condition, which is pretty much two members of every football team," says Theresa. "There are some conditions where, sadly, you will never get a good outcome, but more treatments are developed all the time. Increasingly, there are many more positive stories, such as Ashleigh's – conditions that can be cured or managed, or from which there is full recovery – and the more funding we get, the more solutions we can come up with to help future patients."

Fit for the future

HAVING ALREADY TRANSFORMED THE LIVES OF COUNTLESS LEEDS RESIDENTS, THE HAMARA HEALTHY LIVING CENTRE IS EXPANDING ITS SPORT FACILITIES

www.hamara.org.uk

From the start, when it consisted of two members of staff working in a single office, the Hamara Healthy Living Centre has grown to become the largest ethnic-minority organisation in Leeds' voluntary and community sector.

In those early days, the centre worked on a single project to improve the lives of elderly people. It now employs more than 30 staff, working on projects to help children, older people, those with learning disabilities and others in the Leeds area looking for education and training opportunities, as well as delivering healthy-living projects.

Hamara is an Urdu term that means "ours", reflecting the founding principle that the organisation belongs to its community. Before embarking on any new projects, the team asks residents what they need. "We have come a long way," says Project Lead Arnie Sajad. "From our flagship building alone, more than 10,000 people in our community access this centre per year and, since the pandemic, Hamara has supported more than 100,000 individuals through our city-wide work."

Based in a purpose-built £1.2 million centre in Beeston, the charity now plans to open a further site, which will include a sports hall and community centre. "We really want to expand on the service that we're giving Leeds," says Raheem Mohammad, Interim Director. "We want to offer so much more to those who are less fortunate and living in deprivation in the area."

Initial funding for the new sports hall came from the local authority, impressed with the work the Hamara Healthy Living Centre does with girls, older people and adults with learning disabilities, focusing on physical activity. Football, tennis, cricket and other sports help these groups to stay fit and connected with others – but the current building has reached full capacity. "The space we've got now is dated, and has no windows," explains Mohammed Iqbal, Chairman of Hamara. "It isn't the best facility to serve our community."

More than £2 million has now been raised through ten different funders, with £1.6 million still to go. Hamara is in talks with the Football Foundation about further financial support. "These projects can be challenging, like climbing a mini-Everest," says Arnie. "A lot of people in our sector struggle with them because of lack of investment or lack of knowledge, but we have shown that, with perseverance and commitment, we can succeed.

"I'm a big believer that communities should work together, and that together we are stronger. This building will allow us to bring together a lot of different organisations with the same agenda, which is to try and improve people's lives."

The sports hall is set to open late summer 2024, with the aim of improving the wellbeing of residents in Leeds and the wider area through better physical health. Arnie also hopes it will start to generate income and make the charity less reliant on donations. "We want to become sustainable and have the opportunity to flourish," he says.

The new facility will include a five-a-side pitch that can be hired out on evenings and weekends. Its multi-use games area will also be rented out, and tenants in the building will contribute to the charity's funding. "It will generate money that we can put back into sport," says Arnie. Users can access the facilities for free or, in some cases, at subsidised rates, and this self-sufficient model is one that they believe could be emulated by other charities.

"Sport is such a universal language," says Raheem. "It has the power to bring people from all backgrounds together."

COCKBURN CENTRE

COCKBURN CENTRE

Creating future citizens

WITH ITS PROGRESSIVE, EMPATHY-LED EDUCATION, GROWING PLACES ENHANCES LIVES, RAISES ASPIRATIONS AND CREATES OPPORTUNITIES FOR CHILDREN, FAMILIES AND COMMUNITIES

www.growingplaces.org.uk

Jackie Warren came to Portsmouth from Liverpool 27 years ago as a navy wife with a desire to develop a shared vision for early-years care and education. It involves the whole family and community in understanding the capability of children, and recognising the vital role they play in developing the future citizens of the world. Jackie is now CEO of Growing Places (Community Childcare Centres), a charitable group of seven nurseries that provides early-years care and education, as well as five after-school and holiday clubs for five- to 13-year-olds in the Hampshire region.

Growing Places began as a single nursery in Havant, Hampshire, which Jackie felt needed to change to better serve the local community. "With the support of trustees and parents, I made the hours more flexible and developed a more representative social mix to encourage connections, raising aspiration and empathy," she says. Jackie's approach is led by strong values, underpinned by theory and cutting-edge global educational research and practice, including the Reggio Emilia approach to education developed in Italy. This relationship continues to develop and inform change in practice for Growing Places.

But Growing Places is much more than a nursery group. Inspired by Jackie's vision and belief in children, it has become central to the local community; a place where children and adults can belong, and feel safe and valued for their individual contributions. Growing Places has extended and developed to meet the changing needs of its communities over the past few years, offering a community pantry, various parent and family workshops, professional training and youth groups. During the pandemic, its nurseries stayed open for all who needed them while others closed. They became essential to the local area, helping to maintain social interaction.

"We saw the best in everybody," says Jackie. "We took hampers to the community and cooked meals for parents." Growing Places continues to act as a community hub with a pantry where parents can get food and supplies. "People often need support or want to help other people but don't know how – but they know they can trust us," says Jackie. "We don't judge our families because we don't walk in their shoes, but we are there with open arms when they need us."

The group's research and its knowledge of its communities has highlighted a gap in opportunities outside school for children aged 5-16 years. The current opportunities on offer are not accessible to all children and families because of social deprivation. "We are worried about our five- to 16-year-olds, and we want to develop a community hub based around creativity and sport that they can easily access," explains Jackie, citing Marcus Rashford as a role model. "Who knows what our children are really capable of? We want to give them the opportunity to grow into people who contribute to society. We want to create a place for them to go where they can be themselves. We want to do this on a big scale, but we need help to make it a reality." Growing Places is currently seeking support, guidance, funding or patronage from like-minded individuals who believe in children as much as Jackie does.

The ultimate vision for the Community Hub (CH 5-16) is to develop kindness, tolerance, understanding and empathy in children, helping them feel they have a valued contribution to make to their communities. "We don't want our children to blindly follow," says Jackie, "but to know what is right and respectfully challenge when things are wrong."

mitre

A force for good

CAUSEWAY WORKS TO HELP MARGINALISED INDIVIDUALS START A NEW LIFE, RECOGNISING THE ROLE PLAYED BY FOOTBALL IN GIVING THEM A VOICE

www.wearecauseway.org.uk

When Chris – not his real name – emerged from a scarcely comprehensible traumatic experience that saw him enslaved and forced to live in a shed, it was football that provided a crucial aspect of his long journey towards recovery. This came through the engagement of Causeway, a charity that works to deliver a thriving future for marginalised and vulnerable people, including survivors of slavery and exploitation, and those with experience of the criminal justice system.

"We've found that football can play an important role in the recovery of our service users," says Amy Bond, Causeway Chief Operating Officer. "Chris had been forced to live in a shed for 40 years and was exploited that entire time. He came to our service and part of his recovery has been watching all the World Cup matches that he couldn't see during the time he was enslaved. This was something he really missed, and it's played a really important role in his recovery journey."

Indeed, football has helped highlight problems with exploitation. This became a topic of public debate during the 2022 Qatar World Cup, with many commentators drawing attention to the living and working conditions of the migrant workers who built the facilities. For Amy, this illustrates the need for industries such as football to examine decision-making relating to working practices and conditions, to prevent exploitation, for example, of people making the kits or building the grounds. But it also demonstrates the unique platform that football provides to raise concerns and speak up for marginalised individuals.

"Football has a duty to be aware of this problem and that doesn't just mean the players; it means the entire supply chain," says Amy. "There is a real opportunity for football, with its money, power and influence, to look at this area. Football has raised the profile of issues like mental health and racism, and that has had a huge effect, particularly among working-age men. We know that 70 per cent of slaves are men – and it's not just an international problem; a lot of victims, like Chris, are from the UK. People are often shocked when they learn this."

Causeway also supports those with experience of the criminal justice system who are looking to rehabilitate and step away from criminality, helping them to adapt to normal life while ensuring their voice is heard by society. This often involves combating prejudice, misinformation and stereotypes, amplifying the experiences of individuals so they are seen as people. For those with experience of the criminal justice system, that means explaining that people who make bad choices are not bad people. For those who have faced slavery, it means showing how easily people can end up in situations where they are exploited.

Looking ahead, Causeway is working to encourage more people with lived experience to get into positions of influence in industries such as football. "With football, you cannot find a more diverse and international group of people, who come from a variety of backgrounds and experiences," says Amy. "But the decision-makers don't always reflect that diversity. Ultimately, our goal is to elevate the voices of this community so they can have an impact on policy and influence the narrative. It is about celebrating the value of the individual rather than seeing them as a single collective of marginalised people and having other people make decisions for and about them.

"Every individual voice matters and that is how we operate as an organisation. We want to show that each of these individuals has every bit as much value as you or me."

Relationship support

RELATE HAS BEEN OFFERING PROFESSIONAL COUNSELLING FOR 85 YEARS AND IS THE LARGEST RELATIONSHIP SUPPORT CHARITY IN ENGLAND AND WALES

www.relate.org.uk

At its best, football can inspire, excite and entertain – but the emotions it evokes are not always so positive. Research has shown that after England's men's team have played in an international tournament, cases of domestic violence across the country increase. Studies show this is true even if England win. In 2014, a report by Lancaster University showed that reports of domestic violence rise by 38 per cent after an England defeat and 26 per cent following a win or draw. In 2021, research by the London School of Economics (LSE) showed that alcohol is a key contributor to this violence. The LSE found there is a 47 per cent increase in reported alcohol-related domestic-abuse cases on days that feature an England win, peaking in the three-hour period following the game. "We want to raise awareness of this issue among footballing organisations," says Carol Florin-White, Assistant Director, National Partnerships, at Relate, the charity that specialises in relationship counselling.

Domestic abuse is one of many issues that lead people to seek support from Relate. Many people reach out to Relate when their relationships are at breaking point.

"At Relate, we offer services to support people with a diverse range of relationship issues," says Carol. "Relationship issues often impact negatively on mental and physical wellbeing, but the majority of our clients report improved wellbeing after accessing our services."

Relate has been providing expert relationship support since 1938, offering people help to overcome a range of relationship difficulties. Although traditionally known for couples counselling, the charity's practitioners support individuals, families, friends, roommates, co-parents and colleagues, while also providing counselling for children and young people struggling with a range of issues, and providing relationship support beyond counselling.

The Relate Federation is made up of the national charity and 24 independent local Relate charities. Around 150,000 individuals access support each year, while 5.7 million people receive advice through the Relate website, which features articles, tools and quizzes. The organisation now offers innovative digital sessions, including 30-minute online chats with counsellors that can be booked at short notice. The 60-minute one-session therapy – either for an individual or a couple – is another digital option, while further assistance is provided through online services or email. All Relate counsellors are highly trained, skilled and experienced, and not only help those who are struggling with relationship problems, but also those who want to improve their communication or listening skills in order to strengthen a relationship. Indeed, over 75 per cent of Relate clients report that counselling leaves them with improved coping strategies.

There is an increased demand for Relate's services, particularly when it comes to children and young people, who face a wide range of challenges. With further funding, Relate is keen to support more people, particularly those from diverse backgrounds, and to make services available in ways that work for them. The organisation is always open to prospective partners that provide funding to enable their beneficiaries to access free counselling. "We are always looking for ways to find funding to support more people. We are committed to supporting more people and securing funds to enable us to provide free or low-cost support where clients struggle to pay," says Carol. "We want to be their for anyone who needs our support."

Playing, and moving, away

WHEN THE TRANSFER WINDOW OPENS, PREMIER RELOCATION IS READY TO HELP FOOTBALLERS MOVE HOME OR COUNTRY AT A MOMENT'S NOTICE

www.premier-relo.com

The first time Andrew Wells and Vladimir Piskla helped a footballer move home, they were not told who their client would be. The pair had formed Premier Relocation, a VIP relocation service that offered security, privacy and reliability; but when they arrived in Spain for the initial survey, they discovered no chances had been taken – every single photograph of the player in the house had been covered over. "But they forgot to cover the framed football shirt in the hallway with his name and number on the back," says Andrew. "That allowed us to make an educated guess."

The possessions of that footballer, who moved from Barcelona to Chelsea, were expertly, discreetly and quickly handled by Premier Relocation. Since then, the company has assisted countless professional footballers undertake huge and complex moves. Many have used Premier Relocation on more than one occasion.

Moving is a constant possibility for any footballer, often at short notice, and CEO Andrew can call on a team of expert removal people and a fleet of vehicles to ensure everything runs smoothly. The company has developed

close relationships with Europe's leading clubs and agents, establishing offices in Barcelona and Madrid, and is preparing to open another in France. While most moves are predominantly within Europe, players are regularly moved to different continents. The logistics team are well versed on all of the requirements for each country on the planet, says Andrew. "We have moved hundreds of footballers. Quite often, if they know they are leaving their current club they will go on holiday for the summer and leave us with the key. We have to plan meticulously for each transfer window – the closer you get to deadline day, the shorter the notice, and there are times when we have to move a player in one day. Sometimes we get more of a warning from the agents because they know that they can trust us, which is why they continue to work with us."

Before setting up his company in 2011, Andrew operated a first-class airline check-in service in central London. When that was forced to close after a change in flight rules, he started working for a friend's removal company, which is where he met Vladimir. The two then utilised their expertise in customer service and ability to form excellent relationships with high-net-worth clients, including stars from the entertainment industry. Success has come from a relentless focus on customers' needs and the ability to move everything from expensive sports cars to pets.

"Privacy, security, trust and reliability – those are the qualities we offer," says Andrew. "We do so much more than moving." Although Premier Relocation is not a concierge company, it has had requests to help with everything from plumbing and interior design, to building a swimming pool and landscaping a garden.

The company works hard behind the scenes to ensure each move is a success. "It is a privilege to work with the players. There's a lot of paperwork to do and we help the player through that process, because the most important thing for us is that as soon as the player lands in his new country he can concentrate on what he is there for, which is to play football. We take the pressure off the player but also off their partners and families. We support them and get them set up as quickly as possible, so they feel like they are at home."

Chapter Three

1993|94 – 2002|03

So much of what we refer to as the modern game in England was forged in the third decade of the PFA Awards, from the influx of international stars to the drama of transfer deadline day. The rise of global television broadcasting supercharged this period of rapid change, which was characterised by the need for the PFA to stand up for the rights of its members, and the actions of a little-known Belgian midfielder by the name of Jean-Marc Bosman.

Bosman, who played for RFC Liège in the Belgian First Division, had come to the end of his contract in 1990. He wanted to sign for French side Dunkerque, but they couldn't afford the 12-million-franc fee. Unable to leave his club, Bosman took his case to the European Court of Justice, claiming it restricted his right to work. In December 1995, the European Court found in Bosman's favour, ushering in the era of free transfers upon the expiry of a contract.

The ruling was indicative of how the sport was modernising. Players from overseas, Irishmen aside, had been rare in English football until the '90s. Foreign managers were even less common. By the end of the decade, the Premier League had played host to the magic of Gianfranco Zola, Juninho and Eric Cantona, the first PFA Players' Player of the Year from the European continent. Similarly, Arsène Wenger had defied his critics to become the first manager from the continent to win the English top flight, bringing a new brand of professionalism to the game in the process.

Attitudes were changing on the terraces, too. In 1991, the Football (Offences) Act made "indecent or racialist chanting" a specific criminal offence for the first time. Two years later, the campaigning charity Kick It Out was founded to fight discrimination in football, working in partnership with the PFA, the FA and the Premier League.

The very edifices we watched football in changed as well, with all-seater stadiums compulsory in the Premier League for the 1994/95 season. The decade ended on a bittersweet note when the original Wembley Stadium, immortalised by Pelé as "the cathedral of football, the capital of football and the heart of football", was closed in 2000.

On the pitch, Manchester United and its Class of '92 dominated the Premier League to lift seven of the ten titles, the crowning achievement being the treble-winning 1998/99 season. Also of note was one Alan Shearer, who became the first person to be named PFA Players' Player of the Year with two different clubs.

For the PFA, providing a voice for its members would mean taking a firm stand. As the trade union for footballers, the PFA had received a share of television revenues from the Football League, and later the Premier League, in recognition of its central role in representing players. After broadcasting rights were renegotiated in the summer of 2000, there was disagreement over how the PFA and its members would benefit from the new and lucrative television deals when the existing PFA agreement expired in 2001. As a result, PFA Chief Executive Gordon Taylor announced he would be consulting his membership on possible strike action, believing that the new offer did not reflect a satisfactory increase in the players' share of the "pot".

A ballot was sent to members in October 2001, and of the 2,496 ballot papers sent, 2,315 were returned, with 2,290 in favour of action. With a strike looming, the PFA, Premier League, FA and Football League met and agreed that the PFA and its members would benefit from a new deal worth over £50 million.

asics
McEWAN'S
LAGER
LETS

Arsenal

Carlsberg

HOLSTEN

1993|94

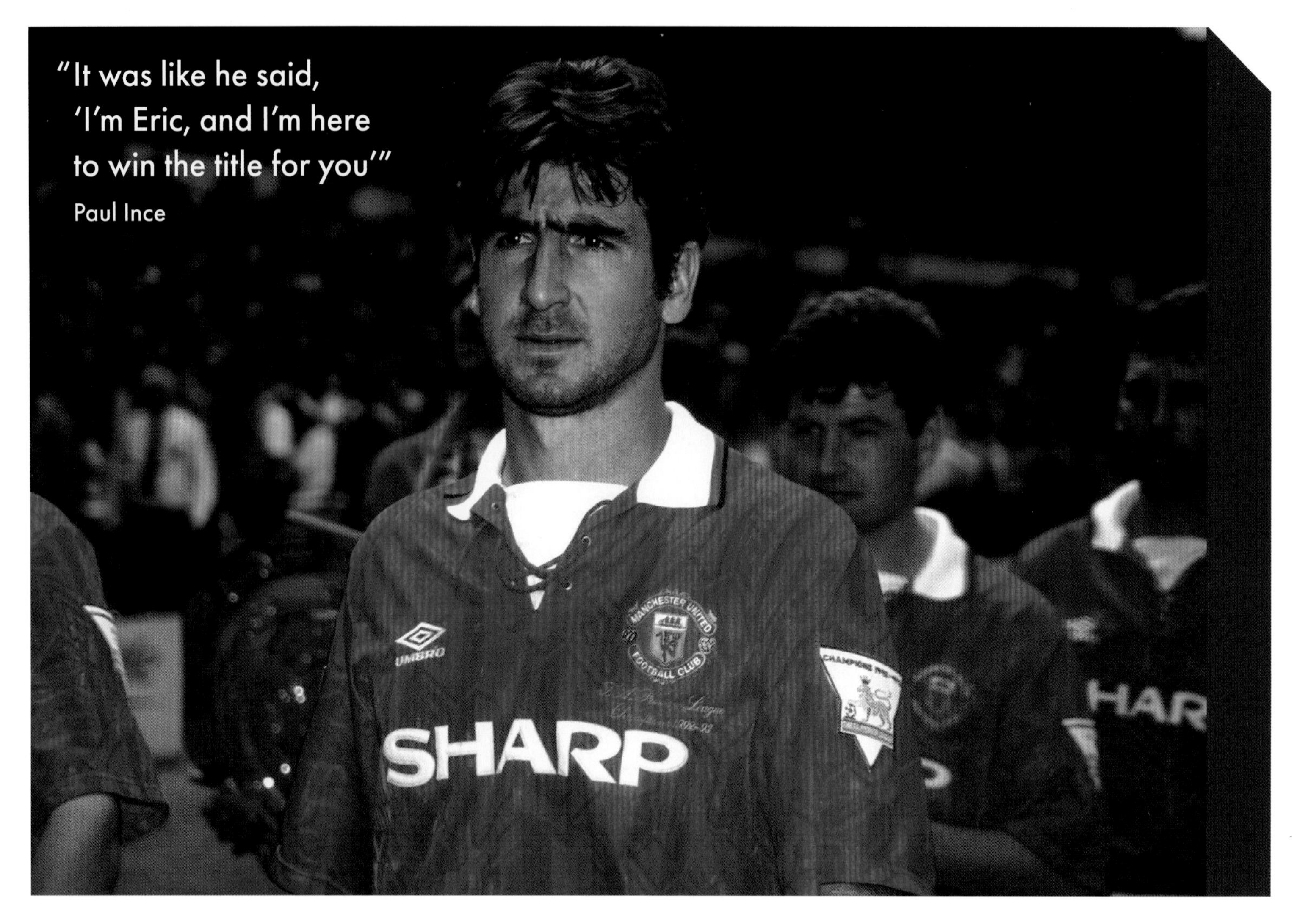

PLAYERS' PLAYER OF THE YEAR

Eric Cantona

THE MANCHESTER UNITED TALISMAN BAGGED A CAREER-BEST 25 GOALS IN HIS PFA AWARD-WINNING SEASON

Above | Cantona at Wembley following United's defeat of Arsenal in the Charity Shield, 1993

The year 1966 was seminal for English football. Eric Cantona was born.

Twenty-six years later, in November 1992, Cantona and Manchester United needed each other – the former on the naughty step at Leeds and for France, the latter desperately seeking a leader to scratch a quarter-century title itch.

"He just had that aura," recalled midfielder Paul Ince. "It was like he said, 'I'm Eric, and I'm here to win the title for you'." Cantona did just that in 1992/93, but it was his first full Old Trafford season that created a trophy-winning monster.

The French forward strutted his way to 25 goals in all competitions in 1993/94 but not even his career's most prolific campaign fully illustrates his transformative, standard-setting impact at Old Trafford. "It was like the messiah," recalled Sir Alex Ferguson.

A free-kick missile against Arsenal in September 1993 took United top, a position they would never relinquish to retain their title by eight points. If a sublime volley at Wimbledon in the FA Cup fifth round was Cantona's best goal, his two penalties in the final against Chelsea were the most important in sealing the double.

Though three red cards were a harbinger of the fireworks to come, 1993/94 provided another Cantona first – the number seven popped his infamous collar, citing sciatica in his shoulder on a cold day. Two–nil down at half-time to Manchester City, United roared back to win 3–2 thanks to a Cantona brace, delivered from a deeper role just to prove he really could do what he pleased.

"I'm very happy and very proud to win this prize," said Cantona, the first continental player to win the PFA Players' Player of the Year Award. "I want to thank Alex Ferguson, my coaches, my teammates and congratulate the players who didn't vote for me, for all the pleasure they've given me in playing in this magnificent English football."

Enigmatic and unmistakably Eric.

YOUNG PLAYER OF THE YEAR

Andy Cole

"I'm going to sign a player just for you," Newcastle United manager Kevin Keegan told Andy Cole in the summer of 1993. The Magpies had won promotion to the Premier League and King Kev's perfect foil for his electric 21-year-old striker was to spend £1.5 million on a 32-year-old.

It worked. Cole and Peter Beardsley scored 65 goals between them in all competitions, the former plundering 41 to break Hughie Gallacher's 70-year club record. Cole really hit his straps in October and November, scoring eight goals in five games, including a deadly hat-trick against Liverpool at St James' Park, and finished with a then joint-Premier League record 34.

According to Keegan, Cole was "the country's most exciting player", whose canny movement and unerring finishing helped the Magpies to third. Fittingly it was Cole's unlikely strike partner Beardsley who presented the nascent forward with his PFA Young Player of the Year award – 68 per cent of Newcastle goals that season stood on the stage. Lethal.

Above | Cole unleashes a shot against West Ham in the Premier League fixture at St James' Park, 1993

MERIT AWARD

Billy Bingham

Right | Northern Ireland manager Bingham at Windsor Park, 1981

As a player, Belfast-born Billy Bingham was a slippery outside right who won the 1962/63 First Division with Everton and helped Northern Ireland to the 1958 World Cup quarter-finals. Yet it was Bingham's two spells in charge of his beloved country, particularly his 13-year tenure from 1980, that ensured his status as Northern Ireland football royalty.

Distilling the disparate talents of Martin O'Neill, Sammy McIlroy and Gerry Armstrong into a cohesive unit, Bingham not only claimed the 1980 British Home Championship – the first time Northern Ireland had won the competition outright for 66 years – but also qualified for successive World Cups in 1982 and 1986.

At Spain '82, Armstrong's famous strike beat the hosts 1–0 to top their group. "He was a genius, the best manager we ever had," Armstrong later said, "there is nobody can get anywhere near him."

Bingham resigned in November 1993, and was the obvious candidate five months later to receive the PFA Merit Award for his services to football in Northern Ireland. A master tactician.

PLAYERS' PLAYER OF THE YEAR

Alan Shearer

THE PREMIER LEAGUE'S GREATEST GOALSCORER NETTED 37 IN ALL COMPETITIONS DURING THE 1994/95 SEASON, AS BLACKBURN ROVERS CHARGED TO THEIR FIRST LEAGUE TITLE IN 81 YEARS

PFA: You're in a very elite club, one of only seven who have won the Players' Player award twice. If we roll it back to the first year you won it, in 1995, what do you remember from that season?

Alan Shearer: I remember almost everything, from start to finish. How we were under pressure as a team because Manchester United were hunting us down. We were sitting at the top of the league, playing some good football, but we'd never crossed that line, if you like, in terms of winning something. For a smaller club like Blackburn Rovers to come into the Premier League and take on the might of Manchester United and be above them and be pushed all the way, it was pretty nerve-racking. But we had an unbelievable manager in Kenny Dalglish, who was experienced, who had been there before, had done it both as a player and a manager, so he helped us a lot. We got over the line, just, on the final day of the season.

PFA: The best way to do it!

AS: Yeah, it was tough. I remember going 1–0 up at Anfield, I scored the goal and we should've gone two, three up. I missed a big chance. Chris Sutton missed a big chance. And, of course, Liverpool came back and got two goals late on. And we thought "That's it, we've blown it, after all that hard work."

PFA: Hard for Kenny, too...

AS: At Liverpool, I know. It was a really strange atmosphere because Anfield wanted Kenny to win it ... we know what Kenny means to Liverpool.

PFA: The chance to put one over on Manchester United?

AS: Exactly. We owe West Ham a favour because going to Upton Park, United had to win, couldn't win and we got over the line, that was it.

PFA: Everyone talks about the mindset of Premier League-winning teams. At Blackburn, were you expecting to go

Right | The striker adds to his tally against Newcastle during a league match at Ewood Park, 1995

Opposite | A beaming Shearer scored against Chelsea in Rovers' 2–1 home victory, 1995

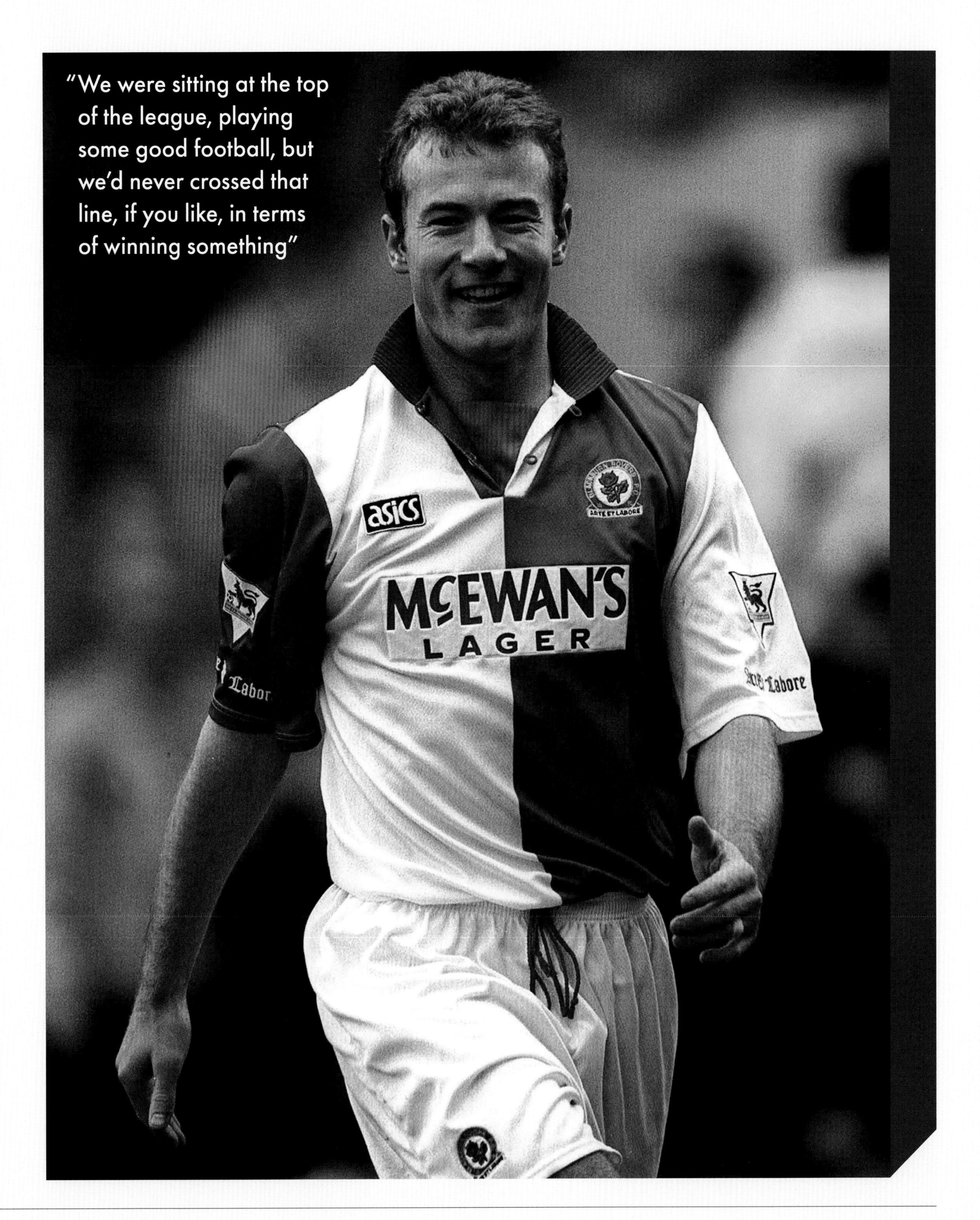

"We were sitting at the top of the league, playing some good football, but we'd never crossed that line, if you like, in terms of winning something"

McEWAN'S
LAGER
McEWAN'S
LAGER
CARLING

McEWAN'S
LAGER

"Jack Walker, Kenny, they all said to me, 'We hope to win the league within four years'. That was one of the main reasons why I went there, because of that ambition"

and win it or was there a point in the season where you thought, "Come on, we can do this"?
AS: No, we were expecting to win it. When I signed for Blackburn in '92, that was what was put to me. Jack Walker, Kenny, they all said to me, "We hope to win the league within four years". That was one of the main reasons why I went there, because of their ambition. Jack Walker was hugely successful as a businessman and with the experience of Kenny and Ray Harford, who is sadly no longer with us, with his expertise on the training field as a coach, it was all set up to win. And we did it within three years. It was an amazing achievement.
PFA: So, you had that incredible season, you win the league with Blackburn, and then after another year you move to your boyhood club. How easy a decision was it to go back home and play for Newcastle?
AS: It wasn't easy at all, it was a really, really difficult decision. One minute I was going to Manchester United, Blackburn were desperate for me to stay and there were other clubs interested. Obviously, with Newcastle there was the pull of going back home because I left there as a 15-year-old kid to go and start my dream and be a professional footballer down at Southampton. But I just woke up one morning and I thought, "You know what? I'm going back home. I'm going to go and play for the club that I support." I wanted to wear the number nine shirt, I wanted to score goals at the Gallowgate End, at my football club, the team that I'd supported as a young boy. My hero was the manager, Kevin Keegan, at the time. So it all felt right. And don't forget, the previous season, Newcastle had lost that 12-point lead, I think it was, to Manchester United, so it wasn't as if I was going to a club who weren't ready to challenge. It was the best decision I ever made. I had ten unbelievable years there.
PFA: In 1996/97, the season you received your second PFA Award, you topped the Premier League goalscoring charts for a third year. When you're in that kind of form, are you confident of scoring every week?
AS: Yeah. I mean you obviously need very good players around you and a system that suits you. That was definitely the case with me, both at Blackburn and at Newcastle. I had wingers who were prepared to put the ball in for me. I needed that, that's what I wanted. But I just felt supremely confident going onto the pitch in every game. I had belief in my ability, although I did miss a few – I always felt that, more often than not, when the chances came along, I was gonna stick them away. And luckily for me, that was the case. I know you often hear it but there is no better feeling than hitting the back of the net with that ball, scoring goals, it's just incredible. It doesn't get any better than that. So once you've had a taste of that, certainly in my experience, I just wanted more and more, and that's where that hunger came from.
PFA: All the top strikers seem to be in the right place at the right time. Obviously you work on patterns, you train hard, but how much of it is instinct?
AS: Yeah, a lot of it is instinct but you can get better, you can improve your technique, you can improve your shooting, you can improve your left foot or right foot, your touch and all of those things. But a lot of it is instinct, yeah – it can't be coincidence that forwards end up in the right place at the right time every single time, time and time again, so you just sort of have that knack of sniffing it out, where it's gonna land. Don't ask me how, it just happened.

Opposite, clockwise from top | The deadly "SAS" strike partnership of Shearer and Chris Sutton lift the Premiership trophy, 1995; at an England training session with Barry Venison (left), manager Terry Venables (centre) and John Barnes (right), 1994; Shearer celebrates winning the title at Anfield, 1995

Right | On England duty, 1994

YOUNG PLAYER OF THE YEAR

Robbie Fowler

Fowler (left) and Jamie Redknapp lift the 1995 League Cup after a 2–1 victory over Bolton Wanderers at Wembley

Robbie Fowler wasn't strong, tall or particularly quick but there was one very good reason why his Liverpool teammates christened the teenager "God". "Nobody," recalled Reds midfielder Jamie Redknapp, *"nobody,* could finish like him."

Fowler scored on his Liverpool debut in September 1993, but it was in the Toxteth terror's first full season that the 19-year-old went stratospheric. The percussive ratatat of his August 1994 hat-trick against Arsenal was emblematic Fowler, a study in low backlift, unerring finishing and achieved in just four minutes and 33 seconds. It stood as a Premier League record for more than 20 years.

By the turn of the year, Fowler had scored 18 Premier League goals and he went on to finish the season with 31 in all competitions as Liverpool won the League Cup under the avuncular Roy Evans. A beaming Ian Rush presented his goalscoring protégé with the PFA Young Player of the Year award, a prize the born-and-bred Scouser, a natural finisher, would retain 12 months later.

Strachan playing for Leeds, 1990

MERIT AWARD

Gordon Strachan

Not even Gordon Strachan's retirement in 1995 could persuade the 38-year-old to hang up his boots. When the tireless midfielder left Leeds United for Coventry City that March it was to be Ron Atkinson's assistant, claiming to have run himself "to a standstill". The tenacious Scot went on to play another 33 games over two-and-a-half seasons, mainly as player-manager.

Strachan's competitive fire always burned strong. The one-time watchmaker won eight major honours in Aberdeen's "golden era" – including two Premier Divisions and the 1983 European Cup Winners' Cup final against Real Madrid – plus the 1984/85 FA Cup with Manchester United, before reviving Leeds's listing fortunes from Second Division also-rans to top-flight champions in three full seasons.

"You could video him and sell it as what you expect from a player," said Leeds boss Howard Wilkinson. Strachan received the 1995 PFA Merit Award from fellow legendary Scot Denis Law for services to football, later winning six trophies as Celtic boss.

PLAYERS' PLAYER OF THE YEAR

Les Ferdinand

THE PROLIFIC LONDONER, WHOSE 25 GOALS FOR NEWCASTLE SECURED HIM THE PLAYERS' PLAYER AWARD IN 1996, TALKS TRAINING, CLUB CULTURE AND THE CHANGING FACE OF FOOTBALL

Above | Ferdinand celebrates after scoring against Arsenal at St James' Park, 1996

PFA: Hi, Les. You completed the PFA Effective Board Member Programme a year before you took on the role of Director of Football at QPR. What was the most important thing you gained from it?
Les Ferdinand: It was seeing the other side of the fence. When you're a footballer, you're quite selfish – you've just got to keep yourself as fit as you possibly can and you go out and perform for the team. Whatever goes on in the football club, the other side of the football club, you think the club will take care of it. What it gave me was an insight into the fact that football clubs have budgets and have to work to those budgets and no matter what you think as a player, those budgets are still in place. One of the amazing things was when you look outside the Premier League – at the Championship, League One, League Two – nine times out of ten, teams finished within their budget. It was uncanny to look at how much this team spent and where they finished and so on. It gave me a really good insight into what goes on on the other side of the fence.
PFA: During your playing career, which clubs had the biggest impact on you in terms of creating a cohesive, successful culture?
LF: When I was at QPR at the beginning, we had a really good culture. Everyone understood where the club was, we had a couple of good managers in place who identified with the culture of the football club and kept things on an even keel. But going to Newcastle was probably the eye-opener for me. I always remember the late, great Ray Wilkins said to me, "When you go to a big club, you understand how things are run." I went to Newcastle, and they saw themselves as a big club – the way they ran the football club in line with what the manager wanted and what the club needed, that opened my eyes.
PFA: What did that approach feel like?
LF: Listen, we should have won the league in the first year I was there, and that was because of the culture and the togetherness and the understanding, not just about what the football club wanted, but what it meant to the people of Newcastle as well. Everything was entwined. Everything we did was for them.
PFA: I'd imagine the culture and type of player is quite different today from when you were playing?
LF: The way you used to be able to talk to players in the dressing room has changed. That side of things in football has changed, but that side in society has changed, so it's not just football. People communicate a lot differently now than they used to. We never had mobile phones in the early part of me being a footballer, so we had to communicate by talking to each other and getting on with each other. Like I said, that societal change obviously impacts football.

MERIT AWARD

Pelé

Edson Arantes do Nascimento wanted his father to stop crying. Brazil had just lost to Uruguay in the de facto 1950 World Cup final and the nine-year-old made his dad a promise. "Don't cry, dad," he said. "I'll win the World Cup for you."

Two decades later, having adopted the childhood nickname Pelé as his chosen epithet, that youngster became the only player to win three World Cups. Just 17 for his first world crown, Pelé scored 1,281 goals in his 21-year playing career for Santos, Brazil and finally New York Cosmos before his 1977 retirement. Numbers, however, are irrelevant.

"I told myself before the game, he's made of skin and bones just like everyone else," said Tarcisio Burgnich after Pelé turned the Italian defender inside out in the 4–1 1970 World Cup final defeat to Brazil, "but I was wrong."

Descriptions of Pelé tend to focus on the ethereal because it's the only way to rationalise the most complete footballer in history. The Brazilian could play as a number ten or centre forward – he beat opponents with either sickle or scythe.

A quarter of a century on from that third world crown, football's first superstar received the PFA Merit Award. That it was England goalkeeper Gordon Banks, whose "save of the century" from a Pelé header in 1970 sparked a lifelong friendship, who presented the honour only added to the sense of occasion.

"I told myself before the game, 'he's made of skin and bones just like everyone else'. But I was wrong"

Tarcisio Burgnich

A jubilant Pelé after Brazil's defeat of Italy in the final of the 1970 World Cup at Estadio Azteca, Mexico City

YOUNG PLAYER OF THE YEAR

Robbie Fowler

Fowler with his second consecutive Young Player of the Year Award, 1996

"It was clear straight away that he had an amazing knack for scoring goals, and all sorts of goals; left foot, right foot, headers. In that sense he reminded me of John Aldridge, but as great as Aldridge was, Robbie was better; without doubt the most naturally gifted goalscorer I have ever played with."

John Barnes

PLAYERS' PLAYER OF THE YEAR

Alan Shearer

"England have had many great strikers over the years who have excelled in certain parts of the game but there is no chink at all in Shearer's armour, even to the point of magnificent mental strength. He works so hard. He's not afraid to put himself around physically and won't be intimidated by aggressive tactics. He is a clever player, who is capable of understanding tactical instructions and then carrying them out, even if it means defensive duties."

Glenn Hoddle

Shearer with his second Players' Player of the Year award, 1997

YOUNG PLAYER OF THE YEAR

David Beckham

David Beckham changed his life wearing someone else's boots. Look closely when the 21-year-old scored from inside his own half at Wimbledon on the opening day of the 1996/97 season and you'll see the word "Charlie" stitched into the Manchester United midfielder's Adidas Predators. The only size eights available were a custom-made pair for Rangers' Charlie Miller.

"That moment was the start of it all: the attention, the press coverage, the fame," he wrote in his autobiography, *My Side*. "When my foot struck that ball, it kicked open the door to the rest of my life."

Did it ever. By season's end, Beckham was an England regular, Premier League winner and PFA Young Player of the Year, and had a Spice Girl on his arm. But that goal against the Dons, his first of 12 in all competitions – which also included a curling drive against Derby, deft chip against West Ham and trademark free-kick at Southampton – encapsulated the midfielder's peerless ball-striking ability and relentless training ground application.

No one has ever crossed a football better.

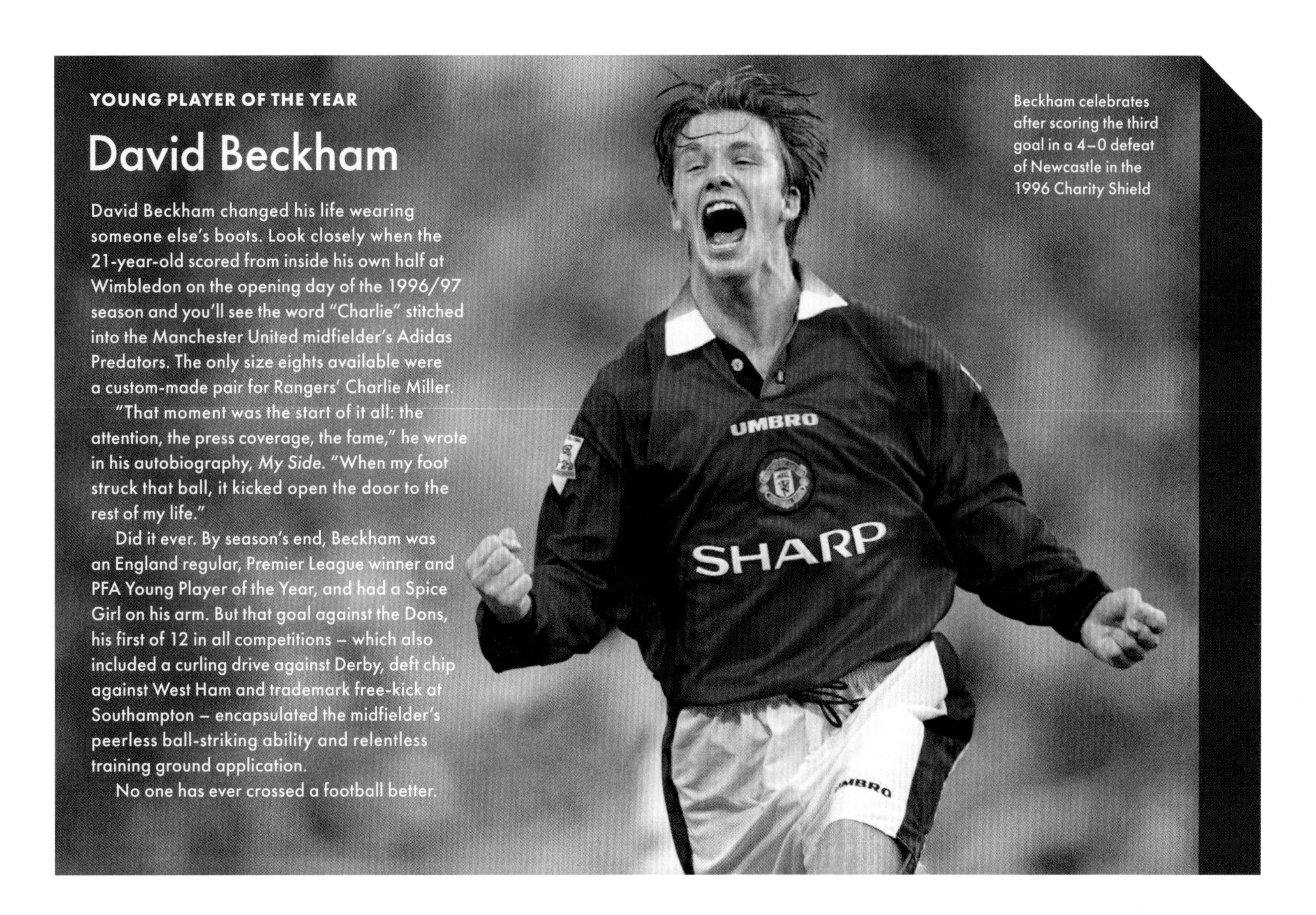

Beckham celebrates after scoring the third goal in a 4–0 defeat of Newcastle in the 1996 Charity Shield

MERIT AWARD

Peter Beardsley

Right | Beardsley playing for Newcastle United, 1984

Peter Beardsley's diminutive frame may not match the profile of the typical English forward but the Liverpool, Everton and Newcastle United goalscorer was as stylish as they come with the ball at his feet. English football has produced few players with a greater appreciation of space or deftness of touch.

Beardsley's innate ability and love of hard work earned a record transfer fee, two league titles and an FA Cup. His peers' appreciation, though, was priceless.

"My colleagues in the West German team are excellent players, but Beardsley is world class," 1990 World Cup-winning striker Rudi Völler once said, despite his side beating England in that tournament's semi-finals.

Though 32 when signed by Kevin Keegan for a second Newcastle spell in the summer of 1993, he became the conduit through which much of the Entertainers' play passed and received the PFA Merit Award at the end of his final Magpies season for services to football.

PLAYERS' PLAYER OF THE YEAR

Dennis Bergkamp

THE DUTCH MASTER'S SUBLIME SKILLS GUIDED ARSENAL TO THE DOUBLE IN 1998 AND EARNED HIM A WELL-DESERVED PFA PLAYERS' PLAYER AWARD

Wim Bergkamp loved Denis Law so much, he named his fourth son after the Manchester United forward. As a boy, young Dennis pored over videos of Tottenham Hotspur playmaker Glenn Hoddle. Yet something made him look across North London in the summer of 1995.

"I saw Highbury for the first time ... wow! This was football," Bergkamp later recalled. "You don't support a football club because of the trophies, or a player, or history, you support it because you found yourself somewhere there; found a place where you belong."

The Dutch forward had never settled at Inter, one Italian newspaper having renamed its "Donkey of the Week" award the "Bergkamp of the Week" after just three Serie A goals in 1994/95. They also gave Bergkamp the nickname "Beavis" after the sniggering blond-haired cartoon character of limited intellect. When Arsenal boss Bruce Rioch offered £7.5 million, the Nerazzurri couldn't say "ciao" quickly enough.

One of the most cerebral players to ever commit boot to leather, Bergkamp thrived as Arsenal's creative fulcrum. "I knew that if I get the ball over in his general direction there's a chance he'll do something I haven't even thought of," recalled Ian Wright of a new strike partner who averaged a goal every other game in his first two Highbury seasons. Yet it was following Arsène Wenger's arrival as manager in September 1996 that the number ten's holistic influence began to reveal itself.

"Dennis has intelligence and class," said Wenger. "Class is, of course, most of the time linked to what you can do with the ball, but the intelligence makes you use the technique in an efficient way."

As a child, Bergkamp spent hours kicking a ball against a wall outside the Amsterdam family home, studying its every movement. "I wanted to see how it bounces, how it comes back," he recalled, "how the spin worked, what you could do with spin. Behind every kick of the ball there has to be a thought."

At 28, the former Ajax youngster distilled that knowledge into his finest individual season in 1997/98. Part of a run of ten goals and six assists in his opening ten league games, Bergkamp also delivered arguably his greatest performance at Leicester City that August. The Foxes had cancelled out the Dutchman's stunning 25-yard curling opener and stabbed second, but his hat-trick goal was a footballing Vermeer.

Left | Bergkamp receives the PFA Player's Player of the Year trophy

Opposite | The Arsenal man celebrates after scoring against Wimbledon, 1998

First, he controlled David Platt's 40-yard through ball, then juggled over Matt Elliott to finish into the top corner. Leicester boss Martin O'Neill called it "the best hat-trick I've ever seen". A runaway Goal of the Month winner – ahead of Bergkamp's solo goal four days earlier at Southampton and his Leicester opener, the only time the same player has finished first, second and third in the same month – it also topped the end-of-season list. It didn't matter that the game finished 3–3.

Most incredible of all was Bergkamp's foresight. "The Leicester [hat-trick] goal was pure," he said. "When the pass came I knew what I wanted to do: control, ball inside, finish." He made it sound simple. For mortals, his teammates included, it was anything but.

"Dennis did plenty of things we didn't think were humanly possible," said left back Nigel Winterburn. "I still talk about that hat-trick all the time, while his class wasn't confined to specific matches but over a very long period of time."

With the balletic Bergkamp as Nureyev, Nijinsky and Baryshnikov all rolled into one, sixth-placed Arsenal went 18 games unbeaten from Boxing Day to surge ahead of Manchester United to the title with two fixtures to spare. Patrick Vieira and Emmanuel Petit were a complementary midfield duo, Marc Overmars added raw pace and Tony Adams indefatigable leadership, but Bergkamp was the star turn. There was the only strike in a 1–0 win against Sheffield Wednesday and another goal of the season contender at Barnsley as the Dutch master scored 22 goals in all competitions and laid on a further 13 assists. He missed the FA Cup final through injury as Arsenal sealed the double, but won the Football Writers' Association Player of the Year and also collected the PFA honour from Sir Tom Finney.

Though he would never scale the same goalscoring heights again, Bergkamp's influence on the club until his 2006 retirement was such that he would go on to be immortalised in bronze outside the Emirates. His statue? A mid-air first touch, the sort of momentary piece of skill that so captivated Wenger.

Calm, efficient and understated. Bergkamp at his purest.

JVC

Owen and David Beckham pictured after the striker opened the scoring in a 1998 World Cup group game against Romania

YOUNG PLAYER OF THE YEAR

Michael Owen

Terry Owen knew straight away. "Jeanette," the former Everton and Chester forward said to his wife after a back garden kickabout with his infant son, "I think we've got something special here."

Prodigious doesn't begin to describe Michael Owen's early years. At nine, he didn't just beat Ian Rush's 20-year goalscoring record for Deeside Area Primary School's Under-11s, he destroyed it, firing 97 in a single season – 25 more than Rush. At 16, he scored 11 goals in five FA Youth Cup games to beat Rio Ferdinand and Frank Lampard's West Ham to the title.

Another record fell on his senior Liverpool debut at Wimbledon in April 1997. Owen's goal off the bench in a 2–1 defeat that gifted Manchester United the title provided quite the consolation – searing, brutal, eye-watering pace to get beyond the last man, followed by the calmest of finishes. At 17 years and 143 days old, he was the Premier League's youngest goalscorer.

In his first full season, he flew. Wearing an oversized shirt, the teenage hitman's early goalscoring form didn't quicken the pulse – three goals in his opening 16 league appearances – but Owen's raw speed certainly did. Liverpool's so-called Spice Boys of Robbie Fowler, Steve McManaman, Jamie Redknapp, Jamie Carragher and Jason McAteer had a new member.

A superb dinked finish in a 3–0 defeat of Crystal Palace in early December began a run of 15 goals in Owen's remaining 20 Premier League games of the season. On Valentine's Day, he became the youngest player to score a Premier League hat-trick, in a 3–3 draw at Sheffield Wednesday. Three days earlier, he'd made his senior England debut and broke the great Duncan Edwards's record as the Three Lions youngest player of the 20th century.

"I was born to score goals, I feel," said Owen. "It bothers me when I don't."

Everything seemed to come so easily to Owen, who revelled in denying table-topping United the title with a 1–1 draw at Old Trafford. The obvious candidate for the PFA Young Player of the Year Award with 23 goals in all competitions, Owen would also light up the World Cup that summer with a memorable solo goal against Argentina in England's eventual last 16 exit.

MERIT AWARD

Steve Ogrizovic

Still a Premier League regular at the age of 40, Steve Ogrizovic was the obvious candidate to pick up the PFA Merit Award for 1997/98. That the Coventry City goalkeeper received the honour from Pat Jennings, a fellow gloveman whose playing career spanned three decades, only made it more special.

Unable to dislodge Ray Clemence at Liverpool in the early '80s, Oggy was the Sky Blues' first-choice keeper for 14 seasons from 1984 and a cult hero like no other. Tall, imposing and a born leader, Ogrizovic was voted the club's Player of the Season in 1986/87 as Coventry lifted the FA Cup, their only major trophy.

"He is one of the finest pros of the modern era, a superb example to all players and a thoroughly decent and pleasant man," said Coventry boss Gordon Strachan after Ogrizovic's final senior appearance – a 4–1 defeat of Sheffield Wednesday – two years after picking up his PFA award.

His club appearance record – 601 games in all competitions – may never be beaten.

Above | Steve Ogrizovic, winner of the 1998 PFA Merit Award

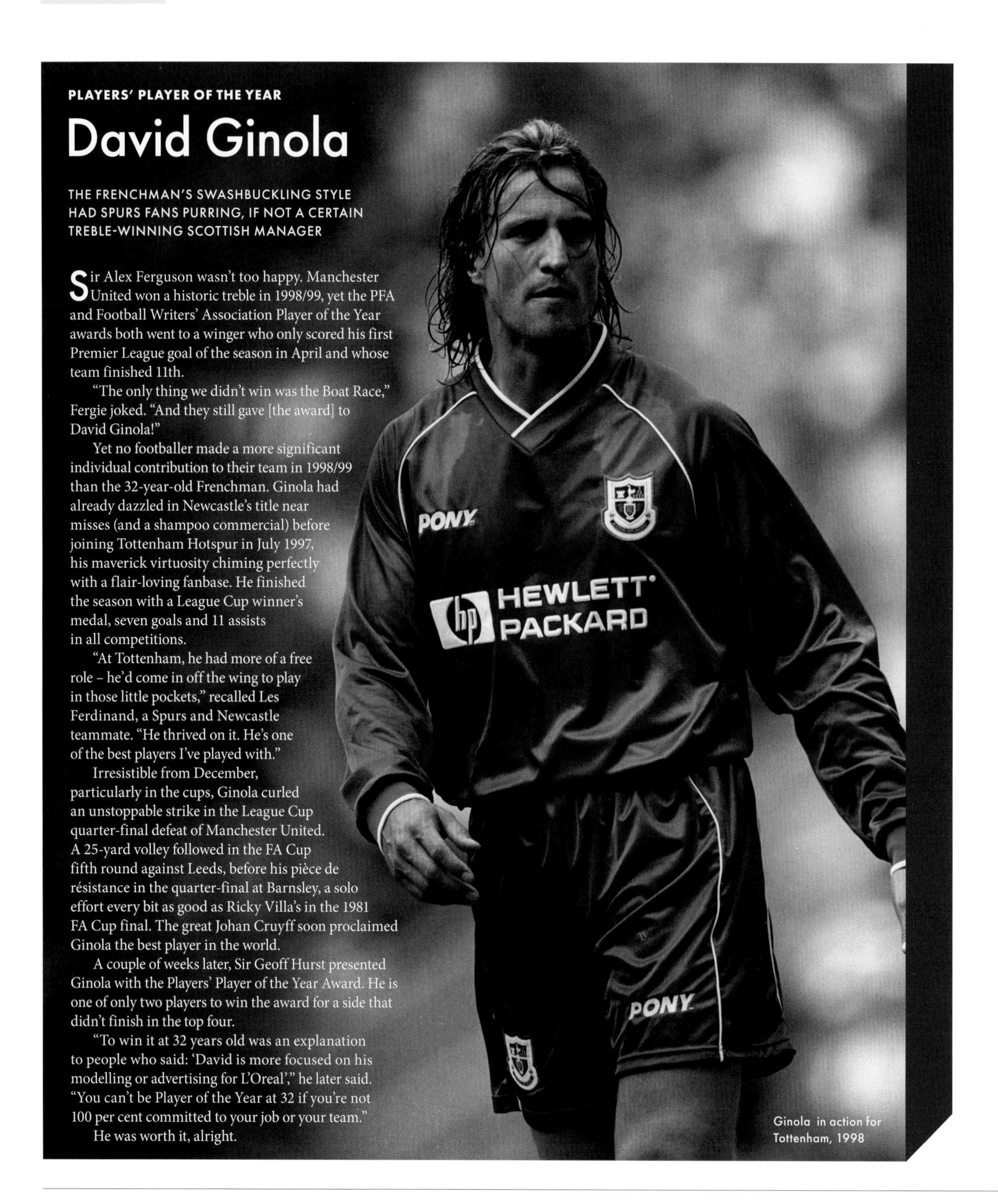

PLAYERS' PLAYER OF THE YEAR

David Ginola

THE FRENCHMAN'S SWASHBUCKLING STYLE HAD SPURS FANS PURRING, IF NOT A CERTAIN TREBLE-WINNING SCOTTISH MANAGER

Sir Alex Ferguson wasn't too happy. Manchester United won a historic treble in 1998/99, yet the PFA and Football Writers' Association Player of the Year awards both went to a winger who only scored his first Premier League goal of the season in April and whose team finished 11th.

"The only thing we didn't win was the Boat Race," Fergie joked. "And they still gave [the award] to David Ginola!"

Yet no footballer made a more significant individual contribution to their team in 1998/99 than the 32-year-old Frenchman. Ginola had already dazzled in Newcastle's title near misses (and a shampoo commercial) before joining Tottenham Hotspur in July 1997, his maverick virtuosity chiming perfectly with a flair-loving fanbase. He finished the season with a League Cup winner's medal, seven goals and 11 assists in all competitions.

"At Tottenham, he had more of a free role – he'd come in off the wing to play in those little pockets," recalled Les Ferdinand, a Spurs and Newcastle teammate. "He thrived on it. He's one of the best players I've played with."

Irresistible from December, particularly in the cups, Ginola curled an unstoppable strike in the League Cup quarter-final defeat of Manchester United. A 25-yard volley followed in the FA Cup fifth round against Leeds, before his pièce de résistance in the quarter-final at Barnsley, a solo effort every bit as good as Ricky Villa's in the 1981 FA Cup final. The great Johan Cruyff soon proclaimed Ginola the best player in the world.

A couple of weeks later, Sir Geoff Hurst presented Ginola with the Players' Player of the Year Award. He is one of only two players to win the award for a side that didn't finish in the top four.

"To win it at 32 years old was an explanation to people who said: 'David is more focused on his modelling or advertising for L'Oreal'," he later said. "You can't be Player of the Year at 32 if you're not 100 per cent committed to your job or your team."

He was worth it, alright.

Ginola in action for Tottenham, 1998

YOUNG PLAYER OF THE YEAR

Nicolas Anelka

Signed for £500,000 with little more than a shrug's acknowledgement by Arsenal fans, Nicolas Anelka's £22.3 million move to Real Madrid two-and-a-half years later provoked Gunners fans to spit pure fury.

Anelka's searing pace, sublime skill and lethal finishing had earned him a starting spot in the 1997/98 double-winning season – scoring an FA Cup final goal – but it was in his second full campaign that the Frenchman announced himself as one of the brightest prospects in Europe. The 20-year-old struck 17 Premier League goals – a February 1999 hat-trick against Leicester the highlight – as the Gunners finished runners-up to treble winners Manchester United in what would be his final season at Highbury.

Former winner Tony Adams picked up the PFA Young Player of the Year Award on Anelka's behalf, the striker's absence on the night a first sign that all was not rosy in England. His relationship with the Gunners would never heal, particularly when winning the Premier League with Chelsea over a decade later.

Above | Anelka poses with the PFA Young Player of the Year award before Arsenal's home Premiership fixture against Aston Villa, 1999

MERIT AWARD

Tony Ford

Right | Ford playing for Mansfield, 1997

Ordinarily, Tony Ford wouldn't have fond memories of a 3–0 Mansfield Town defeat at Plymouth Argyle. Yet that January 1999 day, the 39-year-old midfielder broke Terry Paine's Football League appearance record for an outfield player, his 825th fixture.

David Essex was Number One with "Hold Me Close" when a 16-year-old Ford had made his debut for hometown club Grimsby Town in October 1975. It was "Praise You" by Fatboy Slim when he broke the record.

"There seems to be some unwritten rule that when you get to 32 or 33 you should start thinking about packing up," the former Stoke, West Brom and Scunthorpe man said. "Rubbish. My body will tell me when it is time to give up. Until then I'll carry on."

He was as good as his word. Ford, 42, made his 931st and final Football League appearance in a 2–0 Rochdale win at Torquay United in November 2001. It remains an outfield record.

Nobody deserved the 1999 PFA Merit Award more.

PLAYERS' PLAYER OF THE YEAR

Roy Keane

ONE OF THE ALL-TIME GREAT CAPTAINS, MANCHESTER UNITED'S SKIPPER LED HIS TEAM ON THE TROPHY TRAIL ONCE AGAIN

Roy Keane with a point to prove was as dangerous as a ravenous lion. Missing the blue riband Champions League triumph of the previous season's treble through suspension consumed Manchester United's apex predator.

Restless, relentless and driven by a fanatical will to win, the 28-year-old resolved that only total domination would suffice in 1999/2000. Four games in against bitter rivals Arsenal, Keane produced arguably his finest display in a United shirt. He squared up to opposite number Patrick Vieira, snapped into tackles and marauded forward to score twice in a come-from-behind 2–1 win that ended the Gunners' 20-month unbeaten Highbury record.

"He was intimidating – terrifying, even – but he was the ultimate captain," said Luke Chadwick, who made his United debut that season. "If we gave everything, then he would fight for every last one of us."

Keane missed much of the following six weeks with a knee injury. When he returned in mid-October, United had just lost 5–0 to Chelsea and slipped to second. It wasn't just that United beat Watford 4–1, the squad's standards immediately improved.

"If he thought you were slacking, you were going to get it," Wes Brown said. "He knew what it took to make it at the highest level, what it took to win."

With the return of their fit-again leader, Sir Alex Ferguson's side lost just two more league games, winning their last 11 to lift the title in record time by 18 points. Only eventual winners Real Madrid denied United in the Champions League, a competition in which Keane scored an impressive six goals in 12 games.

Already voted the Football Writers' Association Player of the Year, Keane was a near-unanimous choice for the PFA award, presented by FIFA president Sepp Blatter. Other United vintages won more, but never with the remorseless belligerence demanded by peak Keane in 1999/2000. And not a prawn sandwich in sight.

Keane celebrates with the Premiership trophy, Old Trafford, 2000

YOUNG PLAYER OF THE YEAR

Harry Kewell

Precocious, skilful and tough – training with David Batty and David Hopkin will do that to you – the 1999/2000 Leeds United side was the unmistakable product of the club's vibrant academy. Jonathan Woodgate, Paul Robinson, Ian Harte, Stephen McPhail and Alan Smith were all FA Youth Cup winners just three years previously, but it was Harry Kewell's stardust that elevated the Whites to a third-place Premier League finish, Champions League qualification and the UEFA Cup semi-finals.

"Harry and Ryan Giggs were probably the best left wingers that played in England for a long, long time," said left back Harte.

Kewell was good and he knew it. His insouciant outside-of-the-left-foot flick from 20 yards out in a 3–0 April 2000 defeat of Sheffield Wednesday was the cocksure strut of a 21-year-old who scored a career-best 17 goals in all competitions.

Cruelly robbed of his peak years by persistent injuries, the future Champions League winner with Liverpool was an obvious choice to pick up the PFA Young Player of the Year award.

Above | Kewell in action during Leeds United's 2–0 victory over Sheffield Wednesday at Elland Road, 1999

MERIT AWARD

Gary Mabbutt

He's too humble to admit it, but Gary Mabbutt is an icon to millions. The stately centre back made 611 appearances for Tottenham Hotspur – second only to 1983/84 UEFA Cup-winning teammate Steve Perryman – but it's the awareness he gave those who live with diabetes that makes the Bristolian so inspirational.

Since his diagnosis at 17, Mabbutt has had to administer four daily injections of insulin, but never let his condition clip his ambition to become the first diabetic to play for England. He also raised millions for charity.

"We roomed together for three years and I saw what he had to go through to play the game," recalled Gary Lineker. "He was a model professional and so many players today could learn from him."

Spurs' 1991 FA Cup-winning captain who nearly lost the sight in his right eye after a sickening clash of heads with Wimbledon's John Fashanu in 1993, Mabbutt was a worthy winner of the 2000 Merit Award, two years after his retirement.

Above | Mabbutt of England and Tottenham, c. 1989

2000 | 01

PLAYERS' PLAYER OF THE YEAR

Teddy Sheringham

THE OLDEST WINNER OF THE PLAYER'S PLAYER OF THE YEAR AWARD AT THE TIME, THE EVERGREEN FORWARD CHIPPED IN WITH 15 LEAGUE GOALS TO FIRE MANCHESTER UNITED TO THEIR THIRD CONSECUTIVE TITLE

PFA: Teddy, where does winning the Players' Player award in 2001 rank among the achievements in your career?
Teddy Sheringham: At the time you won the awards for the team, but when you look back on it 22 years later, to be alongside all those names that have won it before and after me is a real privilege. There are some big names there that you just look at and go "wow." It's a real honour.
PFA: You were the oldest player to have won the award at the time. What do you make of how you evolved as a player to win it at the age of 35? Most people have got their feet up on the sofa by then…
TS: Well, it's quite surreal really, because initially people go, "Oh, that was the treble year because you scored in the FA Cup and in the Champions League final." And I say, "No, it wasn't, actually I only scored five goals that year and it wasn't so good the year after that." But then I got back in the team, started the season, scored a few goals and the whole thing just spiralled from there. It was my way of showing that I wasn't done just yet. I was still at Manchester United, I still wanted to play a big part and I did that. We won the league convincingly that season and I scored a few goals, and to get the awards that I did was fantastic.
PFA: You mention the 1998/99 season and that famous Champions League final – that's got to be up there for you as the standout moment in your career.

Below | The Manchester United man with his PFA Players' Player of the Year trophy

Opposite | Sheringham after scoring against Leicester City in the Premier League fixture at Filbert Street, 2000

TS: First of all, playing for Manchester United is massive – bigger than anything you could imagine when you're playing for other clubs. People want to beat you week in, week out, and I don't think that's changed even now. So to play for United and win things, especially the way we did, winning the treble in the last days of that season, beating Newcastle in the FA Cup and then beating Bayern Munich in the last two minutes, you know, people remember where they were at that specific moment. They come up to me and tell me all the stories and just ask me what it was like to score and to set up the winner for Ole.
PFA: Do you ever get tired of talking about it?
TS: Not at all. Everyone has their stories that they want to tell me and I'll tell them how it felt, you know, celebrating in front of the United fans, right in front of them. It was just the perfect place to win the Champions League and the treble that year.
PFA: A few years down the line, do you get the chance to reflect on your success?
TS: I was coming to the end of my career when I won this PFA award, but I still carried on for another six or seven years. It's a privilege to be a professional footballer, the way I saw it, and I loved every minute of it, so I didn't want to give it up.
PFA: When you moved to United, did you have to change your mindset to fit in with the culture at the club?
TS: You could feel the vibe as soon as you went to Manchester United, that we're here to win. This is what we do. Sir Alex actually said to me, "You won't believe what it's like to play for Man United." I was like, "Well, you know, I've played for Tottenham for a few years now and I've played for England." But he was right, the expectation levels go up at Manchester United. People want to beat you, they want to take a point off you. So your game has to rise with that.
PFA: Thinking about the year that you won the PFA award, what was so special about that season? You were in great form, scoring 21 goals in all competitions.
TS: I still had belief in my own ability. I'd signed a three-year contract and Sir Alex asked me to sign an extra year. I said to Steve McClaren – he called me while I was away in Dubai – "I'm going to sign, but I'm just letting you know that I don't want to be a bit-part player." And he said, "Okay, I'll tell the manager." I wanted to get back in the first team. I still had faith that I could score goals at the top level and that's exactly what I did.

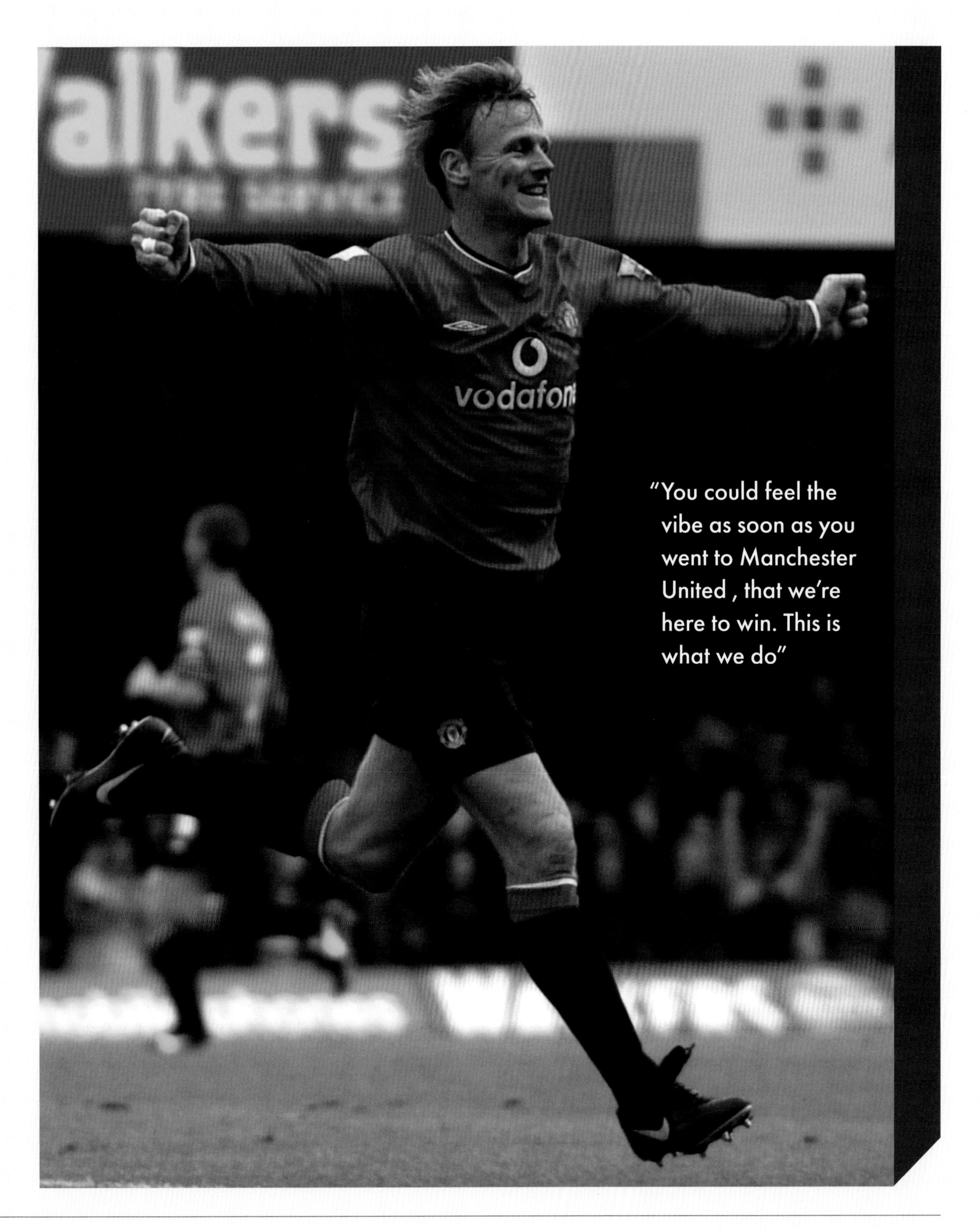

"You could feel the vibe as soon as you went to Manchester United , that we're here to win. This is what we do"

YOUNG PLAYER OF THE YEAR

Steven Gerrard

Steven Gerrard had scored eight Liverpool goals in his nascent career, but this was different. This was against Manchester United. This was a thunderbolt that nearly detached the net from its moorings. This was the moment the 20-year-old midfielder's career took off.

"If you were looking for the player you would replace Roy Keane with, it would be Gerrard," Sir Alex Ferguson later said of his fiercest rivals' new star. "Everywhere the ball is, he seems to be there. He's got that unbelievable engine, desire, determination."

Growing pains had limited Gerrard's first full season in a Liverpool shirt, but 2000/01 seemed a breakthrough even before that late-March Anfield cracker. A regular for Gérard Houllier whether on the right of midfield or through the middle, Gerrard made 50 appearances in all competitions as the Reds won a famous cup treble, scoring his 10th goal of a superb season in the seesawing 5–4 UEFA Cup final defeat of Alavés.

Presented by new England boss Sven-Göran Eriksson, the PFA Young Player of the Year award was also Gerrard's.

"I was in contention for the award last year and I really wanted to win it this year," said Gerrard.

Above | Gerrard receives the PFA Young Player of the Year award, 2001

MERIT AWARD

Jimmy Hill

Jimmy Hill earned his nickname "Castro" because of his trademark beard, yet it could just as easily have come from his revolutionary zeal. Hill's was a life dedicated to reform, his first act in becoming the Players' Union chairman in 1957 was to change its name to the more fitting Professional Footballers' Association.

Three points for a win. Goal difference. Matchday programmes. Ex-players as TV pundits. All-seater stadia. The lyrics to 1971 top-ten hit "Good Old Arsenal". Hill came up with them all, yet it's the gift he gave his fellow professionals six months before his own retirement as a player in 1961 that improved footballers' rights forever.

The maximum wage had been part of football's fabric for six decades, but £20 a week hardly set up players for life following a transient career. Articulate, confident and whip-smart, Hill campaigned tirelessly to abolish the archaic imposition, outmanoeuvring the Football League with the threat of a January strike. Within weeks, his Fulham teammate Jonny Haynes became the UK's first £100-a-week footballer.

Hill went on to manage Coventry City, winning two promotions to take the Sky Blues into the First Division, before moving into broadcasting and presenting more than 600 editions of *Match of the Day*.

"He was football's equivalent of Christopher Columbus, a great explorer of ideas," said PFA Chief Executive Gordon Taylor after Hill's death in 2015.

Forty years on from the moment he gave footballers a voice, Hill received the 2001 PFA Merit Award. English football would be nothing without him.

Hill at Fulham, 1960

"He was football's
equivalent of Christopher
Columbus, a great
explorer of ideas"
Gordon Taylor

Van Nistelrooy scores in a 3–2 win against Fulham, 2001

PLAYERS' PLAYER OF THE YEAR

Ruud van Nistelrooy

FOLLOWING A FALSE START AT MANCHESTER UNITED, THE DUTCHMAN BURST ONTO THE SCENE IN 2001/02, SCORING 36 IN ALL COMPETITIONS

PFA: Looking back to the year 2000, you're about to join Manchester United but the transfer is cancelled due to injury concerns, then you suffer a serious knee injury. Two years later, you score 23 goals in the league and become Players' Player of the Year. How do you explain such an impressive turnaround?
Ruud van Nistelrooy: Strong rehab. Also, the support from United as a club at the time, and then from Sir Alex in particular. He said, "Okay, one day you'll be a United player." Of course, at that moment you think, "It's kind of him to say it to support me, but probably won't be true." But then every month he phoned me. "How's the rehab going? How is the knee doing?" And I started believing "Okay, I can actually get fit again and signed again." So, I started training, you know, nine months of sort of Olympic training. And in the end, I did it, with the really great team of physios and doctors behind me. I was able to sign for United a year later.
PFA: How does winning Players' Player rank among your footballing achievements?
RvN: There's nothing better than to get the recognition of your colleagues.
PFA: At the time, the club was fighting Arsenal for the title, and you were battling Thierry Henry for the Golden Boot. Did that rivalry drive you on?
RvN: Speaking for myself, Thierry was pushing me. Our rivals at the time were Arsenal, Chelsea and many more, and they were pushing us as a club and also as individuals. So, all the great players in those teams, they push you. And, of course, when you are competing for the Golden Boot against a striker like Thierry, then it pushes you to your limit.
PFA: Thinking about your earlier career, you were a midfielder who switched to striker around the age of 21 when you were at Heerenveen in the Netherlands. How did the transformation to one of the top scorers in Europe come about?
RvN: Well, it took developing, of course. The manager of Heerenveen said, "Ruud, you're a striker, you can be a nine." We started working, playing with my back towards goal and I had a quick connection with that position and started scoring goals. Sometimes I missed playing in midfield, but in the end, I think my strength was to be there when it mattered and score the goals at the highest level.
PFA: Is there an art to goalscoring?
RvN: I don't know. It's also a connection with your teammates. If you start to link up and connect with them and use each other's strengths, then you can get a real force. They benefited me and vice versa, and that's why I got in in a lot of good positions.

YOUNG PLAYER OF THE YEAR

Craig Bellamy

"Everyone was like, 'What have they signed him for?'" Craig Bellamy recalled of his £6.5 million transfer to Newcastle United from relegated Coventry City in the summer of 2001. "I thought: 'I'll show you in a good arena.' I just took off, but I was angry."

Rage proved the firebrand Welshman's stimulus. "A great player wrapped round an unusual and volatile character," according to Magpies boss Sir Bobby Robson, Bellamy's wheel-spinning acceleration complemented the line-leading experience of Alan Shearer to score 41 goals between them in all competitions. The 22-year-old junior partner struck 14, his goal and assist in a 3–1 defeat of Leeds United in mid-January sending the Magpies briefly top.

A knee injury deprived Newcastle of their irrepressible youngster from March, but Bellamy's earlier form was enough to secure Champions League football and the PFA Young Player of the Year Award.

"To win that award basically says you are one of the best young kids in Europe," said Bellamy, who represented Team GB at the London 2012 Olympics. "That was huge for me."

Above | A happy Bellamy shows off his 2002 PFA Young Player of the Year award

MERIT AWARD

Niall Quinn

Completing the 2001/02 PFA Awards' striking triumvirate, Niall Quinn received the Merit Award in recognition of a 19-year senior career at Arsenal, Manchester City, Sunderland and Ireland. Better than Adam and the Ants, Quinn's eponymous "Disco Pants" chant ensured the genial striker's cult-hero status wherever he went, his decision to donate the £1 million proceeds from his May 2002 testimonial to hospitals in his hometown of Crumlin and adopted home of Sunderland testament to his generosity.

"While it was a tremendous gesture that Niall opted to give his testimonial money to worthy causes, the Merit Award is mainly for his fantastic career," said PFA Chief Executive Gordon Taylor after Quinn, then Ireland's record goalscorer, received the honour from international manager Mick McCarthy.

A future Black Cats chairman, his 163 goals in 551 club appearances proved the lofty forward was as adept on the (dance)floor as he was in the air. Quinn could have turned professional at hurling, Gaelic football or Aussie rules, but the beautiful game was always his first sporting love.

Above | Quinn on international duty at the 2002 World Cup finals

PLAYERS' PLAYER OF THE YEAR

Thierry Henry

THE GUNNERS GREAT REGISTERED A STAGGERING 24 LEAGUE GOALS AND 20 LEAGUE ASSISTS TO PUT THE PLAYERS' PLAYER AWARD BEYOND DOUBT

Above | Henry in control during the FA Cup final win against Southampton, 2003

In 2002/03, arguably the Premier League's most complete player delivered his most complete season. Thierry Henry's 24 Premier League goals and record 20 assists remain a holistic creative benchmark that has never been beaten. The only other player to manage 20 goals and assists in the same season in Europe's top five leagues is Barcelona's Lionel Messi in 2019/20.

Henry was at once Arsenal's deadliest finisher and selfless architect, combining the imagination, elasticity, balance and blinding quickness of an artistic gymnast in an Olympic all-around final. It was a heady mix.

"When he hit top gear and ran past you," Liverpool defender Jamie Carragher said of peak Henry, "it was like trying to chase after someone on a motorbike."

The 25-year-old began the season with six goals in his first seven league games and though calm side foots, low fizzers and a solo wonder goal against Tottenham Hotspur in the North London Derby were archetypal Henry, it was his artifice for creation that most shone. The number fourteen's formative years as a winger in Monaco's academy had forged a roaming centre-forward who not only released spaces into which Freddie Ljungberg and Robert Pires could surge but also despised strikers' traditional greed.

"I'm not only a goalscorer," he recalled. "Sometimes people put me in the same league as [Michael] Owen or [Ruud] van Nistelrooy, but I'm not at all like this type."

Mentioning Van Nistelrooy was instructive. The Dutchman was driven by an almost fanatical determination to score. Manchester United and Arsenal's leading men spent much of 2001–03 in a two-man tug of war for Premier League, Golden Boot and PFA Players' Player of the Year prizes.

In 2002/03, Henry took only the latter (and the FA Cup) but registered five assists in his final two league games, including three at Sunderland, to reach 20. It was as if he were proving a point. Van Nistelrooy's season tally? Four.

"To me, the most beautiful thing is making the pass when you are in a position to score yourself," said Henry, who became the first player to win consecutive PFA awards the following season. "You know you're good enough to score, but you give the ball. You share. And you see that joy in the eyes of the other guy. You know, he knows. Everyone knows."

YOUNG PLAYER OF THE YEAR

Jermaine Jenas

There was one overwhelming favourite to win the Young Player of the Year award in 2002/03 and it wasn't Jermaine Jenas. A 16-year-old Wayne Rooney seemed a shoo-in after his Arsenal rasper in October 2002, yet such was Jenas's consistency, he succeeded Craig Bellamy to become the second successive Newcastle United player to take home the honour.

"This means a lot to me," admitted the former Nottingham Forest midfielder little more than 12 months after becoming British football's second-most expensive teenager. "To win this shows me what the other players think of me."

Beginning with a superb volley against West Ham in January 2003, Jenas registered six goals in 32 appearances by the end of a stellar first full Premier League campaign, and made his senior England debut alongside Rooney against Australia.

"What JJ has achieved in the space of one year between the tender ages of 19 and 20 is of huge credit to him," said beaming Magpies boss Sir Bobby Robson.

Above | Newcastle United's Jenas, 2002

Robson as manager of Ipswich Town, 1971

MERIT AWARD

Sir Bobby Robson

Sir Bobby Robson's last job in football was also his most personal. Robson had played for his country, managed them to the World Cup semi-finals, led Barcelona, PSV, Porto and even Ipswich Town to domestic and continental trophies, yet nothing made this son of a County Durham miner prouder than taking charge of Newcastle United in September 1999.

"Football," he said, "is a small boy clambering up stadium steps for the very first time, gripping his father's hand, gawping at that hallowed stretch of turf beneath him and, without being able to do a thing about it, falling in love."

There was barely a dry eye at the Grosvenor House Hotel as Robson, in his sixth footballing decade, accepted the 2002/03 PFA Merit Award in honour of his incredible longevity.

"This is a wonderful surprise and a trophy I will treasure," said the 70-year-old. "It is overwhelming, really."

Robson understood football's inherent beauty like no other. "He was," said Sir Alex Ferguson, "a genuinely colossal human being."

Levelling the pitch

SIMONE POUND, THE PFA'S DIRECTOR OF EQUALITY, DIVERSITY AND INCLUSION, REFLECTS ON TACKLING UNDERREPRESENTATION IN FOOTBALL AND THE IMPORTANCE OF PRACTISING WHAT YOU PREACH

Simone Pound, PFA Director of Equality, Diversity and Inclusion

The goal of a level playing field for its members is at the core of what drives the PFA, but the Equality, Diversity and Inclusion (EDI) department's work transcends every branch of the players' union.

"The game evolves, but at the heart of it the idea of everyone being treated equally and fairly remains," says Simone Pound, PFA Director of EDI. "It's having someone on your side who can support you. Our amazing team have built extensive relationships across the game, some of them have also navigated similar issues related to discrimination in their careers, which means they can relate to a player's experience."

For more than a decade, the PFA has taken workshops to clubs nationwide to help players understand more about discrimination, microagressions and bias, increasingly aimed at those for whom English isn't a first language. In a post-Black Lives Matter, George Floyd and Taking-The-Knee world, the focus is now on encouraging players to speak out.

"Discrimination exists across society and is systemic," says Pound. "It's important that our members know what a line of reporting looks like, how to whistle-blow and what will happen if they speak up. Going through an FA hearing can be quite harrowing and even if you're a victim or alleged victim, it's a lot like a court of law. We provide support at every point."

Pound's department has also helped shape the Online Harms Bill, which is working its way through government thanks to the 2019 #Enough campaign, a social media boycott that reached 90 million social-media users worldwide to highlight increasing levels of online racist abuse.

"It's about real-life consequences for online behaviour," Pound says. "Players are held accountable for what they say online via the FA's rules and yet, every day, the same players are subjected to barrages of abuse online with no punishment. While there have been tweaks, blocks and filters from social media platforms, it's still happening and players are still seeing it."

Helping members to be their authentic selves is also at the heart of the PFA's work surrounding LGBTQ+ inclusion. "We work with Stonewall and other partners in the game and pushed for the media to be responsible in their reporting to create a culture and climate that embraces and celebrates all sexualities," says Pound, whose department worked with Blackpool's Jake Daniels when he became the first men's professional in a generation in the UK to come out as gay in March 2022.

"Prior to Jake's decision, we had already spoken to the Australian PFA and it was fascinating to hear how they worked with Josh Carvalho and his club as he went through the process of coming out to his squad, the game and then the world. It was a snowball effect. It worked well for Jake and that was the most important thing. He spoke to the PFA, his club Blackpool were really supportive, and we managed it alongside Jake and his family. The game really came together."

Addressing underrepresentation and inequality across football is key to EDI's work. "I've been working in this field for more than 20 years and the injustices that we were dealing with then are still prevailing," says Pound. "I'm talking about racial injustice and not racial equality because we're not there yet, but there are also significant positives we've brought to the game.

"Previously we've created dual roles with coach educators who work with black players to create a mass of black coaches over ten years. We've provided opportunities within the game via Elite Coaching Placement, Player to Coach Scheme and voluntary codes for clubs to interview black managers, but we need something more mandatory for real progress. The time of doing things for the right reasons has gone and we now need very strong, enforceable actions.

"Led by Riz Rehman, the PFA's Asian Inclusion Mentoring Scheme [AIMS] has been a great success in turning the narrative from the negative of underrepresentation in the men's and women's game to focus on the players who are in the game and build relationships with them and their families. We've held a series of events where experienced professionals such as Neil Taylor and Danny Batth meet younger players and their families, so they can see what success looks like."

The PFA itself leads from the front when it comes to representation at boardroom level. Chief Executive Maheta Molango is one of the most influential black leaders in the game, current chairman Omar Beckles is the latest in a long line of senior black player representatives, and Geoff Thompson, Trevor Johnson and Ebru Köksal sit on the Operational Board.

"We're the only organisation in football that has this representation," says Pound. "We have a black CEO, a black chair of our players and operations board. It's important our members see us as a union that's for them. Equalities is the golden thread of the organisation – everything we do, we must ensure it's for everyone."

Opposite, clockwise from top | Raheem Sterling was just one of the players who championed the #Enough campaign in 2019; the likes of Neil Taylor have helped change the narrative for young Asian footballers; Norwich City players show their support for Blackpool's Jake Daniels, 2022

"I've been working in this field for 20 years and the injustices we were dealing with then are still prevailing, but there are also significant positives we've brought to the game"

Simone Pound

Cause for thought

THE PFA'S COMMITMENT TO CHARITY SPANS EVERYTHING FROM NATIONWIDE CAMPAIGNS SUCH AS KICK IT OUT TO INDIVIDUAL PLAYER FOUNDATIONS, ENABLING ITS MEMBERS TO USE THEIR VOICE FOR THE GREATER GOOD

At the heart of the PFA's values is a firm belief in "the unifying power of football in society" and a commitment to "empowering footballers to recognise their value as people, not just players". This deep-rooted dedication to the players' importance as individuals and their place in the wider societal picture is championed by the union's many charitable partnerships and connections.

The PFA supports nationally recognised charities, as well as causes and foundations created by its individual members, with the latter often set up to address a personal or localised issue. It strives to inspire and support its members to use the influence of the game and its players to deliver the maximum positive impact in society.

The union's principal charitable partnerships reflect its emphasis on engagement, access and equality, as exemplified by Kick It Out, which was founded in 1993 to campaign against racism in the sport. The PFA immediately recognised the importance of the charity and its goals and signed up as a founding partner.

Kick It Out expanded to encompass all forms of discrimination in 1997, and the PFA is to this day represented on the charity's board and continues to work to support its mission and initiatives. These include the running of educational programmes for academy players, parents and fans, while campaigning to make sure football is welcoming, whatever an individual's race, religion, gender or sexuality.

Kick It Out is instrumental in calling out discrimination wherever it occurs – from a Sunday League fixture in the local park to the packed stands at the elite professional levels and, increasingly, on social media. As well as having a strong media profile and the support of countless players current and retired, the charity provides fans and players with a means to report incidents of abuse while working alongside other organisations to raise awareness. The impact of social media upon football-related hate crime is just one example of the importance of its work – of the 380 incidents reported in the past season, almost 50 per cent involved racism, while a further 28 per cent referred to sexual orientation.

As the PFA's Director of Equality, Diversity and Inclusion (EDI), Simone Pound, who represents the players' union on the Kick It Out board is all too aware of the challenges faced. "Football has the power to do so much good in the world," she says. "We must always try to use the sport's popularity and influence to make positive change. The PFA has always been at the forefront of tackling racism and we always look to reaffirm that commitment to all of our members. We will do all we can to put an end to the abuse players face on the pitch and online."

The PFA's other main charitable partnerships include Sporting Chance, Show Racism the Red Card and The Prince's Trust. Founded by Tony Adams following his own struggles with addiction, Sporting Chance provides free mental health support for professional sportspeople, as well as a rehabilitation programme for addiction or behavioural issues. Players who need to access these services often come to the charity via the PFA.

Former Manchester City and Northern Ireland midfielder Jeff Whitley is the PFA's Player Welfare Executive. As part of the union's wellbeing team, he comes from a position of experience, having won his battle with alcoholism with the help of Sporting Chance. "When I made that call to the PFA, that was the hardest part, because as a professional sportsman you don't want to admit defeat," he says. After leaving the clinic, he wrote a letter of thanks to the PFA. "I wanted to thank my union for their incredible support. They changed my life and going into the Sporting Chance clinic saved my life, no question. It is 13 years without a drink – and how I live my life is completely different, thanks to Sporting Chance and the PFA."

Show Racism the Red Card, which has enjoyed the backing of the PFA and its members since it was founded in 1996, combines education and football, using professional footballers and the game to promote inclusion and celebrate diversity. It was founded following a donation by then Newcastle goalkeeper Shaka Hislop, after he was racially abused by supporters near St James' Park – who then asked Hislop for his autograph when they realised who he was. Following this experience, Hislop and other Newcastle players began to visit local schools to talk to young people, establishing the educational model that is essentially still used today. The charity's strategic priorities are to maintain and further strengthen partnerships with players, clubs and sporting institutions, and the charity delivers training to more than 50,000 individuals each year.

The PFA also works closely with the Prince's Trust through the Football Initiative, which was launched by Prince Charles in 1997 to help young people develop their confidence, motivation and team-working skills through football, allowing them to attain qualifications for jobs, education or training. The Prince's Trust realised that many of the young people who needed their support lived in the same inner-city areas as leading football clubs and began shaping courses around football and developing relationships with the Premier League and PFA.

Opposite, clockwise from top | Romelu Lukaku joins a Kick It Out event, 2017; Sporting Chance's founder Tony Adams; getting the Kick It Out message across loud and clear at Stamford Bridge, 2018

"The PFA has always been at the forefront of tackling racism. We will do all we can to put an end to the abuse players face on the pitch and online"

Simone Pound

"When I made that call to the PFA, that was the hardest part, because as a professional sportsman you don't want to admit defeat"

Jeff Whitley

"There's nothing better, in football and in life, than seeing a young person come through and make a success of themselves against all the odds"
Gordon Taylor

More than 170 professional footballers have now supported young people taking part in programmes delivered by clubs, demonstrating the power footballers and football clubs have to change lives. "There's nothing better, in football and in life, than seeing a young person come through and make a success of themselves against all the odds," said former PFA Chief Executive Gordon Taylor of the charity's involvement. "That's why I feel very proud that we are one of the longest-standing partners of the Prince's Trust. I'm also proud that so many current and former professional footballers have pledged their support to the Prince's Trust by becoming official ambassadors."

As well as these headline charities, the PFA has important links with the Premier League Charitable Fund, the EFL Trust and the National League Trust. The Premier League Charitable Fund was formed in 2010 and has enabled 1.5 million young people to participate in programmes, festivals or community activities delivered through the community arm of Premier League and English Football League clubs. The charity works with the PFA Community Fund to enable Club Community Organisations to respond to local need and develop projects, engaging with players and scholars to enhance the impact on participants. The PFA contributes more than £8 million each season to the charity.

The EFL Trust and National League Trust both deliver a wide range of community initiatives to improve people's quality of life. As well as providing important financial contributions – £2.8 million per season for the EFL Trust and £1.2 million for the National League Trust – the PFA has a senior, visible presence at the organisations, with Community Liaison Executive Dave Palmer holding a place on the EFL Trust's board and Community Equalities Executive Terry Angus being a trustee of the National League Trust. This ensures that the PFA has a voice to share the concerns and needs of its members via the activities of both charities.

In addition to such large-scale bodies, in recent years, the PFA has had the privilege of supporting several charitable foundations set up by players or their relatives. Those looking to develop their own foundation often require legal advice and guidance, and the PFA offers professional support to ensure that such formalities are completed correctly, providing the player and charity with a sound base to progress from. Examples include the Bobby Moore Fund, the James Milner Foundation, the Russell Martin Foundation, the Jason Roberts Foundation, the Darby Rimmer MND Foundation and the JE3 Foundation, founded in memory of former Tottenham player Justin Edinburgh, who died in 2019 after a cardiac arrest.

All of these player foundations and charities address important personal causes: the James Milner Foundation and Russell Martin Foundation both promote healthy recreation for young people; the Jason Roberts Foundation invests in local communities to change outcomes for the most marginalised in the United Kingdom and Caribbean; and the JE3 Foundation seeks to change outcomes in the face of cardiac arrest. The Darby Rimmer MND Foundation was created by former Liverpool, Bradford City and Bolton Wanderers player Stephen Darby and army veteran Chris Rimmer, who both have motor neurone disease. The foundation raises awareness of MND, funds and assist research into the illness, raises funds, offers grants to those with MND and creates a support network for those diagnosed with the disease.

Of all these foundations, the PFA has had the longest association with the Bobby Moore Fund, which was founded by the family of England's legendary World Cup-winning captain to raise funds for research into bowel cancer – the disease that he died of aged just 51 in 1993. Bobby had expressed his wish to start a charity to his wife Stephanie Moore just weeks before his death and the PFA has supported the fund since 2005. Since it was founded, the charity has raised more than £23 million and supported international school-building projects in remote areas of Brazil, South Africa, Ecuador and Namibia through the activities of former players.

"One of the great things about our partnership with the PFA is that we reach men of a certain age who perhaps wouldn't listen to health messages but do through football," says Stephanie. "What is important to me is that the Bobby Moore Fund, the charity set up in his memory just after he died, is doing so much to help others suffering from the same disease."

From nationwide campaigns such as Kick It Out to the efforts of individual players, the extensive support that the PFA provides its host of charitable partners and associates mirrors its principle of supporting individuals, the game and society as a whole in tackling, and overcoming, many of its toughest challenges. As the union's motto puts it so succinctly, "For Football, For Life".

Opposite, clockwise from top | England's Lionesses demonstrate their support for Show Racism the Red Card following a training session at St George's Park, 2023; a Manchester City player wears a James Milner Foundation T-shirt at the Etihad, 2013; a poster for the Bobby Moore Fund

Leading edge

PEARSON IS A FRONT-RUNNER IN THE RACE TO BUILD MORE DIVERSE CAREER PATHWAYS INTO SPORT

qualifications.pearson.com

Sport and physical activity contribute £39 billion to the UK economy and a sizeable portion of this comes from grassroots sport. Pearson's sports qualifications play a pivotal role in preparing learners from across all communities to enter this exciting industry. From sports science to sports therapy, event management to coaching and even journalism, Pearson has created a range of qualifications that allow students to access career-focused pathways, including the Pearson BTEC Sport and a variety of apprenticeships.

"The importance of skills and continuous learning will be crucial in supporting young people to build careers in key industries such as sport" says Freya Thomas Monk, Managing Director, Vocational Qualifications & Training at Pearson. "Today's workplace is evolving so rapidly that continuous learning and career readiness is critical. But it's not just about training for the jobs of the future – it's also about staying relevant with the soft skills necessary in work and life.

"A young person may be drawn to a BTEC in sport because of their passion for football," says Freya. "They might not become a footballer but could continue to work in the sporting industry as a nutritionist, coach, sport psychologist, or in media, promotions or hospitality. The skills they will need to future-proof their career in the industry, such as leadership, collaboration, problem-solving and teamwork, are all the sorts of skills taught on a BTEC or our other vocational qualifications."

Pearson is using high-profile ambassadors from the industry to promote the vocational route and attract young people from diverse backgrounds. Britain's most famous gymnast, triple Olympic gold medallist Max Whitlock MBE, has worked with Pearson to launch a new series of short videos to support BTEC Sport learners, explaining key themes and topics in an accessible, bite-sized way. He is an excellent example of how BTEC qualifications can be a launchpad for a successful career. "Taking a BTEC showed me that there were different ways of learning and many paths to success" says Max. "And I'm proud of my BTEC, because of the skills and confidence it gave me."

Similarly, Tunji Akintokun MBE, business leader and Senior Independent Director at England Athletics, is passionate about diversity, the arts, science and technology, sport and social mobility. "I want to raise awareness of the value that my BTEC vocational qualification gave me, both in university and in the workplace" says Tunji.

Pearson has focused its recent marketing campaign, BTEC Works, on careers and the skills gap in the sport, engineering, technology, health and creative industries. As part of the campaign, individuals from diverse backgrounds tell positive stories of their vocational journeys in videos, social media campaigns and advertising.

Like Max and Tunji, Freya is keen to talk about how BTECs and other vocational qualifications can increase diversity in high-profile industries such as sport. "We support campaigns such as Kick It Out, which promotes inclusion in football, and attracting a diversity of new recruits into sport is essential if we are going to eradicate discrimination. The BTEC Sport is powerful because it attracts kids from all backgrounds.

"The qualifications we offer in sport attract learners regardless of background, and provide an opportunity to develop their passion for sport. We are extremely proud that our qualifications are shaping the future of UK sport and helping young people from all kinds of backgrounds to flourish."

BARCLAYS
sky
sports

The sky's the limit

WITH RECORD VIEWING FIGURES AND TOP-LEVEL PLAYER PUNDITRY, SKY SPORTS IS MAKING, AS WELL AS BREAKING, THE NEWS

www.skysports.com

As a Middlesbrough fan, Steve Smith has seen more than his fair share of ups and downs since the Premier League formed in 1992. But in his role as Executive Director of Content at Sky Sports, there has only been a series of spectacular "ups", with record-breaking audiences in 2022–23, including the Premier League season; the Women's Super League (WSL) fixture between Arsenal and Chelsea; and the Carabao Cup Final between Newcastle United and Manchester United. There was also renewed and expanded coverage of Scottish football and a multimillion-pound deal with the English Football League (EFL). Despite continued competition, Sky Sports and football remain as closely connected as a referee and his whistle.

"We support the entire football ecosystem and partnerships are very important to us," says Steve. "Sky Sports' partnership with the Premier League is one of the oldest and strongest in our portfolio, as it has been since the very beginning; and over more than 30 years, we have seen a huge increase in popularity in British football around the world. We feel very much part of that growth and narrative. Through those partnerships, we have the best access and strongest relationships with players. We tell their stories both on and off the pitch, and if you look at the growth in the game and the benefits the players have received from that, it's extraordinary."

As well as bringing huge audiences to the Premier League, EFL and the Scottish Premiership, Sky Sports has been instrumental in the growth of women's football, with viewing figures up by more than 50 per cent in 2022–23. Smith highlights the fact that the network is the largest domestic investor in women's football, offering an essential platform to the clubs and working with the FA to improve scheduling and create cross-promotion between the men's and women's games. This has allowed women footballers to become household names and role models.

As Sky Sports prepares to unveil a new London studio, fresh pundits and further innovation in its coverage, Smith sees his role as being like that of a football manager, identifying talent and then finding the right partnerships to deliver the best insight and make the greatest impact on screen. Pundits such as Jamie Carragher and Gary Neville have grown up on, and with, Sky Sports, first showing their knowledge, personalities and gift for communication through post-match interviews. Moreover, Steve is intent that the channel does more than simply deliver match coverage; he wants it to tackle the issues that matter to players and fans. He can do this because Sky Sports has earned the respect of the game's biggest assets – the players. "Our presenters can explore important issues in documentaries that illustrate the role that sportsmen and women can play in society," he says. "We can use our players to tackle subject matter that would have been unimaginable just a few years ago."

Steve's pundits really understand the game, as well as how to communicate and find different ways to talk to fans. This is not only through high-level analysis, but also through knowing what it is like to be a player. "We don't just want to break news through Sky Sports News, we want to make the news, and often the comment and debate of our talent is what leads the agenda. That creates our record audiences across the entire football world, as well as in cricket, F1, golf, netball, boxing, NFL, tennis and more, as Sky Sports goes from strength to strength."

One Nation, one vision

HUMANITARIAN AID CHARITY ONE NATION CARRIES OUT LIFE-CHANGING WORK AROUND THE WORLD, WITH THE GOAL OF DEVELOPING EMPOWERED COMMUNITIES

www.onenationuk.org

"We see ourselves as first responders to emergencies," says Muhammad Luqmaan Vania, trustee and co-founder of UK-based One Nation, an international, non-profit humanitarian aid relief and development organisation, which currently operates in over 30 countries. "We can put teams on the ground there within 72 hours, whether it's floods in Mozambique, an earthquake in Turkey, or a migrant crisis in Lesbos. We are ultra-fast to respond, setting up tents, infrastructure for toilets, electricity, heating and food distribution."

One Nation was founded in 2014, providing food, water and shelter to Syrian refugees caught up in the country's brutal conflict. Today, the charity is active around the world. However, while emergency aid remains key to its activities, it is looking at starting up what Luqmaan calls "empowerment-related" projects. "You find in places that have been stricken long-term by war, like Syria, that there's a generation growing up who have known nothing but to wait for a food parcel each month and not do very much with themselves beyond that. They're victims of the war, but if you can take a handful of them, you can create a more successful culture for them," he says. "So, in terms of empowerment, one of our latest projects in Pakistan is our Pakistan 'Super Village'. We're building homes, relatively basic but efficient homes, at £1,000 each. And within that village, we're also going to have a community centre, a school – the idea is to build communities upwards, enabling them to become self-sustainable."

One Nation also proposes to set up another Super Village, in Syria, which it describes as a "mini ecosystem", building 200 homes, a school, a mosque, as well as shops and workshops, creating jobs for local people, making items that can be sold – and even constructing a football stadium. "Don't get me wrong, it's not going to be Old Trafford," says Luqmaan. "It's not going to be a 70,000-seater with corporate seating – it'll be a football pitch with a couple of hundred seats around the side. It's all about increasing the quality of life for communities. That's something that really sets us apart as a charity."

Football is a big passion among the One Nation team, not least since the Premier League extended its global reach, attracting an international audience by touching and enthusing communities worldwide. They already work with various academies, but this is just the start. With this in mind, the charity plans to create networks with footballers and football clubs to garner interest to help with their projects, whether it be sponsorship, donating boots and kit, surplus stock that would otherwise go to waste, or helping fund football pitches.

One Nation has experienced rapid growth since 2014, from £500,000 in donations in its first year to an expected £19 million in 2023. The charity is transparent about its work, stressing that donations are not swallowed up by excessive administration costs. "We work to a 100 per cent donation policy," says Luqmaan. "And we work in a very efficient manner with the charity truly being run on staff and volunteer passion. Not a single penny donated will ever go to our UK administration costs. We're just a vessel for their charity to get to the recipients."

In keeping with UK law, One Nation discloses its annual report, which details the countries it has

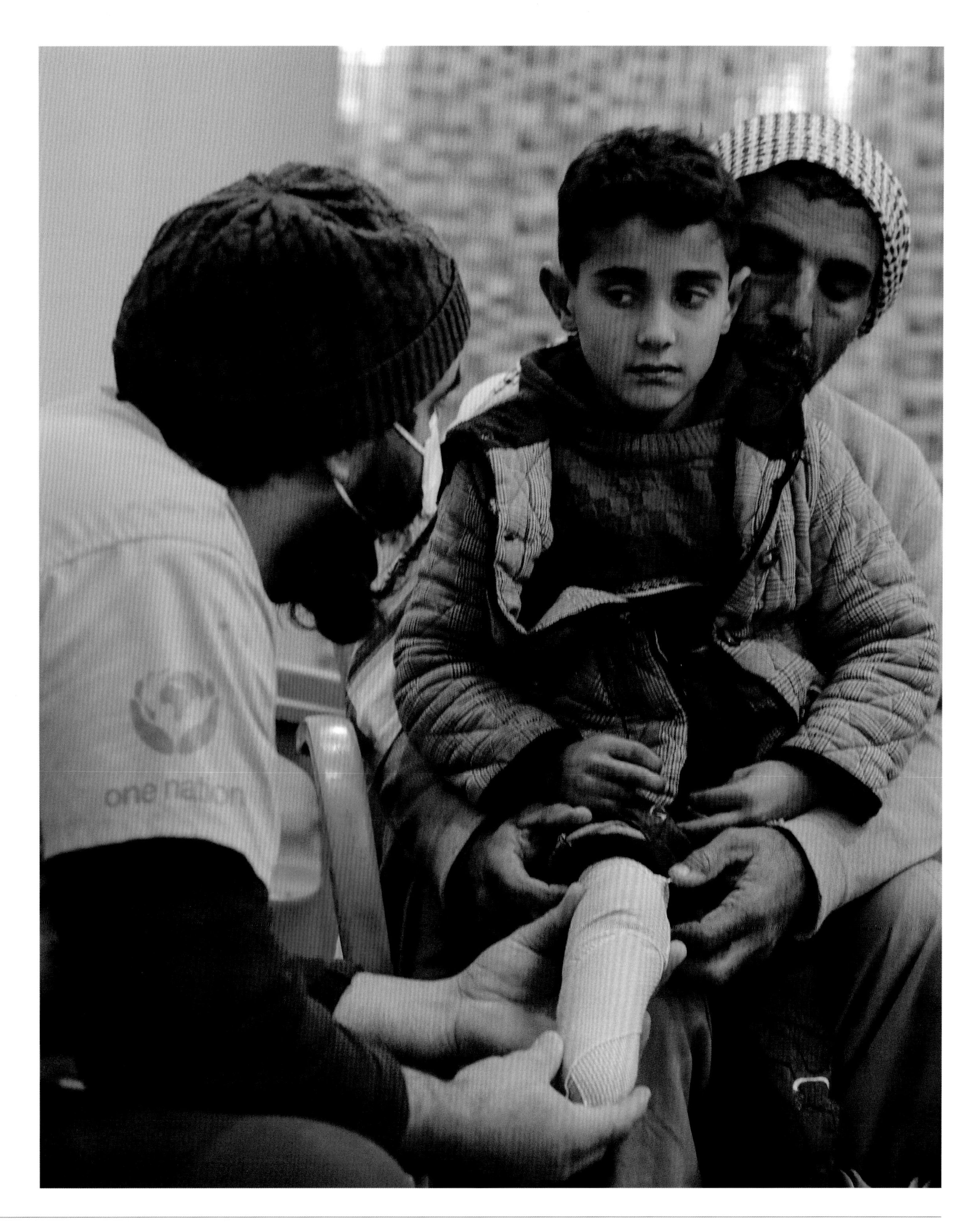
one nation

"The idea is to build communities upwards, enabling them to become self-sustainable"

operated in, how much money it has spent in those countries and any administrative costs. It also posts a large amount of video and stills footage on various social media platforms. "I think that really resonates with donors in the current day and age. We're keen to give them as much transparency as we can."

An team of volunteers help One Nation carry out its work. This input at grassroots level plays a significant part in fundraising. Alongside the volunteers is a staff of around 30 who are involved in the day-to-day running of the organisation. As Luqmaan explains, it requires a tightening of the purse strings to run the charity at this level, with longevity and sustainability. In addition to donations, funding comes from government grants and the Gift Aid scheme.

Such funding supports One Nation projects like Gift of Water, which has seen one million bottles of water handed out to communities since 2014 (in addition to the 20 million food packs it has distributed worldwide) and the building of hand pumps close to homes so that people do not have to travel for water. The charity has also provided cataract surgery, of which there are thousands of beneficiaries so far in Asia and Africa. "It's not a massively complex surgery, but it gives people the gift of sight back instantly." In addition, there are plans to create homes for the elderly, a group particularly neglected in times of war and displacement, with those without family left to fend for themselves.

Based in West Yorkshire, One Nation not only cares for those overseas, but also the immediate community, too. During the Covid pandemic in 2020, it responded with typical rapidity, cooking 200 hot meals a day for the elderly and isolated, with the charity's volunteers making the deliveries across local towns Batley, Heckmondwike and Dewsbury. "The local authority was initially overwhelmed and struggled in the first few months of the pandemic," explains Operations Manager Javed Rafiq. "We liaised with them, giving information on the scale of the vulnerability. We didn't ask for guidelines, we did it ourselves because we could see what was going on in our community."

One Nation is keen to expand on its success to date to meet even greater needs worldwide. "One or two Super Villages are fine," says Javed, "but what about the millions of people who aren't able to be part of that? But with more funds, we can create more villages. The long-term aim is to create that sustainability for everybody."

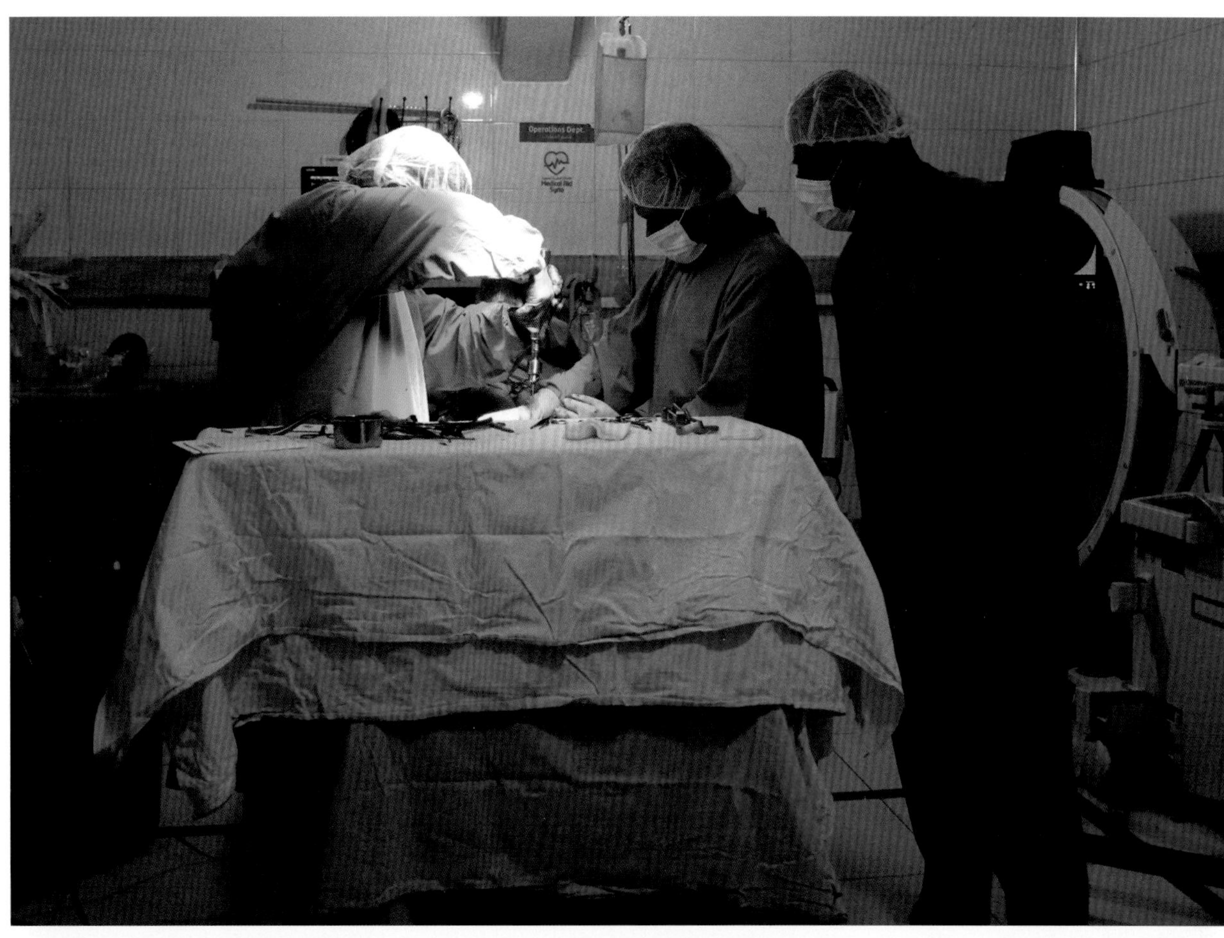

one nation
SYRIA
FOOD PARCELS
OCTOBER 2022

Equal opportunities for all

FROM BUSINESS TO SPORT, BLUEPRINT FOR ALL HELPS YOUNG PEOPLE FROM UNDERPRIVILEGED BACKGROUNDS TO SUCCEED AGAINST THE ODDS IN THEIR CHOSEN CAREERS

www.blueprintforall.org

Modern football academies search the land for the best talent, leaving no school playground, park or playing field untouched as they attempt to secure the finest young footballers. But access for young players is far from equal. Underprivileged children might not have the time, parental support or financial resources required to make the sort of commitment demanded by academies. This is where the Blueprint for All charity steps in.

The organisation works with young people of diverse ethnic heritages and from disadvantaged backgrounds, between the ages of 13 and 30. Nurturing talent, it not only inspires young people, but also provides tangible opportunities for them to thrive in a career of their choice. It does this entirely through donations and the support of corporate partners, ensuring that an unprecedented 85 to 90 per cent of all donations go directly to help those who need it most. "This means that anybody who donates knows their donation will have an impact," says CEO Sonia Watson. "We are now phasing in a digital access platform that is the first of its kind to have this sort of reach. That will transform the lives of young people by making sure everything we do is accessible through digital means."

The new digital platform – My Blueprint for All – allows the charity to offer more targeted support at different stages of an individual's journey. The impact on its participants is measured and is set to continue after the high-impact programme or workshop has been completed. An essential part of the charity's work involves engaging with school-age children, to plant a seed of aspiration.

"People can feel they do not belong in an organisation or profession and that is the first barrier we tackle when we intervene with young people," says Chelsea Way, Strategic Director. "We work with them to the age of 30, tackling the barriers that arise at all these different stages through workshops, bursaries and internships. We can now enhance participant journeys by sharing relevant and dynamic opportunities. Sport and fitness is one of our key sectors, as we could see from our research there was a big gap in knowledge about this sector. We have created resources to break down common myths and show how to access opportunities."

Creating equal opportunities for all remains a difficult but vital task. In the world of football, for example, there is equal opportunity on the pitch, but not necessarily in positions of responsibility off the pitch. It is a similar story across the business world, as almost 70 per cent of FTSE 250 boards have no ethnic minority representation. The ethos at Blueprint for All is that race, ethnicity or social background should not limit what anybody achieves in life. The charity strives to break down barriers and ensure all young people receive the education, training and support they need to reach their potential.

"There is huge synergy between what we do and what we hear the football world speak about as being important in terms of equity for all and anti-racism," says Sonia. "We know this demographic very clearly, and we know that football is a very powerful tool for them.

"We receive donations from around the world, allowing us to help young people, whatever stage they are in their career. As a small charity, we are proud of the impact we make. Last year alone, we directly helped more than 3,000 young people into opportunities that might change their lives."

Levelling the field

EAST MIDLANDS CHARITY BACA IS USING THE BEAUTIFUL GAME TO CREATE A BETTER LIFE FOR YOUNG REFUGEES

www.bacacharity.org.uk

Football has an incredible capacity to unite people from different cultures and offer tremendous opportunities to those who come from challenging backgrounds. The sport transcends barriers of language, race and social class, building a sense of community while encouraging personal responsibility and teamwork. These positives are wholeheartedly embraced by Baca, a charity that provides essential and empathetic support for young refugees in the East Midlands. The organisation runs several initiatives to support young people, and some of the most successful and popular have revolved around football.

"Our funding comes partly from the government as our young people have arrived without parents or guardians, and we deliver therapeutic support on behalf of social services to enable each young person to thrive," explains CEO Jimmy Zachariah. "We take additional funding from individuals and organisations to deliver support in areas such as education, enriching trips, sport and therapy, and have formed a seven-a-side football team that our young people called 'Bacalona'. We have found football helps with language and emotional wellbeing, plus it allows them to let off steam – girls as well as boys. Some of our young people join local football clubs, which is a great way to understand the community, and some have been offered trials at local clubs, which is great for their self-esteem."

Baca takes its name from the biblical Valley of Baca – a fertile place where travellers could rest and gather strength during their pilgrimage to Jerusalem. And this reflects the role that the charity plays for young people who have travelled from across the world to find sanctuary in the UK, often impacted by the trauma of what they have experienced. The staff at Baca believe that, with sufficient care, support, understanding and belief, these young people will thrive as they face the next stage of their journey through life. "We believe young people don't just need a safe place to live – they need a family. For a lot of our young people, we are that family," says Jimmy.

First and foremost, the charity provides young people with a safe home. Previously, many were placed in hostels among adults – an unsuitable environment for vulnerable children. Baca assists with asylum applications as well as training and education, and then starts to build a new life for these young people, putting in place the scaffolding that will allow them to contribute to the country they hope to call home. Football is one element of this – a shared love that unites and inspires people across the world. Many young refugees are aware of role models such as Victor Moses and Alphonso Davies – both former refugees who became international footballers.

Having proven a success in the East Midlands, Baca hopes to extend its offering to other parts of the country, either by helping other charities or by taking responsibility for young refugees in different regions. "We come across young people who are incredibly resilient in many ways," says Jimmy. "They are brave and determined to make the most of life, but they have had some horrible experiences. Given the chance, treated well, and presented with opportunities, we know that they will contribute to society. There is a huge opportunity for anybody to get involved and support that journey, whether it's a football club or an individual. We believe these children will contribute to life in this country, if they are given the chance."

Chapter Four

2003|04 – 2012|03

The women's game grew rapidly throughout the PFA Awards' fourth decade. The FA introduced central contracts for 17 England players in 2009, three months before the UEFA Women's Euro finals kicked off in Finland – a tournament in which England finished as runners-up following a 6–2 defeat to Germany in Helsinki. Two years later, the Women's Super League was launched, replacing the FA Women's Premier League National Division as the pinnacle of women's domestic football. A further two years on and Arsenal's Kim Little became the first PFA Women's Players' Player of the Year, confirming a new era in the game and the PFA's own commitment to achieving parity for female footballers.

In the men's game, the ten-year period began with the jaw-dropping dominance of the Gunners' Invincibles season, during which Arsène Wenger's team fought and finessed its way through 38 league matches unbeaten. The fundamentals of Premier League football were changing, however. Having taken over Chelsea in the summer of 2003, Roman Abramovich invested heavily in the squad, and introduced manager José Mourinho to the English game in June 2004. The team put together one of the great title runs the following season, led by PFA Players' Player John Terry, seeing off Arsenal and beating Manchester United home and away to win the league.

That same season, Liverpool produced one of the all-time great comebacks in the Champions League final, overturning a 3–0 deficit at half time to defeat AC Milan in a penalty shootout. English clubs went on to enjoy further success in the competition, with Manchester United and Chelsea facing off in the 2008 final in Moscow; Sir Alex Ferguson's charges coming out on top on that occasion. In the wake of this success, and for the first time since English clubs were banned from Europe in 1985, UEFA's coefficient rankings placed the Premier League as the best in the world.

At the same time, the English league system was restructured, with the First Division becoming the Championship, and the divisions below renamed as League One and League Two. As if to mark the beginning of a fresh chapter, the new Wembley Stadium was completed in time to host the 2007 FA Cup final. Some elements of the game, however, proved reassuringly durable. Sheffield FC, the world's oldest football club, celebrated its 150th anniversary in October 2007, and the PFA, the world's oldest professional sport union, marked its centenary that December.

To protect homegrown talent, the 2010/11 season heralded the introduction of a new rule that required clubs to name at least eight players in their 25-man squad who had been registered domestically for a minimum of three seasons prior to their 21st birthday. The move was designed to ensure there would continue to be a pipeline of players with top-flight experience coming through to the national team, and to lay the groundwork for a period of English success at international level.

The decade ended with the departure of the era-defining Sir Alex Ferguson. If his 1,500th and final match in charge of Manchester United – a tumultuous 5–5 goalfest at West Brom in May 2013 – was anything but storybook, his team's results in the ten-year period prior to his send-off were the stuff of legend. The Red Devils won half of the Premier League titles on offer, finishing runners-up on three occasions – a level of consistent success that few if any managers can hope to replicate in the modern game.

20|13
CHAMPIONS 20|13
HANKYOUSIRALEX
CHAMPIONS 20|13
20 TIMES CHAMPIONS OF ENGLAND. 13 PREMIER LEAGUE TITLES.
Private Charter

Fly Emirates
Fly Emirates

Aurasma

2003 | 04

PLAYERS' PLAYER OF THE YEAR

Thierry Henry

THE CATALYST FOR THE INVINCIBLES' UNBEATEN SEASON WITH 30 LEAGUE GOALS, THE FRENCHMAN ALSO WON HIS SECOND SUCCESSIVE PFA PLAYERS' PLAYER OF THE YEAR AWARD IN RECOGNITION OF HIS RELENTLESS PURSUIT OF SUCCESS

PFA: Hi Thierry. You're the first person to win the Players' Player of the Year award in consecutive years. You've won everything, but that must rank right up there for you?
Thierry Henry: Yeah, it does. No disrespect to the other trophies that you can win individually, but when the players are voting, they know exactly what the player is about and how tough it is to play against him. But when you play with the players that I played with – I have to mention them – because it wouldn't have been possible for me to win it twice, or even one time. So, it's who you play with, and yes, it makes it extra special when players are voting.
PFA: When you look at the first season you won it, you didn't win the Premier League, but you broke the record for assists and were one goal off being top scorer.
TH: Individually, it's one of my best seasons ever. To score 24 goals and have 20 assists, it just doesn't happen like that. I didn't know at the time that the 20 assists would go down in history. It's so funny because I always say to people, "I care more about my assists than my goals". If not, I wouldn't have had 20! If I was shooting on sight and staying in the box to just wait for my goals, then I wouldn't have had 20.
PFA: How did you redefine that forward position?
TH: You have to recognise what you're good at and what you're not good at. I was always trying to make sure that you're never going to see my weaknesses. I wasn't a target man, I wasn't a guy that was going to break his neck to out-jump someone at the first post. But I was a guy that used to come and try to play, make things happen, go down the wing, try to beat people, shoot from outside

Right | Henry scores his second against Inter in the Champions League group stage at San Siro, 2003

Opposite | The Arsenal man in action against Celta Vigo in the Champions League at Highbury, 2004

14

2003|04

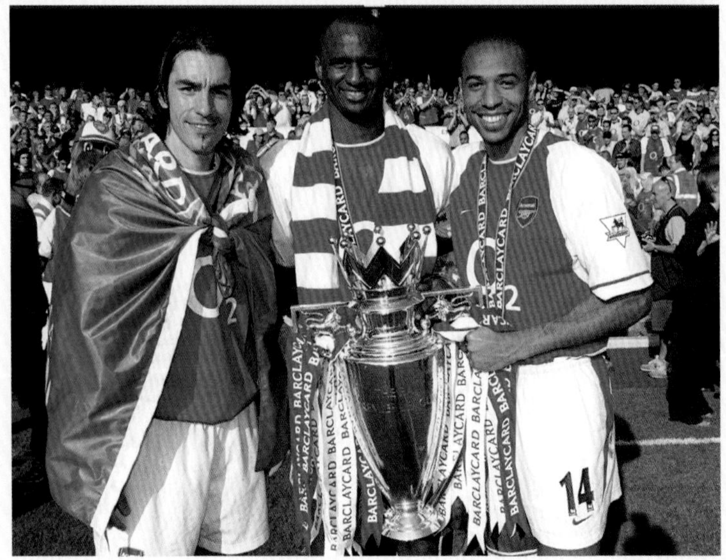

"I wanted to make people understand that it is a team effort. Sometimes I put the goalkeeper down and I pass it back. I could have scored but what message do I send to my teammates?"

the box, finishing a movement in the box. So, I was like, "Okay, what can I do for everyone to understand that I'm not a box player?" Even at Arsenal, I used to drift off the centre backs and try to stay on the left, and I used to hear the Arsenal fans saying, "What are you doing? Get in the box." I'm like, "I'm not that guy." You have to perform first. You have to deliver. Then everyone was like, "Oh, well okay, let him do what he has to do."

At the beginning of my career, it was, "How can I make people understand that giving is also important and it's as important as scoring?" How many players can score without an assist? How many players can go and get the ball alone and score? It doesn't happen often. So that means a pass matters. But how do you arrive at the goal? You pass the ball, right? You don't dribble, apart from some players. Why are we telling kids all the time, "The most important thing is to score"? The most difficult thing in the game is to score, yes, but what about the pass? It's always "Who's gonna win the Golden Boot?" Yeah, that's important, but who's gonna win the assists chart?

I wanted to make people understand that it is a team effort. And if you look at some of my assists, sometimes I put the goalkeeper down and I pass it back. I know I could have scored more goals, but what message do I send to my teammates? Are we together? Do I share? Yes. So how did I change the game? I wanted to make people understand that when you play as a winger you go up and down the whole game and you break your neck to cross the ball back for the striker and he scores a tap-in and he runs on the other side like he won the game, but *we* won the game. Right?

PFA: How did you go into the following season after the disappointment of missing out on the title that year?

TH: First and foremost, we lost it, so we wanted to win it again. It was just one day at a time, one game at a time. I didn't want to go on holiday, I didn't want to go to a tournament, I just wanted to come back and go to our pre season and be ready to get what belongs to us. That's where my spirit was, that's what I wanted to do, and obviously everyone was on the same page.

PFA: You oozed confidence. Was that key to how you led the team?

TH: I liked to play letting people know it's on. I wasn't good all the time, we all know that it can happen, but my demeanour was going to tell you, "It's going to be tough for you today". Whether I was going to do it with the ball, the way I looked at you, the way I used to look at the fans – I think that's why people always say there was an understanding with me and the fans. It's simple. Any Arsenal fan will tell you that when I was upset, I couldn't hide it, I was transparent. I wasn't an actor so you could see people could relate, I guess. I wasn't good all the time, like I said, but I always tried to give 100 per cent. I think that's one of the most important things.

Call it cocky, call it confident, but you need to have an edge when you arrive at the top. If you look at me on the field, you need to have the feeling, "Oh, oh." That's what you need to see in my eyes. The eyes will tell a lot and you need to feel that. A lot of the guys had that. When you look at Patrick [Vieira], when you look at Gilberto [Silva], Sol Campbell, they had that. And that's why I think that season was particular, because we had a real edge.

PFA: Is there a goal that stands out for you from the two seasons that you won the Players' Player award?

TH: The Liverpool goal at Highbury in 2004. I think [Sami] Hyypiä scored the first goal and then Michael Owen made it 2–1. I think it's the first time I felt the stadium ... everyone stopped breathing, it was like, what's happening? And when I scored that goal. We all started to breathe again together. I scored later, it could have been anyone, but it was the 3–2 and I felt everyone breathing at the same time. That's why for me that goal is special. Not only because of how I scored it, but the impact that it had on people.

Opposite, clockwise from top | Henry celebrates putting the ball past David James of Manchester City at Highbury, 2004; three of Arsenal's Invincibles, Robert Pires, Patrick Vieira and Henry, pose with the Premier League trophy, 2004; the Frenchman, pictured with Sol Campbell, scores the equaliser against Manchester United in the 2003 Charity Shield

Right | Henry with his second PFA Players' Player of the Year award, 2004

2003|04

YOUNG PLAYER OF THE YEAR

Scott Parker

Scott Parker first gave an indication of his supreme skill and close control when performing some back-garden keepy-uppies as a 13-year-old in a 1994 World Cup advert for McDonald's. A decade on, the precocious midfielder was voted the country's best young player by his fellow professionals.

Parker had been the beating heart of the Charlton Athletic midfield for two and a half seasons, but even by the 23-year-old's standards his 2003/04 form was extraordinary. He made his senior England debut that November. "I don't think I've ever seen a player be so wholehearted in a challenge and making tackles like Scott in training in my whole career," recalled Parker's midfield partner Matt Holland.

By January 2004, the Addicks were fourth in the Premier League and chasing Champions League football, having beaten Liverpool 3–2 and Chelsea 4–2. The Blues were so impressed, they paid £10 million for Parker's services. Without their irreplaceable best player, who beat new teammate John Terry to his PFA honour, Charlton limped home to seventh.

Parker battles for the ball with Alan Smith of Leeds United at The Valley, 2003

MERIT AWARD

Dario Gradi

Dario Gradi received the Merit Award in 2003/04 in recognition of his long spell as manager at Crewe Alexandra. He managed Sutton United, Wimbledon and Crystal Palace before taking over at Crewe where, between 1983 and 2011, he oversaw 1,359 first-team matches across two permanent and one caretaker stints in charge.

2004|05

Above | Terry with his Players' Player of the Year trophy, 2005

PLAYERS' PLAYER OF THE YEAR

John Terry

THE INDOMITABLE DEFENDER CAPTAINED CHELSEA TO THE CLUB'S FIRST TITLE IN 50 YEARS, CONCEDING A MERE 15 LEAGUE GOALS ALONG THE WAY

PFA: How would you describe a young John Terry coming through the Chelsea ranks?
John Terry: I'd describe myself as very hungry, very ambitious and determined to get right to the very top. I did all I could as a youngster to stay out on the pitch, do all the extra bits as a kid, both on and off the pitch, to give myself the best opportunity to break through in the first team. I'd ask the likes of Marcel Desailly and Frank Leboeuf questions, constantly being there, going and sitting next to them at the training ground and just picking their brains. I had the best players in the dressing room at the time, and it was important for me to go and learn off them.
PFA: What qualities would you attribute to making that leap from academy football to becoming one of the world's greatest centre backs?
JT: That's very kind. I had the utmost respect for all of my peers, but once I got on the pitch with the first team players, it was a level playing field and I was renowned as tough tackling so, if there was an opportunity to win a tackle, I would win a tackle. Gianluca Vialli was manager when I first come through, and I remember this one training session, I smashed him and he's gone up in the air over me and everyone's gone "oh no". Vialli got up and said, "That's exactly what I want on the pitch." And from that moment, it was like, "Yeah, I'm okay to do what I need to do." I was there to win that game on the training pitch, and I was the same in the games of a weekend. That really served me well.
PFA: Fast forward to the 2004/05 season. You're renamed captain by José Mourinho and you win the Premier League in record-breaking fashion – most clean sheets, most points accrued at the time. How does it feel to look back on that season?
JT: I certainly remember José announcing himself as "the special one". We'd never seen a coach work as well as he did, give us as much tactical information as he did, and make us believe that we were the best players. He was telling me constantly, week after week, I was the best defender in the world. He was telling me that personally, but he was telling the world that in the press conferences as well. It made you feel that you were invincible. It was a great achievement to get the armband and to go and win the title. Like you said, we broke some records that I don't think will be beaten. I mean, the 25 clean sheets and 15 goals conceded I don't think will ever be beaten in the Premier League.
PFA: You have a long list of individual achievements – UEFA Club Defender of the Year in 2005, 2008, 2009, in the FIFA Pro World 11 for five consecutive seasons. Where does being named Players' Player of the Year rank?
JT: Right up there at the very top. The PFA one stands above all of them because it's decided by the players in the Premier League, which is the best league in the world. When I look back at the players that were up for winning it at the time, it's incredible to go and win that, especially as a defender.

YOUNG PLAYER OF THE YEAR

Wayne Rooney

Rooney bagged a hat-trick on his Champions League debut against Fenerbahçe in 2004

You've just become the most expensive teenage footballer in the world. How do you react? If you're £27 million Wayne Rooney, you imagine you're back on the Croxteth streets and thump home a Champions League hat-trick on your Manchester United debut in September 2004.

"Nothing fazes him, not the fee, not the club, nothing," said Roy Keane of the new signing.

The first of 17 goals in all competitions in 2004/05, Rooney saved his best for the April 2005 day he picked up the first of two successive PFA Young Player of the Year awards from England manager Sven-Göran Eriksson. Nursing a dead leg and about to be substituted, he hit a venomous top-corner volley against Newcastle United that crystallised his myriad gifts. If ever there was a goal for the YouTube generation, the platform having hosted its first video 14 hours before the 19-year-old's own internet-breaking effort, this was it.

"Eventually, he'll have all the United records," said prescient United icon Denis Law. A star was born.

Hislop in goal for West Ham against Bolton Wanderers, 2006

MERIT AWARD

Shaka Hislop

One nondescript day in 1995, Newcastle United goalkeeper Shaka Hislop stopped at a petrol station.

"These kids started shouting racist abuse," recalled the ex-West Ham and Portsmouth shot stopper, who went on to appear in two FA Cup finals and for Trinidad and Tobago at the 2006 World Cup. "Then after a bit one of them realised who I was and told his friends. Then they came over looking for autographs."

Soon after, Hislop and anti-racism campaigner Ged Grebby formed Show Racism the Red Card, using the power of sport to educate about all forms of discrimination and eradicate the cancer still grimly endemic in a predominantly beautiful game.

"It's overwhelming in many respects and I'm not quite sure what I have done to deserve this," he said, humble almost to a fault, after receiving the 2005 PFA Merit Award to mark the charity's tenth anniversary.

Hislop continues to campaign tirelessly against racism. No PFA Merit Award has been more deserved.

PLAYERS' PLAYER OF THE YEAR

Steven Gerrard

LIVERPOOL'S CAPTAIN LED BY EXAMPLE, DELIVERING GOALS AND SILVERWARE IN A DEFINING SEASON

Only one word describes Steven Gerrard in 2005/06. Inevitable.

Liverpool's homegrown skipper had already produced one of the all-time great displays in the previous season's seemingly impossible Champions League final comeback against AC Milan, but the 25-year-old's 23 goals and 15 assists provided consistent perfection. "One-man team" is a facile term but Gerrard came as close as anyone to becoming Roy Race incarnate.

He wasn't even playing in his preferred position. With Xabi Alonso and Mohamed Sissoko as coach Rafael Benítez's central midfield pair, Gerrard was accommodated out wide, but given freedom to drift inside and cause mayhem.

"He's not a winger, but he's not playing as a winger," explained a miffed Benítez later in 2006. "Which has been his best season? Last year, when he scored 23 goals from the right-hand side."

It was the variety, too. Sure, there were trademark long-range howitzers against Aston Villa and Newcastle United, but Gerrard also scored calm side-footers against Crystal Palace in the League Cup and Sunderland in the Premier League. He flew into tackles, split defences with one pass and delivered a constant stream of pinpoint crosses.

"I'm still in shock," Gerrard said after picking up the Players' Player of the Year award from World Cup-winning midfielder Alan Ball in April 2006. "To go through to another FA Cup final and win this special award in the same weekend is fantastic for me."

That's right, the crowning moment of Gerrard's jaw-dropping 2005/06 was still to come. He had already scored one and made another as the clock ticked past 90 minutes with Liverpool trailing West Ham 3–2 in the FA Cup final, but with one swish of his cramping right foot, the captain equalised, scoring a penalty in the ensuing shootout to lift the trophy.

"If it was anyone else you'd be screaming at them not to shoot, but when it's Stevie something special will happen," said teammate Jamie Carragher. "It did that day." The Gerrard Final? More like the Gerrard Season.

Gerrard after captaining the Reds to victory in a penalty shootout win against West Ham in the FA Cup final, 2006

MERIT AWARD

George Best

Manchester United scout Bob Bishop was a man of few words. In 1961, he needed just eight to change football history: "I think I have found you a genius."

George Best was 17 when he made his United debut two years after Bishop's succinct telegram to United boss Sir Matt Busby. By 22, his 32nd goal of the 1967/68 season helped secure England's first European Cup. That December, the working-class Belfast kid won the 1968 Ballon d'Or.

At his peak, Best's feints and flicks blended balletic grace with the strength of a prizefighter to "brush aside giants like leaves", according to Manchester City boss Joe Mercer. The Fifth Beatle was football's first rock star, his winking aphorisms inspiring a new generation.

"He was flamboyant and exciting," Diego Maradona once said. "We were very similar players, dribblers who create moments of magic."

Six months after Best's death in 2005, PFA Chief Executive Gordon Taylor presented the forward's surviving family members with the prestigious Merit Award in recognition of the most vibrant of careers.

George Best at The Cliff training ground in Manchester, 1970

YOUNG PLAYER OF THE YEAR

Wayne Rooney

"He was the kid of England, everyone loved him. He was so powerful I was calling him 'Pitbull'. The power of Wayne Rooney is his mentality and strength and he never stops. He's a fantastic team player and he scores. He's a fantastic boy and he helped me a lot when he came to join us in Manchester."

Cristiano Ronaldo

Above | Rooney proudly holds his second consecutive PFA Young Player of the Year award, 2006

PLAYERS' PLAYER OF THE YEAR

Cristiano Ronaldo

THE YOUNG PORTUGUESE ANNOUNCED HIMSELF TO THE WORLD, WINNING HIS FIRST LEAGUE TITLE AND NO FEWER THAN EIGHT INDIVIDUAL AWARDS

Above | On the move as Chelsea's Didier Drogba looks on, 2006

Opposite | Ronaldo delights in scoring the fourth goal in United's 5–1 win over Fulham at Old Trafford, 2006

Cristiano Ronaldo was public enemy number one in the summer of 2006. At the World Cup, the Portuguese had ensured club-mate Wayne Rooney received a red card for stamping on Ricardo Carvalho. CR7's wink to the bench, followed by a match-winning penalty in the ensuing shootout, sealed his fate. Ronaldo wanted out.

Within 12 months, he had won the Premier League, the PFA Players' Player of the Year (presented by United boss Sir Alex Ferguson), Young Player of the Year and the Football Writers' Association Player of the Year. Not since Andy Gray 30 years previously had a player dominated. How?

Ultimately, the winger refused to leave a failure after 27 goals in 137 games, an FA Cup and League Cup from three promising if unspectacular seasons. Working constantly with strength and conditioning coach Mick Clegg, "Cristiano crammed thousands of hours of graft to turn himself into the perfect player" that summer.

"Physically, he changed from a boy to a man," right back Gary Neville later recalled. "He left as a featherweight and returned as a light-heavyweight. That brought him a level of power he didn't have before."

Ronaldo's attitude changed, too. Gone were the peacocking stepovers, replaced by a relentless goalscoring zeal that first showed itself with an opening day half-volley in a 5–1 win at Fulham. By September, he tormented Reading right back Graeme Murty for 90 minutes, including a devilish run and deadly finish.

"You've got no chance because he can go both ways, flick it over your head, nutmeg you and just start laughing," Murty said. "All I could feel was the wind as he rushed past. And he's a brute, as well. Tackling him is like running into a brick wall."

In December, Ronaldo exploded. Beginning with a goal and an assist in the Manchester derby, Ronaldo scored three successive braces against Aston Villa, Wigan and Reading to send United top and become just the third player to win successive Premier League Player of the Month awards.

The milestones kept falling. By February, he'd reached his 15-goal target in all competitions to finally win a bet he'd lost every season with Ferguson. In April, he scored his first Champions League goals – in his 27th appearance in the competition – with a quarter-final brace against Roma. Ronaldo's 50th United goal against Manchester City in May all but secured the title.

"He realised it was about end product," said Rio Ferdinand as Ronaldo finished with 23 goals and 14 assists. "To become the best player in the world it would be all about purely scoring goals or setting them up."

That summer, United's assistant boss René Meulensteen challenged Ronaldo to score 40 goals. By June 2008, Ronaldo had won another league title, the Champions League, retained his PFA crown and scored 42 times. In the ten seasons that followed for both United and Real Madrid, he scored more than 40 goals in eight of them. The best player in the world, all right.

"Cristiano crammed thousands of hours of graft to turn himself into the perfect player"

Mick Clegg

Ronaldo holds his second of two PFA awards for 2006/07

YOUNG PLAYER OF THE YEAR

Cristiano Ronaldo

"It is a special night. It is a big honour to win trophies like this in the Premier League. I am very proud. My colleagues have voted for me and that is fantastic because the players know the qualities of players. I want to keep working hard and getting better because these trophies have now given me more motivation. At this moment, I am consistent. I am more mature now and I am playing better. This great team has helped me as well, because when the team wins it is easier for us all to play with more confidence."

MERIT AWARD

Sir Alex Ferguson

It was probably for the best that Manchester United didn't listen to Pete Molyneux. "Three years of excuses and it's still crap," read the United fan's banner in December 1989. "Ta-ra, Fergie."

Sir Alex Ferguson led his side to the FA Cup less than five months later. By the time he retired in 2013, he'd added another 37 major honours (including 13 Premier League titles and two Champions Leagues) to the bulging Old Trafford trophy cabinet. The inscrutable Scot turned a listing giant without a league title in 26 years into the world's first super club.

"Nobody likes losing but when he came here he was a lunatic," recalled former utility player Clayton Blackmore. "Tiddlywinks, anything. He just wouldn't accept defeat."

Ferguson was always much more than an obsessive workaholic with a hairdryer complex. He created four great United teams and nurtured some of the finest footballers in Premier League history from Giggs to Cantona, Ronaldo to Rooney. And where would the football lexicon be without "squeaky bum time"?

"You may find another Beckham or Ronaldo, but never ever will you find another Sir Alex Ferguson," said Cantona.

Ferguson received the 2007 PFA Merit Award to mark his 20th full season at Old Trafford. Across a 2,155-game managerial career, he won 49 trophies (both records) and managed without a break from the age of 36 to 71.

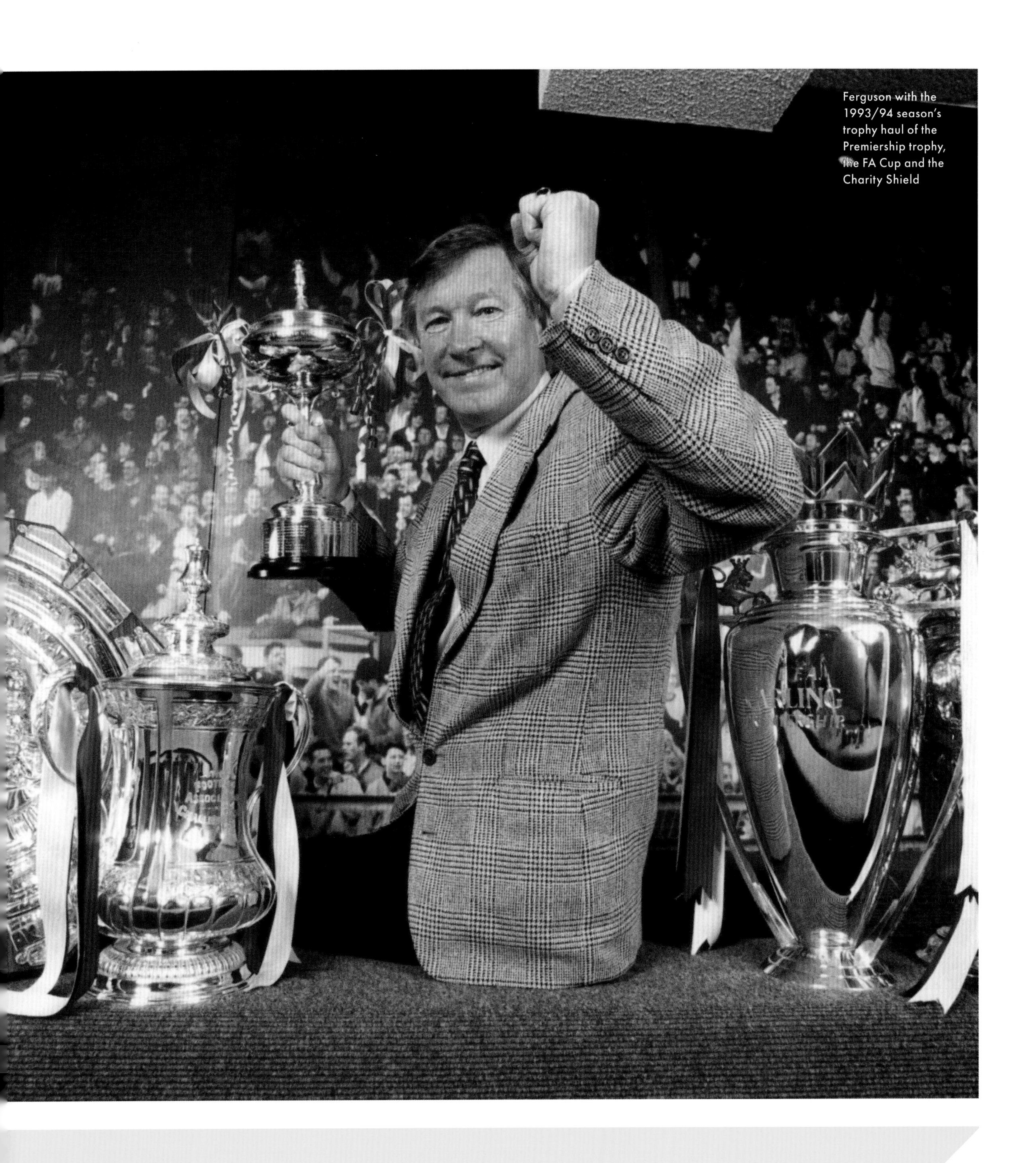
Ferguson with the 1993/94 season's trophy haul of the Premiership trophy, the FA Cup and the Charity Shield

Ronaldo scores Manchester United's fifth goal against Newcastle at Old Trafford, 2008

PLAYERS' PLAYER OF THE YEAR

Cristiano Ronaldo

"In the six years we had him, you just saw his game grow all the time, and he was a fantastic player. Now you see the complete player. His decision-making, his maturity, his experience, plus all the great skills he has got, they all make him the complete player."

Sir Alex Ferguson

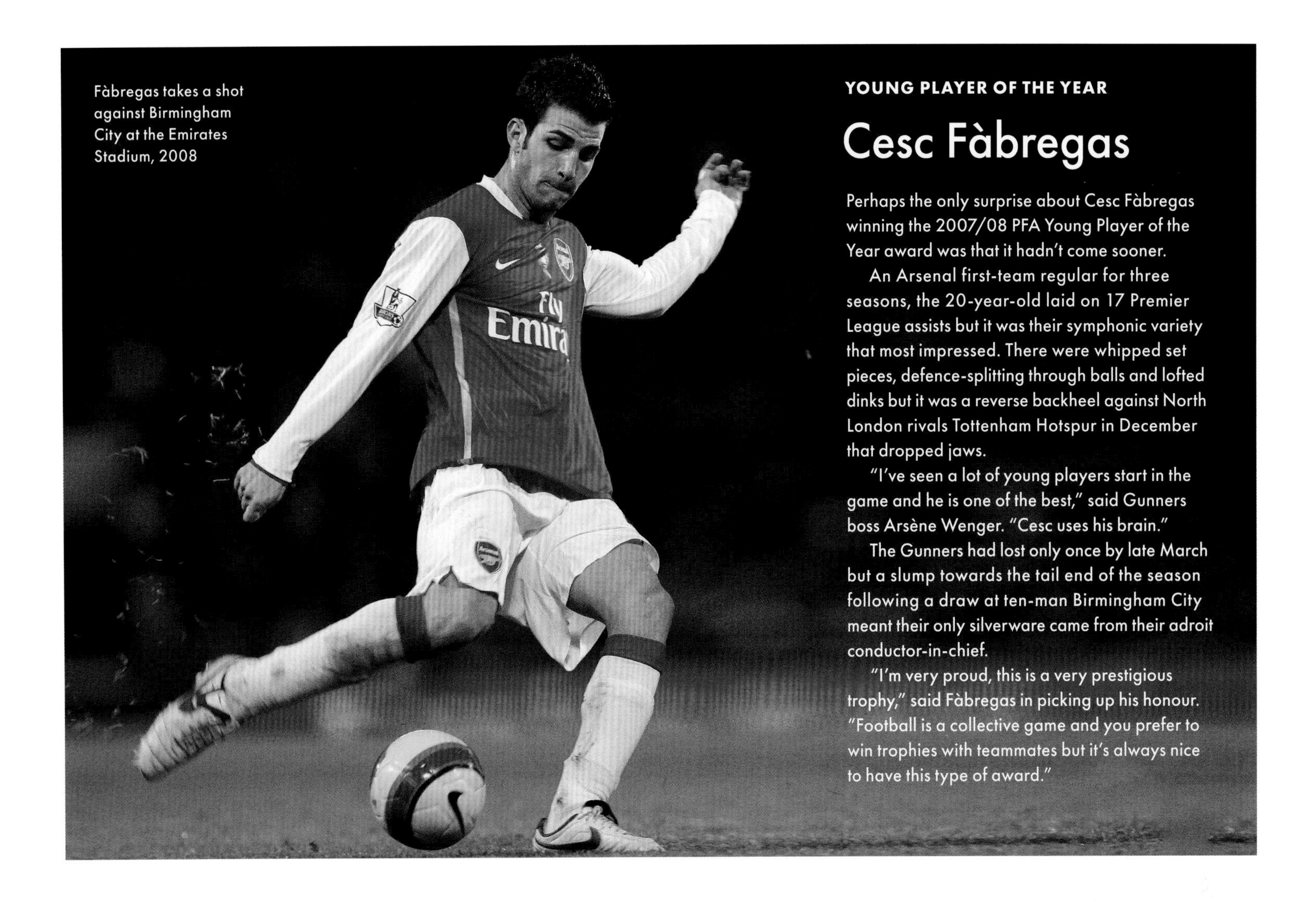

Fàbregas takes a shot against Birmingham City at the Emirates Stadium, 2008

YOUNG PLAYER OF THE YEAR

Cesc Fàbregas

Perhaps the only surprise about Cesc Fàbregas winning the 2007/08 PFA Young Player of the Year award was that it hadn't come sooner.

An Arsenal first-team regular for three seasons, the 20-year-old laid on 17 Premier League assists but it was their symphonic variety that most impressed. There were whipped set pieces, defence-splitting through balls and lofted dinks but it was a reverse backheel against North London rivals Tottenham Hotspur in December that dropped jaws.

"I've seen a lot of young players start in the game and he is one of the best," said Gunners boss Arsène Wenger. "Cesc uses his brain."

The Gunners had lost only once by late March but a slump towards the tail end of the season following a draw at ten-man Birmingham City meant their only silverware came from their adroit conductor-in-chief.

"I'm very proud, this is a very prestigious trophy," said Fàbregas in picking up his honour. "Football is a collective game and you prefer to win trophies with teammates but it's always nice to have this type of award."

MERIT AWARD

Jimmy Armfield

Right | Blackpool and England full back Jimmy Armfield at Bloomfield Road, 1962

At a February 1999 press conference, Howard Wilkinson bristled at the implication he lacked international experience to manage his country on a caretaker basis. "How many England caps have you lot got between you?" he asked the assembled press pack.

"Forty-three," came a voice from the back of the room.

At a stroke, Jimmy Armfield – former England captain, 1966 World Cup winner and BBC radio pundit – had diffused a tense situation and reminded football why he was universally adored.

In a peripatetic half a century at the coalface of football's fierce furnace, Blackpool's record appearance maker – described by Sir Bobby Charlton as "the best right back in Europe in the early 1960s" – also guided Leeds United to the 1975 European Cup final as a manager, became the voice of the game with the BBC and spent two decades as the PFA's coaching consultant.

"He's football royalty, loved by everyone," said Chief Executive Gordon Taylor as Armfield received the 2008 PFA Merit Award. Three standing ovations proved as much.

PLAYERS' PLAYER OF THE YEAR

Ryan Giggs

THE TWO-TIME YOUNG PLAYER OF THE YEAR ADDED THE PLAYERS' PLAYER AFTER AN AGE-DEFYING SEASON AS CAPTAIN OF MANCHESTER UNITED

If there was any doubt that Ryan Giggs would win the 2008/09 PFA Players' Player of the Year award, it vanished as soon as Joe Calzaghe, Wales's recently retired undefeated world boxing champion, took to the stage to present the honour.

"I've been fortunate to win a lot of trophies," beamed Giggs, who would make his 800th Manchester United appearance four days after the ceremony, in the Champions League semi-final against Arsenal. "I won the Young Player Award twice, but this is the big one."

The 35-year-old had only made 12 Premier League starts, with another three to follow by season's end, but there was a very good reason for his lack of game time. Come the biggest moments in Giggs' 11th title-winning season, Sir Alex Ferguson wanted his most trusted of on-field lieutenants ready for battle.

"He's such a valuable player," explained Ferguson of his evolving plan to use Giggs's calm head in central midfield. "At 25, Ryan would shatter defenders with his run down the flank, but at 35, he can play deeper."

Recently departed assistant Carlos Queiroz had come up with the idea of deploying Giggs's reading of the game and still-flawless technique in central areas the season before.

"He makes others play better around him," said Quieroz. "When you understand the game, you can control it. It doesn't matter if he plays left wing or centre midfield, with a few words he can adapt, and always he can create something special."

Sometimes, such as in March's League Cup final defeat of Tottenham Hotspur, it would be to bring final half-hour stability (and score a shootout penalty). When experience was really needed in the Champions League – both legs of the last 16 against Inter or the final versus Barcelona – he'd start. Against Chelsea in January's Premier League 3–0 victory, he was serenity personified, then scored the winner to beat West Ham United a month later. Sixteen assists in all competitions offered further proof, were it needed, that Giggs's metamorphosis was to be celebrated.

"When I arrived, he was playing," said United icon Eric Cantona. "Now, more than a decade after I retired, he's still playing. It's crazy."

Giggs receives his third PFA award, the Players' Player of the Year, 2009

YOUNG PLAYER OF THE YEAR

Ashley Young

At 5ft 9in and tipping the scales at barely 10st wet through, Ashley Young had the kind of build that made him elusive when standing still. He seldom was.

The 23-year-old Aston Villa winger was arguably Europe's most in-form young player in 2008/09 in receiving the PFA Young Player of the Year award from chairman Chris Powell. Seven Premier League goals and eight assists were a fine return, but it was the heady mix of scintillating acceleration, devilish inswinging crosses and sumptuous skill even at top speed that set Young apart.

A December 2008 brace in a 3–2 win at Everton, including a rousing injury-time winner to nip in between two defenders and fire an unerring finish, earned a third Premier League Player of the Month award in the same calendar year, the first player to do so.

"To have that presence of mind, that poise – he's world-class," said manager Martin O'Neill, before comparing Young to "other top-quality 22- or 23-year-olds like [Cristiano] Ronaldo and [Lionel] Messi – he's exceptional".

Above | Young playing against Hull City at the KC Stadium, 2008

MERIT AWARD

John McDermott

There are at least 754 reasons why Grimsby Town fans adore John McDermott. The Mariners' record appearance maker – who is one of just 17 players to feature in more than 600 Football League games for a single club – made his debut against Bradford City in 1987 and was still going strong 20 years later as a diligent right back of rare loyalty.

McDermott won three promotions during his time at Blundell Park, lifted the 1998 Football League Trophy and helped dump Tottenham Hotspur out of the League Cup in 2005. Two years on from his retirement, the ancient Mariner received the 2009 PFA Merit Award for services to football.

"I thought it was one of the lads winding me up, it's a real shock," laughed the 40-year-old after picking up the honour from PFA Chief Executive Gordon Taylor. "To still be recognised, I was flattered and honoured.

"If you care about the football club then people here will look after you. And that's been the case for me for the past 20 years."

Above | McDermott in one of his many appearances for Grimsby Town, 1998

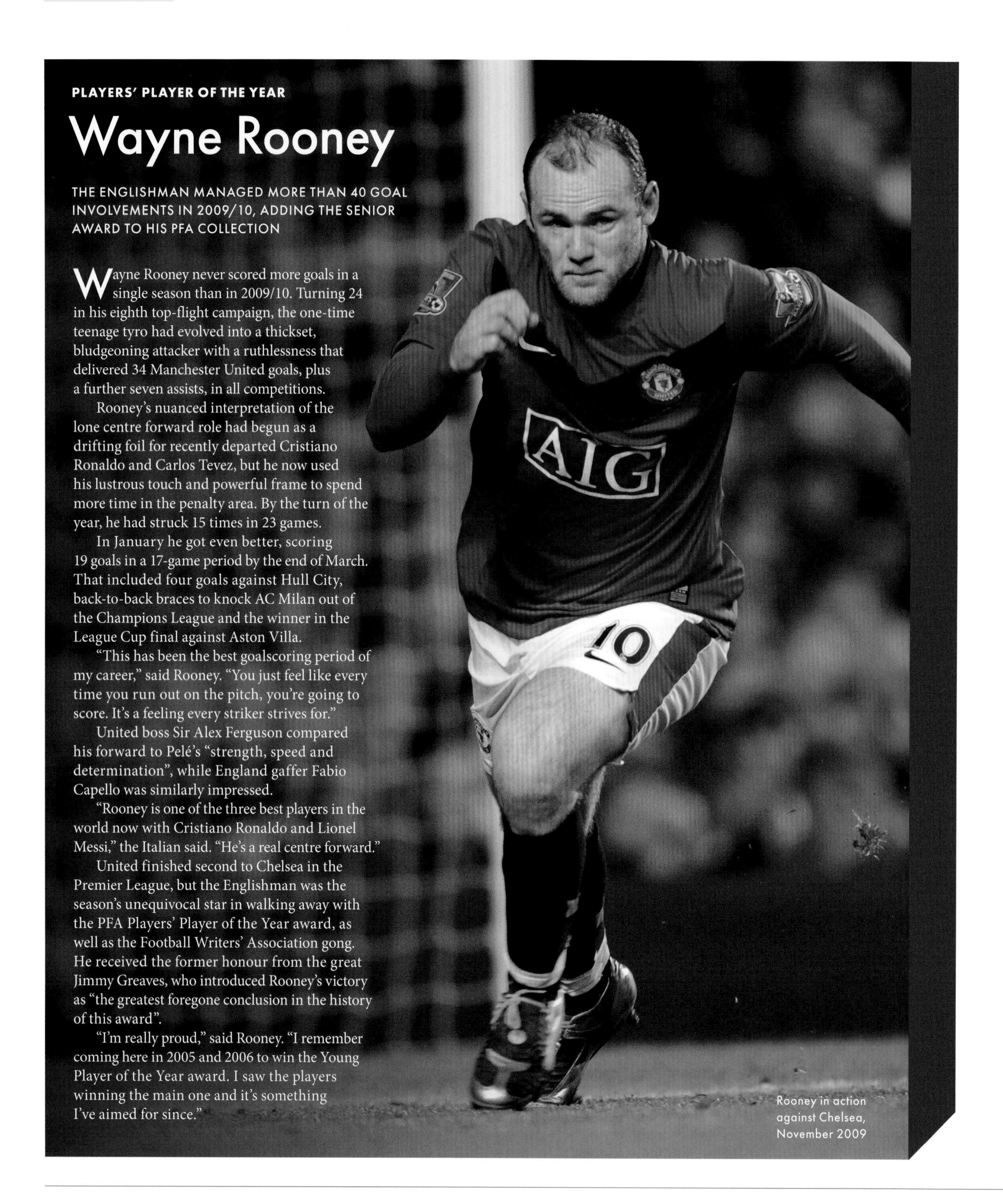

PLAYERS' PLAYER OF THE YEAR

Wayne Rooney

THE ENGLISHMAN MANAGED MORE THAN 40 GOAL INVOLVEMENTS IN 2009/10, ADDING THE SENIOR AWARD TO HIS PFA COLLECTION

Wayne Rooney never scored more goals in a single season than in 2009/10. Turning 24 in his eighth top-flight campaign, the one-time teenage tyro had evolved into a thickset, bludgeoning attacker with a ruthlessness that delivered 34 Manchester United goals, plus a further seven assists, in all competitions.

Rooney's nuanced interpretation of the lone centre forward role had begun as a drifting foil for recently departed Cristiano Ronaldo and Carlos Tevez, but he now used his lustrous touch and powerful frame to spend more time in the penalty area. By the turn of the year, he had struck 15 times in 23 games.

In January he got even better, scoring 19 goals in a 17-game period by the end of March. That included four goals against Hull City, back-to-back braces to knock AC Milan out of the Champions League and the winner in the League Cup final against Aston Villa.

"This has been the best goalscoring period of my career," said Rooney. "You just feel like every time you run out on the pitch, you're going to score. It's a feeling every striker strives for."

United boss Sir Alex Ferguson compared his forward to Pelé's "strength, speed and determination", while England gaffer Fabio Capello was similarly impressed.

"Rooney is one of the three best players in the world now with Cristiano Ronaldo and Lionel Messi," the Italian said. "He's a real centre forward."

United finished second to Chelsea in the Premier League, but the Englishman was the season's unequivocal star in walking away with the PFA Players' Player of the Year award, as well as the Football Writers' Association gong. He received the former honour from the great Jimmy Greaves, who introduced Rooney's victory as "the greatest foregone conclusion in the history of this award".

"I'm really proud," said Rooney. "I remember coming here in 2005 and 2006 to win the Young Player of the Year award. I saw the players winning the main one and it's something I've aimed for since."

Rooney in action against Chelsea, November 2009

YOUNG PLAYER OF THE YEAR

James Milner

Hard work beats talent when talent fails to work hard. James Milner has both by the bucketload. The 24-year-old midfielder was 319 appearances and nearly nine seasons into a staggeringly consistent three-decade career when he picked up the PFA Young Player of the Year Award in April 2010 and forced his way into Fabio Capello's England starting XI for that summer's World Cup.

The assiduous Milner had always demonstrated the versatility of a Swiss Army knife, but in 2009/10 the former winger and occasional full back graduated into an all-consuming central midfield bellwether who contributed 12 goals and 16 assists in all competitions. The square-jawed former Leeds United and Newcastle United man shone even brighter in the League Cup, playing every minute of the Villans' campaign and scoring in four consecutive games, including the final, as the Midlanders fell agonisingly short against Manchester United.

"He's the identikit pro. He puts everything into his training and his game," said Villa boss Martin O'Neill. "You'd take 11 James Milners in your side if that were possible."

Above | Milner makes a crunching tackle against Rapid Wien's Yasin Pehlivan in a Europa League play-off in Vienna, 2009

MERIT AWARD

Lucas Radebe

Right | Radebe playing for Leeds United at Elland Road, 2000

On a visit to the United Kingdom in 2002 to promote South Africa's forthcoming World Cup bid, the country's first post-Apartheid president, Nelson Mandela, pointed at Lucas Radebe and said: "This is my hero." Not bad for someone only included as a makeweight in compatriot Philemon Masinga's 1994 move to Leeds United.

As Masinga failed to settle, Radebe became an adopted West Yorkshire icon. So much so, local band Kaiser Chiefs picked their name in honour of Radebe's first club back home.

The indefatigable centre back was a colossus (and occasional auxiliary goalkeeper) as David O'Leary's bright young things finished third in the Premier League and reached the Champions League semi-finals at the turn of the century, before a chronic knee problem caused his eventual retirement in 2005. Radebe promoted a number of anti-racism causes back in South Africa and received the 2010 PFA Merit Award.

"I'm very proud to get such a great award," he said. "Sport can change the world – football has played such a big part in lifting my community."

PLAYERS' PLAYER OF THE YEAR

Gareth Bale

ONE OF THE GREATEST WELSH PLAYERS OF ALL TIME BURST ONTO THE SCENE WITH TWO UNFORGETTABLE CHAMPIONS LEAGUE PERFORMANCES

Occasionally, an individual performance comes around so captivating it escapes rational analysis. You forget the context. You forget the result. You just see a skinny 21-year-old shredding the reigning European champions in their own back yard with a display of raw savagery. You witness the future.

Ten-man Tottenham Hotspur were 4–0 down to Inter Milan at half-time of an October 2010 Champions League group game when Gareth Bale stepped in. Seven minutes into the second half at San Siro, the Welsh left winger received Peter Crouch's layoff halfway inside his own half and started running. The runaway freight train flew past nerazzurro right back Maicon, captain Javier Zanetti and Walter Samuel and fired low, hard and true across a rooted Júlio César into the far corner. Bale's second was almost identical: run at top speed from deep into space and blast into the net from the inside-left channel. His third featured the same unerring left-footed drill.

Spurs still lost 4–3, Bale's last two goals mere consolations coming as they did in injury time, but that blistering hat-trick was all anyone could talk about for the intervening two weeks ahead of the return fixture.

"Everyone is scared of Gareth," said Spurs playmaker Rafael van der Vaart. "Maicon is the best right back in the world, but Gareth killed him."

He did so again. Bale may not have scored in Spurs's 3–1 victory at White Hart Lane, but he again terrorised Inter. Maicon was on the Ballon d'Or shortlist but Bale's repeated surges around him resembled outright bullying. He was only denied a hat-trick of assists by a contentious call that the ball had gone out of play after yet another dart around the harrowed Brazilian full back.

"You have to put it into perspective," said Spurs manager Harry Redknapp. "Look at who we were playing, Inter Milan, the European champions, and look at who Gareth was up against. It's not just his pace;

Bale surges beyond Inter right back Maicon, 2010

he can run all day, he's got the ability to cross, his left foot is great on the run, he can shoot, dribble, head the ball. The boy has got everything."

At the beginning of 2010, that boy was Spurs's reserve left back. A 17-year-old Bale arrived in North London in May 2007 for an initial £5 million from second-tier Southampton, suffering serious ankle and knee injuries, plus a curious jinx that had taken on a life of its own. Over more than two seasons and 24 Premier League appearances, Bale didn't taste victory once, boss Redknapp admitting "it's difficult" to pick him. With Spurs 4–0 up at home to Burnley in September 2009, Redknapp threw Bale into the fray for the final six minutes as much to end the hex as anything.

It took an injury to Benoît Assou-Ekotto in January 2010 for Bale to get a first-team run. The Welshman kept his starting spot for the remainder of the season, pushed forward into midfield when Assou-Ekotto returned. Nevertheless, Redknapp insisted the youngster's future lay in defence because "he hasn't really got a trick to beat somebody".

That all changed in Spurs' first away game of 2010/11. Bale's head-height volleyed winner at Stoke City featured technical prowess so impressive it merited its own museum, let alone a plinth within one. Incongruous it may have been to watch a left winger of such vibrant speed and effervescent skill wear number three, but Bale had definitively cast aside his reputation as a bad-luck charm.

"It was a bit annoying that people went on about that statistic," recalled Bale. "It was just one of those things that freakily happened. This has been the first time you've really seen me as a player, playing all of the time. I was given my chance and I'd like to say I took it."

Bale's autumn was electric. In back-to-back November fixtures, a brace and magnificent cross dispatched Blackburn Rovers, while his cute finish helped spark a come-from-behind 3–2 North London derby win at Arsenal, provoking serious appraisal.

"He compares to Lionel Messi, Cristiano Ronaldo," said Tottenham great Ricky Villa. "He's playing at that level at the moment."

From his Inter flowering, Bale's card was marked. Every right back in the league was soon asked how they prepared to face Spurs's sensation. After a 4–2 victory, Bolton Wanderers right back Grétar Steinsson explained he "just had a really good chicken korma and relaxed" on the eve of the game. Others resorted to aggressive defending, which eventually brought Bale's season to a premature close with 11 goals and ten assists in all competitions and the PFA Players' Player of the Year award.

"It's an honour, really, when you look at the names that have won it before," said Bale after receiving the award from former champion jockey AP McCoy. "It just makes you go, 'wow'."

Above | Bale picks up his first PFA Players' Player of the Year award, 2011

YOUNG PLAYER OF THE YEAR

Jack Wilshere

Arsène Wenger knew that to hold back 18-year-old Jack Wilshere any longer in the summer of 2010 would be a crime against football. After just two previous Premier League appearances for Arsenal, Wilshere was an overnight regular.

"Jack Wilshere is the best young midfielder I have seen for his age," said an uncharacteristically effusive England boss Fabio Capello after the pugnacious midfielder's August 2010 debut. "He will be England captain one day."

Chronic ankle injuries would leave that prophecy unfulfilled – Wilshere never came close to repeating 2010/11's 49 appearances in all competitions – but there was no doubting his unrestrained gifts. Wilshere played with the abandon of a Victorian street urchin, his atypically English dictating of tempo in both legs of a Champions League exit to eventual winners Barcelona earning the PFA Young Player of the Year award.

"He has a Spanish technique, but an English heart," said Wenger. "What I like as well is he isn't fazed by the occasion; he just plays free off his chest."

Above | An 18-year-old Wilshere playing in the Champions League

Above | Webb issues a yellow card during the 2010 World Cup in South Africa

MERIT AWARD

Howard Webb

It may often be said that the less you notice a referee, the better the job they're doing, but there was good reason that Howard Webb received the 2011 PFA Merit Award, alongside long-time assistants Darren Cann and Mike Mullarkey. The previous July, the trio became the first set of officials to take charge of the Champions League and World Cup finals in the same year.

"It came as a bit of a surprise really," said Webb, who picked up the award alongside Cann and Mullarkey – the first award winners since Jack Taylor in 1977 never to have played or managed at senior level. "It certainly is an honour to be recognised by such an esteemed body as the Professional Footballers' Association. It means an awful lot. It's nice that the playing side of the game has taken this opportunity to mark what happened with us last year."

Widely regarded as the game's finest referee for much of his 534 games, Webb returned to the Professional Game Match Officials Limited as chief refereeing officer in August 2022.

PLAYERS' PLAYER OF THE YEAR

Robin van Persie

THE DUTCHMAN NETTED 37 GOALS IN ALL COMPETITIONS IN HIS FINAL SEASON IN NORTH LONDON

PFA: Looking back to your PFA award-winning season of 2011/12, what memories do you have of that year?
Robin van Persie: Very good memories. I think I scored about 37 goals. We ended up third in the league, but if you look at the way Arsenal played that year, that was very good football. I was having fun, I think everyone could see that. As a kid, it wasn't my target to win the PFA award because it wasn't really realistic, especially in the early days in my career. But then I was like, "Oh, hang on, if I adjust my game a little, if I improve my game, why not?" When I heard I'd won it, that was actually quite emotional, I was very happy. It's the players' award, so that means my opponents were voting for me. I don't think that in the best and the most difficult league to play in there's a bigger compliment than your opponents choosing you to win the PFA award. So it was a beautiful moment of happiness.
PFA: You've obviously achieved so much, where does winning that award rank for you?
RvP: I don't think you can compare it with winning a trophy with your team. It's a different sensation, a different feeling. I don't have many trophies in my living room, but the PFA award is in my living room together with the UEFA Cup and the Premier League.
PFA: Not a bad collection! The season you won the Players' Player award, you didn't score your first goal until January.

Below | The Arsenal man fires in a goal against Borussia Dortmund at the Emirates, 2011

Opposite | Van Persie and Aaron Ramsey celebrate the striker's hat-trick in a 5–3 win against Chelsea at Stamford Bridge, 2011

RvP: That was against Birmingham, right?
PFA: That's right, and then you broke the record for goals from January to May. How did it feel to have a back end of the season like that?
RvP: Yeah, I didn't score for like four months or something. In my mind I was like, okay, I got my first now, now I'm going for it, now I push on. And I ended up scoring loads of goals in that calendar year.
PFA: Do you have a favourite goal from that season?
RvP: Oh, good question. Maybe my hundredth goal for Arsenal? That was a milestone – a good goal at home at the Emirates with my outside left foot. Making a difference, that is what you want to achieve as a player, scoring important goals at home and away from home at the most difficult stadiums, that's always a sweet memory.
PFA: You moved to Manchester United after that season, which means you played under two of the greats – Arsène Wenger and Sir Alex Ferguson. What lessons did they teach you and how did their management styles differ?
RvP: It was a big honour to have worked under them and to have learned so much. Sir Alex Ferguson is the best *manager* there was in terms of keeping 27 players who all think that they're the best happy and keeping them at the highest standards of their game. He was a master of that, and he was a master of influencing intensity in training, keeping everyone on their toes every single day. When there was a boring first half, for example, Sir Alex always triggered us to be more creative, to take more risks, to really go for the win and to excite him and the people in the stadium and the people at home. He always found the words.

Arsène had that same style of triggering us, but he was more of a trainer coach as well, he was always with us on the pitch. He was more patient and he understood as well that when you're young that you make mistakes and that you learn from them. He was managing that, checking if the player was able to learn from his mistakes, and if that was the case, then he would give you that second chance. It is difficult to compare them as a trainer, coach, manager because the way of handling situations, the day-to-day, how they did the training sessions, they were doing it in their own style. In the first couple of years, Arsène was very direct with me and he was very clear about what he expected from me, what I could expect. That was very good for me.

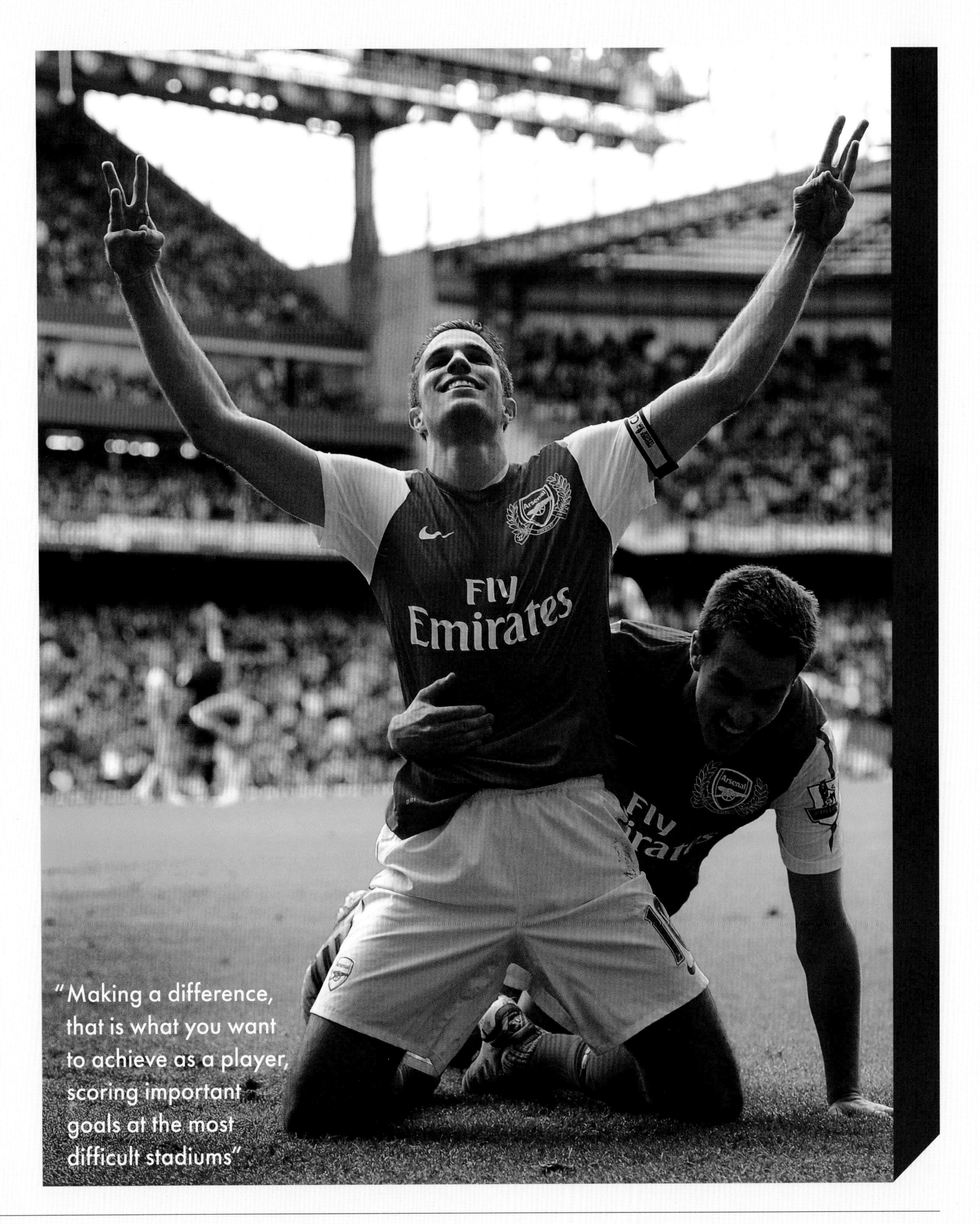

"Making a difference, that is what you want to achieve as a player, scoring important goals at the most difficult stadiums"

YOUNG PLAYER OF THE YEAR

Kyle Walker

Kyle Walker's hitherto itinerant Tottenham Hotspur career had involved three loans in two seasons, but there was only so long boss Harry Redknapp could ignore the buccaneering right back.

Gareth Bale and Luka Modrić were the headliners, but chief support Walker missed just one Premier League game in 2011/12, his long-range winner in October's North London derby win against Arsenal ensuring White Hart Lane adulation, before a superb free-kick set up an April win against Blackburn Rovers and Champions League football.

"It shows you what I know," laughed Harry Redknapp after admitting his surprise at Walker shooting from so far out. "He's got a big future. He's as quick as lightning and has so much ability."

Walker was a one-man rhythm section, fully deserving the PFA Young Player of the Year Award.

"I was a bit surprised because defenders don't normally get these awards and get the limelight as much as the centre forwards," Walker said after beating Bale and future Manchester City teammate Sergio Agüero to the gong. "It's a great honour."

Above | The Spurs man with the Young Player of the Year award, 2012

MERIT AWARD

Graham Alexander

Right |Alexander with Preston North End fans after the First Division play-off semi-final second leg win against Birmingham City, 2001

"I've been a 10-year old for 30 years, going out and playing football with my mates," said an emotional Graham Alexander as he received the 2012 PFA Merit Award. After a 24-year, 1,024-game career – the second outfielder in English football history to reach the milestone – the former Scunthorpe United, Luton Town, Preston North End, Burnley and Scotland right back probably thought a standing ovation from his peers was his footballing peak. He was wrong.

In his final professional appearance six days later, the 40-year-old curled a majestic injury-time free-kick into the corner to secure a 2-2 draw against League One leaders Charlton Athletic. It was the final act of his career.

"Never in my wildest dreams did I think I'd do that," he said at full-time. "I was as nervous as I was when I made my debut at 19 because it was such a big thing for me to stop playing football. To be given this chance to say thank you and goodbye everyone, hopefully I've repaid everyone with the goal."

A consummate professional, Grezza's staggering durability was recompense enough.

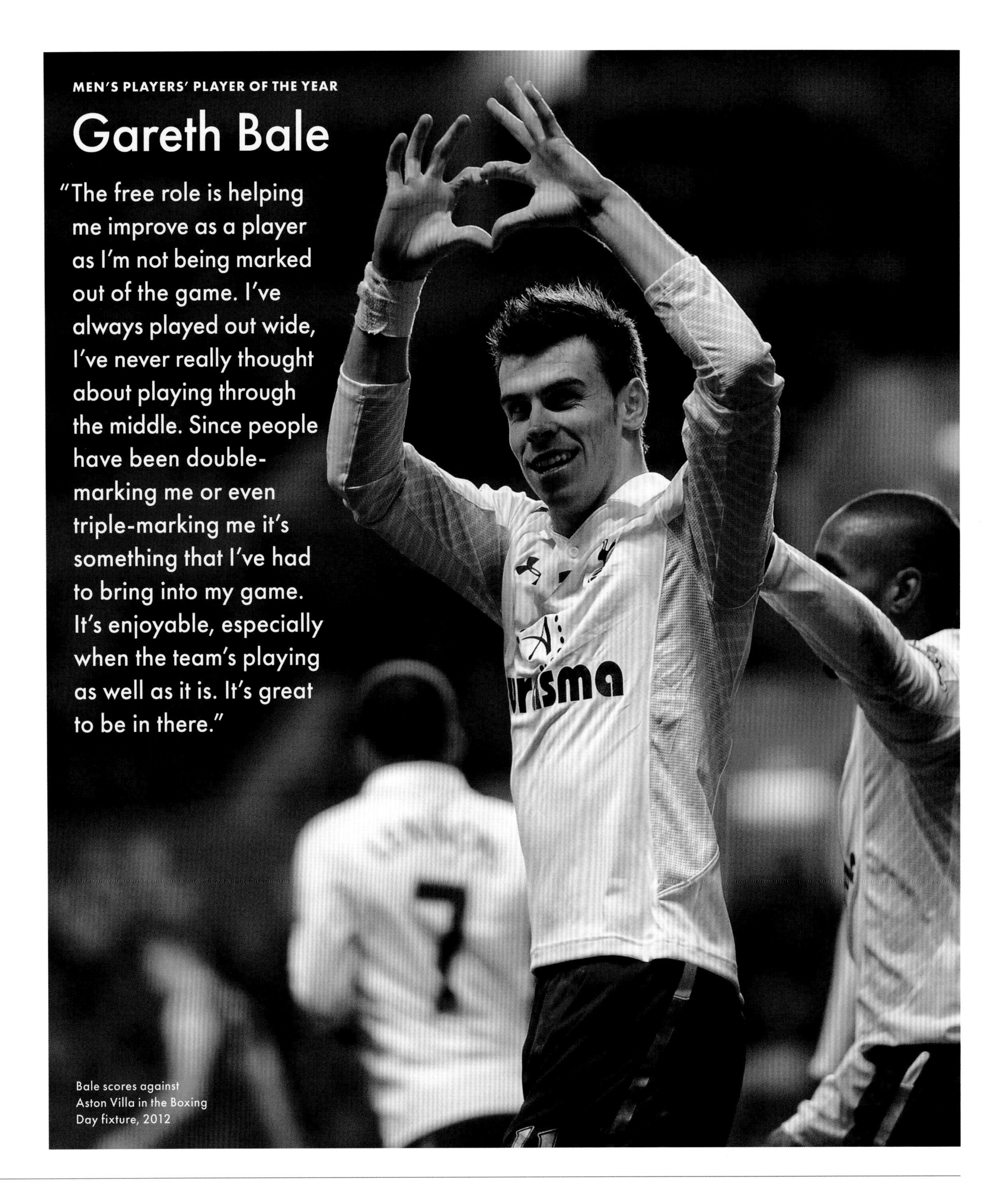

MEN'S PLAYERS' PLAYER OF THE YEAR

Gareth Bale

"The free role is helping me improve as a player as I'm not being marked out of the game. I've always played out wide, I've never really thought about playing through the middle. Since people have been double-marking me or even triple-marking me it's something that I've had to bring into my game. It's enjoyable, especially when the team's playing as well as it is. It's great to be in there."

Bale scores against Aston Villa in the Boxing Day fixture, 2012

WOMEN'S PLAYERS' PLAYER OF THE YEAR

Kim Little

THE FIRST WOMEN'S PLAYERS' PLAYER OF THE YEAR WAS THE DRIVING FORCE BEHIND ARSENAL'S NINTH CONSECUTIVE TITLE

Above | Little playing in the WSL League Cup final against Birmingham City at Underhill, 2012

Opposite | The Scot during the Women's Super League match against Lincoln at Meadow Park, 2012

The Women's Super League was just a year old, professionalism still in its infancy, when the London 2012 Olympics changed women's football forever. All the women's game needed was a platform. Build it and they will come – more than 70,000 of them, it turned out, to watch Team GB beat Brazil in the group stages at Wembley.

Within nine months, women were invited to join the PFA for the first time and in April 2013 voted for their inaugural Players' Player of the Year. Part of Team GB in that previous summer of sporting love, Kim Little was a near-unanimous choice.

It wasn't just that 11-goal Little had won the 2012 WSL Golden Boot as Arsenal lifted a ninth successive top-flight title, winning ten and drawing four of their 14 league games. The Scottish playmaker had come to encapsulate the silverware-winning Gunners juggernaut, filling the creative void left by the great Kelly Smith's 2009 move to US side Boston Breakers with a devastating blend of acceleration over five yards, a rare awareness to bring teammates into play and that eye for goal that averaged better than one a game. And she was just 22.

"What she has done for our football club since she joined is nothing short of fantastic," said recently retired Arsenal captain Faye White. "She didn't flinch. There was a lot of weight on her young shoulders but she rose to the challenge. She has been the playmaker, the person that makes things happen, and has taken on Kelly's mantle so well. On top of that, she just loves the big occasions."

Did she ever. By October 2012's League Cup final against Birmingham City, Smith had returned to the club, but Little remained the star. Eight minutes from time, the Scot cut inside from the left with archetypal ebullience and curled a stunning left-footed curler into the top corner to secure a second trophy of the season.

Little's talent was obvious from an early age. Such was the lack of visibility of the women's game growing up in 1990s Mintlaw, Aberdeenshire, the attacking midfielder was a voracious studier of Zinedine Zidane – "just the ultimate player," she recalled – and added the French playmaker's artistry and vision to her own game. After joining Hibernian's academy at 14 – a three-and-a-half-hour drive one way from Mintlaw – she had outgrown the Scottish top flight within three years, scoring a ludicrous 88 goals in 48 games to attract Arsenal's attention in March 2008.

Inevitably, Little scored on her Gunners debut in a 4–1 defeat of Chelsea. "Make a note of this kid, she's going to be big," said manager Vic Akers.

Arsenal boss from 1987 to 2009, Akers knew what he'd got – a 17-year-old with the world at her feet. "Kim's potential was clear when we first went to see her play as a teenager for Hibernian, and we always believed she could be a world-class talent," he later recalled. "I'm pleased to say that's just what she's become."

By the time she received the inaugural PFA Women's Players' Player of the Year award from her former skipper White in April 2013, Little had few contemporaries.

"For various years I've watched this event on television so to come here and win the first award is fantastic, with so many great players in the room" she said. "Now the PFA membership has been opened up to the whole women's league in England, which is a great step. The formation of the WSL, with promotion and relegation to come [from 2014], has already really pushed things forward in terms of coverage and exposure. The Olympics has put the spotlight on the women's game as well and we have to capitalise on that."

Still an Arsenal regular a decade on from making history, Little captained the Gunners to League Cup glory in March 2023, scoring a typically nerveless penalty in the 3–1 defeat of Chelsea to lift the 22nd trophy of a staggering career that has also included successful spells in the United States and Australia. A bright, pioneering leader with the supreme talent few possess, Little couldn't have been more deserving of winning the PFA's maiden individual honour. History has followed her around ever since.

"For various years I've watched this event on television so to come here and win the first award is fantastic"

YOUNG PLAYER OF THE YEAR

Gareth Bale

If Gareth Bale's 2010/11 Players' Player of the Year award win heralded an exciting new talent, then the Welshman's transformational genius two years on marked a new creative high.

A lithe winger no more, the square-shouldered Tottenham Hotspur powerhouse's Boxing Day hat-trick at Aston Villa took his tally to a solid ten, but it was his late-January redeployment as an all-purpose central attacker alongside Emmanuel Adebayor that unlocked his brilliance. He scored 11 in 11 Premier League games – finishing on a career-best 26 in all competitions – including a brace at West Ham United that featured an injury-time winner so savagely struck it seemed to stick halfway up the net.

By the end of the season – in which he joined Cristiano Ronaldo as the only players to win the top PFA award, Young Player of the Year and Football Writers' Association gong in the same season – Bale became the world's most expensive footballer in joining Real Madrid.

Above | Bale received the Players' Player of the Year and the Young Player of the Year awards in 2013

MERIT AWARD

Manchester United Class of '92

Manchester United love a good Eric. Six months before Cantona's French revolution from the top, another Eric had laid the foundations for nearly two decades' success.

The core of Eric Harrison's 1992 FA Youth Cup-winning squad reads like a roll call of Old Trafford greatness. Ryan Giggs, David Beckham, Gary Neville, Paul Scholes, Nicky Butt and Phil Neville would go on to win every domestic honour possible with the club. Others, Robbie Savage and Keith Gillespie included, became internationals after leaving the club.

If it was Ferguson who trusted his fledglings to soar, it was Harrison who had nurtured them to that point through a mixture of carrot and stick.

"He built character and determination in those young players and prepared them for the future," Ferguson said of Harrison, who died in February 2019. "He's one of the greatest coaches of our time."

Gary Neville, Harrison's captain, agreed. "He taught us how to play, how to never give up, how important it was to win your individual battles and what we needed to do to play for Manchester United Football Club," he said. "Eric, we owe you everything."

Twenty-one years on from their first major honour, the Class of '92, Harrison and Ferguson reunited to receive the 2013 PFA Merit Award in recognition of arguably the finest youth team in history.

You can't win anything with kids? Manchester United could.

The Class of '92 (left to right): coach Eric Harrison, Ryan Giggs, Nicky Butt, David Beckham, Gary Neville, Phil Neville, Paul Scholes and Terry Cooke

UMBRO
UMBRO
UMBRO
SHARP
SHARP
SHARP

On the rights road

AS MARIE-CHRISTINE BOUCHIER, THE PFA'S DIRECTOR OF WOMEN'S FOOTBALL, EXPLAINS, HUGE STRIDES HAVE BEEN MADE IN THE WOMEN'S GAME BUT THERE'S STILL A LONG WAY TO GO

Marie-Christine Bouchier, Director of Women's Football

One word defines the PFA's 20-year-plus support of women's football: parity. The players' union was there in 2009 when the Football Association introduced central contracts for 17 England players to become full-time professionals, and has continued to play a key role in the women's game's stratospheric rise since the launch of the WSL in 2013, which brought about PFA membership. A dedicated department has delivered real, lasting change.

"Historically, we've always been very involved in supporting the women's game," says Marie-Christine Bouchier, Director of Women's Football. "I've been at the PFA for nearly 18 years and have felt completely supported by my male colleagues. We're listened to and the strides that we've made and will continue to make are exactly what's needed for the future of women's football.

"We want to reach the point where we're not having to fight for the basics just because of your gender. What we're striving for is parity. Our women members need the same rights, contractual protections, provisions and professionalisation as their male counterparts."

In January 2022, the PFA concluded 16 months of negotiations to correct significant disparities in WSL and Championship contracts, compared with those for Premier League players. WSL players now receive their basic wage for the first 18 months while injured, and have a 12-month notice period of termination if the problem cannot be fixed, mirroring the injury rights of male players. That had been just three months, followed by a three-month notice period for women. The same settlement also secured vastly improved maternity provision, with women receiving 100 per cent of their wage for 14 weeks before dropping to statutory rate.

"We're just at the beginning with maternity," says Bouchier. "We've made a massive step with putting it into a contract, now we need to work out what return to play looks like, so these athletes don't have to choose between having a career and a baby. That shouldn't be a choice, it should be a given."

The creation of a Women's Professional Football Negotiating and Consultative Committee (WPFNCC), to match what exists in the men's game, is also high on the agenda, which would help ongoing complex discussions surrounding a football-funded pension for female players. Men currently receive over £6,000 a season from a transfer fee levy.

"Changes have felt laborious and piecemeal, but if we had the WPFNCC it would be broader," says Bouchier. "All stakeholders are involved in a forum to debate and agree changes. It would be especially useful in our discussions around pensions, which have been going on for years and we haven't yet found a solution. The funding is within football, we just need to be more creative and find a way because it's not a massive amount of money to give 12 WSL clubs and their players a pension.

"We want standardisation across the leagues and a minimum requirement for what 'professional' looks like," says Bouchier. "Players aren't machines and we need to protect them. It goes hand in hand with funding and the facilities. This is what we're looking at to support all players coming through, not just those at the top."

The next generation, too. Former Brighton & Hove Albion and England defender Fern Whelan's See It, Achieve It programme has been a significant recent attempt to improve black, Asian or mixed-heritage representation in women's football. Just 29 of 300 WSL players are from a minority background.

"New ideas like this are what the PFA do so well," says Bouchier. "Fern is passionate about it as a former England player and you can see the Euro 2022-winning side was very white, quite middle-class and there's obviously an issue there. There was a lot of talk about why this was happening but not enough to change it. Youngsters need to see themselves, which is what this campaign is all about."

Whelan isn't the only big name to back the PFA's work, with former England captain and current Manchester City skipper Steph Houghton having represented her colleagues on the elected Players' Board. Manchester United captain Katie Zelem and Brighton's Danielle Carter are on the board at present.

"It's invaluable having those voices on our board," says Bouchier. "They bring different ideas and perspectives. You can see the work [144-cap Lioness] Karen Carney is doing in the government-led review of the women's game to understand how important it is. Former player, lived and breathed it, she has lots of friends and contacts still in the game and has seen the development herself. The information she and the players provide is accurate. As much as I can sit there and represent them, I'm not a former player so it's my job to listen and make sure their voice is heard.

"We've got the knowledge, we've been working in the game for so long, and we want to make sure the players are central to the game's development. It all comes back to the players, their power as a group. They are football. Who says the women's game can't compete?"

Opposite, clockwise from top | See It, Achieve It campaign instigator Fern Whelan; former Players' Board member Steph Houghton; Karen Carney at the announcement of the government review of the women's game

"We've been working in the game for so long, and we want to make sure the players are central to the game's development"

Marie-Christine Bouchier

Sense of community

AT PLYMOUTH MARJON UNIVERSITY, STUDENTS LEARN ABOUT INCLUSION AND COMMUNITY AS A FORCE FOR GOOD, FROM GRASS ROOTS-LEVEL FOOTBALL TO ELITE

www.marjon.ac.uk

Football has the potential to change lives, not only for professionals, but also for those at a local and community level, such as Sunday league referees, players with disabilities and children's team coaches. Plymouth Marjon University supports football at both professional and community level, often combining the two in an approach that is in keeping with the university's origins. Marjon began life in London as the two separate colleges of St Mark and St John, both of which catered for the underprivileged. After merging in 1923 to become the College of St Mark & St John, known as Marjon, it moved to Plymouth in 1973, receiving full university status in 2013.

"It's 50 years since we moved from London and that's an anniversary we are excited about," says Caroline Westwood, Dean of the School of Sport, Exercise and Rehabilitation. "For us, the institute is so well placed to support all facets of inclusion and disability in sport and football across our region. We do a lot of work in the community right up to high-performance sport. The FA supported us to introduce a high-performance centre for female football, which has seen a lot of success including some who have played for the Lionesses, such as Katie Robinson, who is now at Brighton."

The university holds "Train like a Lioness" days for local primary schools and works closely with national and regional FAs to develop players of all ages for local women's teams. The university has also established a very strong relationship with local football club Plymouth Argyle, where students often undertake placements that see them working on match and performance analysis – the sort of hands-on experience a student would struggle to receive at a bigger club.

Teaching staff include former professional Dr Ian Stonebridge, who retired through injury, and Senior Lecturer Aaron Cusack, who was on Plymouth's books as a youngster. In both cases, grants from the PFA allowed them to return to education, receive formal qualifications and remain involved in the sport, contributing to the game they love. Such an approach aligns with another of the university's ambitions, which is to retain more talent – coaching, teaching and playing – in the South West.

This is helped by the university's role as one of nine FA Women's High-Performance Football Centres (WHPFC), which allows Plymouth Marjon to provide an educational and community-based setting to recruit, develop, deploy and produce quality coaches and inspire player development. In addition, the university has created a dual career pathway so students can continue to study while playing, and has used its formal partnership with the Plymouth Argyle Community Trust to allow students to get involved in community coaching.

"The journey that a lot of our students go on, whether they are fans, coaches or players, is around community," says Senior Lecturer Dr Phil Brown. "A lot of that is about using the power of football to do good, which aligns with our own historical values. Football is the hook, it attracts people and allows us to work with issues around disability, employment and gender. Football is a grass roots activity, and that voluntary effort is so important. We do coach development, we do futsal with Devon & Cornwall FA, we work with those who have disabilities and prosthetics – which is all part of our inclusion and community programme. It's about that community development work. Exceptional talent will go on to fame and fortune, but community work has the potential to change lives."

HOME

PLYMOUTH
MARJON
UNIVERSITY

KUKRI
LOUGHBOROUGH
COACH & VOLUNTEER
ACADEMY
TOTALPOWER
ESP

Ahead of the game

LOUGHBOROUGH UNIVERSITY IS ADVANCING PROGRESS IN INCLUSIVITY IN PHYSICAL ACTIVITY, WHILE MAINTAINING ITS WORLD-LEADING RANKING FOR SPORTS-RELATED ACADEMIA

www.lboro.ac.uk

"The importance of improving inclusion in all aspects of society is widely recognised and sport is no exception," says Mark Lewis, Dean of Loughborough University's School of Sport, Exercise and Health Sciences (SSEHS). "In fact, because being active is key to everyone's health, improving inclusion in sport is paramount. It's a vast, complex area but strides have been made – more recently in women's international football and rugby. But there is more to discover, understand and implement, and we're working with governing bodies, sports clubs, community groups and other organisations to lead research and innovation."

SSEHS is renowned for excellence in teaching, research and innovation in sport, exercise and physical activity, being the major contributor to Loughborough's long-held position as the world's top ranked university for sport-related subjects in the QS World University Rankings. SSEHS is active in fields ranging from medicine, nutrition, biomechanics and cellular and molecular biology to coaching, pedagogy, physiology, psychology and sociology, as well as sport management and economics.

"An inclusive approach," says Mark, "begins with an evidence-based understanding of the positive effects of sport and physical activity – socially and professionally, in participating and spectating, and on physical, mental and societal wellbeing. It is only by committing time and resources to discovering and overcoming any barriers to inclusivity within sport that tangible progress can be made."

To this end, SSEHS has made use of the expertise offered by the Peter Harrison Centre for Disability Sport, and forged strong partnerships with the National Rehabilitation Centre and the Defence Medical Rehabilitation Centre – all of which have helped revolutionise sport medicine as a result of studies into areas such as improving the shoulder health of wheelchair users, reducing injuries resulting from initial military training and managing medical care at road running races.

Recognising the relationship between sport and society, SSEHS works to support sportspeople off the pitch, and attract others onto the pitch. It has teamed up with several organisations: the World Players Association, to launch the first global Census of Athlete Rights Experiences, which protects young athletes; the English Cricket Board, to understand the profile of players within the cricket talent pathway for boys and girls in relation to ethnicity, religion, gender and schooling; Sport England, to identify the determinants of participation in sports and leisure in the UK, and the role of sports clubs in promoting participation; and the charity StreetGames, which brings sport to disadvantaged communities to help tackle youth violence.

Whereas academic research "starts with a question or a desire to understand something," says Mark, "progress comes with change or action taken as a result of gaining that understanding. But if you start from the standpoint that inclusivity fundamentally improves sport and this in turn improves society, you begin to ask the questions, commit the resources, examine the barriers and explore how they can be worked through."

The sporting landscape has transformed over the past decade, with more media coverage and a burgeoning associated industry, says Mark. "I hope investment and resources will be directed towards cross-sector research and innovation to create evidence-based programmes and policies which enhance inclusivity in sport and physical activity, in order for us to deliver a step change in society."

THIS
LSBU
GIRL
CAN

Top-level training

PIONEERING RESEARCH BY THE SPORT AND EXERCISE SCIENCE TEAM AT LONDON SOUTH BANK UNIVERSITY DELIVERS BENEFITS FOR ELITE ATHLETES AND SOCIETY, TOO

bit.ly/lsbu-applied-science

In 2022, the world experienced one of the hottest years on record due to the changing climate. This is especially challenging for elite athletes as performance requires them to acclimatise to the environmental conditions. Responding to this challenge, the sport and exercise science team at London South Bank University (LSBU) established an environmental physiology lab on campus in Southwark. Equipped with state-of-the-art altitude and heat chambers and an "iCool" plunge pool, the lab allows the evaluation of athletes' responses to extreme environmental conditions. "The purpose of the research is to help athletes manage their ability to cope in a range of environmental challenges," says Steve Hunter, Head of Human Sciences Division, and Associate Professor of Sport and Exercise Science.

The research at LSBU – which often involves international collaboration – is not just about individual athletes and teams. There is a strong focus on a wider societal impact. For example, the team is developing a new app that allows people to rate perceptions of how hot and cold they feel – known as their "thermal comfort" or "thermal strain". The app will provide guidance about what actions can be taken. "Going forwards, it will be valuable for individuals who are more vulnerable, such as children and the elderly," says Steve.

Other research at LSBU's Sport and Exercise Science Research Centre (SESRC) includes work in biomechanics and sport psychology. Working with Bristol City FC, researchers led by Kiros Karamanidis, Professor of Ageing and Exercise Science, evaluated the functional capacity of players in terms of motion, muscle quality and tendon structure with the objective of performance improvement and reduced injury risk, more specifically Achilles tendon injuries.

The research carried out by SESRC has been consistently recognised in the Research Excellence Framework (REF). "The REF commends us for considerable impact in terms of reach and significance on health, behaviour change, injury prevention and performance optimisation," says Katya Mileva, Professor in Human Neurophysiology and the research centre's Director. "We pride ourselves in scientific excellence, but we also want our research to be impactful. We are addressing major societal challenges in sport, physical activity and health, and applying science to solve them."

A key aspect of the sport and exercise science team's emphasis on cutting-edge research is how it feeds into the curriculum of their undergraduate and postgraduate courses, and helps students learn and acquire professional skills. "The research motivates undergraduate students – they work with postgraduates and our partners on real-life challenges, and it is relevant to their future careers," says Katya. "They develop hands-on skills, publish [their research] and strengthen their CV."

Students also have the chance to receive training in the assessment of human health and sports performance at the LSBU's Human Performance Centre, which offers services to paying clients such as athletes and sports teams. "We are also very focused on ensuring our students get as much experience as possible in terms of professional development within their courses," says Steve.

The team, of eight permanent staff and around 130 undergraduates, celebrates its 30th anniversary in 2023. Along with the awarding of an honorary doctorate in 2022 to former England footballer Rio Ferdinand for his work on tackling inequality in sport, it highlights how far sport and exercise science at the university has come.

Sense of belonging

THROUGH INCREASING GRASSROOTS PARTICIPATION, THE LONDON BOROUGH OF BARNET IS BRINGING DOWN SOCIAL BARRIERS AND ENCOURAGING WOMEN AND GIRLS TO BE MORE ACTIVE

www.barnet.gov.uk

A north London council with responsibility for 395,000 people and more than 200 parks and green spaces, the London Borough of Barnet understands the importance of sport and physical activity for local residents. Sport improves health and wellbeing, but it is also a great way to increase engagement and promote inclusivity. This is why access to targeted and dedicated programmes such as those delivered by Barnet Nightingales FC, are important in contributing towards placemaking through regeneration. Delivered in partnership with developer Related Argent, London's largest girls' training programme is a project that reflects the borough's approach to "caring for people, our places and the planet".

"We want to harness the power of sport to bring communities together and start to tackle barriers by providing opportunities through participation," says Cassie Bridger, Assistant Director of Greenspaces and Leisure at Barnet Council. "We want to build on the legacy of the Lionesses locally and are launching free coaching sessions and learning courses for girls and women across Barnet for a year. The mission is to connect with communities and clubs at a local level, encouraging diversity and inclusion."

Role models include Somayeh Caeser, who, after realising that local girls were not being offered a chance to play football, started a club for girls at Lymore Gardens FC. "The idea was to create an inclusive space for girls to fall in love with football," she says. "We wanted to offer something more than training and games, creating a community space for girls of all abilities and offering them a sense of belonging within our community." Lymore Gardens now engages more than 100 girls and women ranging from the age of five to 40 years old in the East Finchley area, and Somayeh was recognised for her achievements in BBC Radio 4's Woman's Hour Power List 2023 for Women in Sport.

Somayeh's project is the perfect example of what Barnet Council is seeking to support and facilitate across the borough. The council ran a campaign during the 2023 FIFA Women's World Cup to raise awareness of opportunities in the local area and to challenge some of the stereotypes about women's football. Barnet also engages with the charity Women in Sport to develop a wider understanding of the barriers facing women across different areas of the borough, providing insight that supports a targeted approach to delivery. The council also actively seeks and promotes local people with inspirational stories, such as Davina, who has been playing, coaching and refereeing football since she was 11 years old. Now 61, she thought her playing days were over until she discovered walking football at a local sports facility.

Barnet's commitment to sport is being reinforced through financial investment, with millions being directed to improve facilities and support growing participation. This is good news for Barnet resident Chloe Greenberg, who has been coaching for a decade. In 2021, she founded Beyond the Ball – a place for local women to participate and train – which has already grown into a league with a small number of teams, and raised money for a women's team in Kenya to supply equipment and kit. "Football has always been a passion of mine," she says. "Coaching, playing, managing or refereeing. I've seen and been part of the positive difference football can make, and I am grateful to football for giving me a focus and helping me through some of my toughest mental-health moments."

Women & Girls
Football
Women & Girls
Football
mitre

Brent
Cross
Town

Dreams
15
mitre

Bringing sport to everyone

ACROSS ULSTER UNIVERSITY'S CAMPUSES IS A THRIVING NETWORK OF SPORTS FACILITIES THAT BRINGS THE BENEFITS OF PHYSICAL ACTIVITY TO BOTH STUDENTS AND LOCALS

www.ulster.ac.uk/sport

When Nigel Dobson's apprenticeship at Cardiff City ended in the late 1980s with no offer of a professional contract, he was thankful he was a member of the PFA. The organisation's support and advice set Dobson on a path that – via Loughborough University and Sheffield Hallam University – earned him a PhD, representative honours at the 1995 World University Games in Japan and a position at Ulster University as Head of Sports Services. In this role, he can draw on personal experience to show how football has the capacity to inspire young people in education.

"I know first-hand the opportunities that sport and football presented for me," says Nigel. "The PFA were brilliant to me. They gave me a lot of support and educational opportunities. Their guidance was very clear. After leaving Cardiff, I did my A-levels and then went to university. Now I want to inspire others."

The university – which has campuses in Derry-Londonderry, Coleraine, Jordanstown and Belfast – works alongside organisations such as the Irish FA (IFA), PFA, Harry Gregg Foundation, Manchester United Foundation and local football clubs to educate students while demonstrating the benefits presented by sport. Each of the campuses gives the local community the chance to take part in sport, so schoolchildren and their parents can see what a university looks like and the opportunities available.

Among the university staff is Julie Nelson, who scored Northern Ireland's opening goal in the 2022 Euros. She can be found at the world-class facilities of Jordanstown Sports Village just outside Belfast, which delivers a joint scholarships for female players studying while training part-time. The village is also home to the UEFA and IFA performance academies for boys and girls.

Each campus hosts a different competition for young players each summer – at Jordanstown it is the Belfast Youth Cup, while Derry-Londonderry has the Foyle Cup and Coleraine has the SuperCup NI. Past competitors at Coleraine have included David Beckham and Steve McManaman, and it hosts weekly small-sided games in a league supported by former Manchester United goalkeeper Harry Gregg's charitable foundation.

The university hopes to be both inspiring and integrated. A collaboration with the Manchester United Foundation in Derry-Londonderry delivers an education programme for a dozen schools in the Foyle Learning Community. This enthuses children to think about further education and encourages them to mix with people from different communities in the city.

There are ambitious plans to expand on this already impressive offering, which will see further improvements at each campus, including a new sports centre at the central Belfast campus that will be not only be open to students, but also draw in locals to play and learn sport. "It's 25 years on from the Good Friday Agreement and we want to grow the educational opportunities, inspire and improve the health and physical activity of our local populations," says Nigel. The aim is to collaborate further with governing and commercial bodies, and unions, to ensure the university experience is truly transformative for an Ulster student. The result is that they leave as confident, skilled and highly qualified young people.

"I'm thankful for the opportunities that football and the PFA have given me," says Nigel. "We want to expand on this opportunity in the future and be a part of it, using the inspiration of football as a vehicle to change young lives."

STUDENT

MacBook Pro

Giving back to society

THE UNIVERSITY OF SALFORD'S SCHOOL OF HEALTH AND SOCIETY NOT ONLY HELPS PLAYERS AT THE TOP OF THEIR GAME, BUT ALSO ADDRESSES HEALTH INEQUALITY

www.salford.ac.uk/school-health-society

The cities of Salford and Manchester are home to two of the biggest football clubs in the world, as well as a universe of smaller clubs and related institutions. The University of Salford plays a vital role in nurturing this complex eco-system of sport, culture, society and economics through its School of Health and Society, which assists professional football clubs – including Manchester City, Manchester United and formerly Salford City – with cutting-edge research around performance and rehabilitation.

At the same time, former professionals can start their journey towards a post-playing career by training in physiotherapy as part of the university's decades-long relationship with the PFA. "We partner with clubs and individuals," says Dr Gill Rawlinson, Director of Allied and Public Health. "We can help a professional footballer take their knowledge and experience into a completely new career as a physiotherapist and bring that back to the game. Then there is the work we do for players and clubs around specific problems, using the university's expertise to work towards solving an issue."

The school has developed an expertise in lower limb function – the knee, ankle and hip – and how that translates into performance. This has seen Premier League clubs approach the university for advice about injuries, knee pain and performance. "It is predominantly related to mechanical considerations around performance, injury and rehabilitation, tied in with performance profile and a strength and conditioning focus," says Dr Steve Atkins, Director of Psychology and Sport.

The largest of the university's four schools, the School of Health and Society has 9,500 students and offers a wide range of courses, from Occupational Therapy to Sports, Nutrition and Exercise. It is active in Greater Manchester and beyond. Students benefit from placements at local clubs, while the school delivers a mixture of formal partnerships and consultancy work for industry partners such as the NHS as well as clubs including Manchester City.

Thanks to the school's connection with the PFA (which dates back to the 1990s) and the FA, "we can support professional footballers at that point where they are ending their playing career" says Steve. "We work with the PFA to help those players develop a truly viable vocation."

Since 2012, 98 PFA members have studied at Salford. "We place a strong emphasis on societal value – some people want to make an enormous contribution in a life outside the game, such as working with those requiring rehabilitation after a stroke," says Gill.

This sense of societal value underpins the new clinic that the school is opening in 2025. With £40 million of funding, the aim of the new building is to engage students, the public, community and partners in clinical treatment and research.

"We are in the centre of a city that has many social issues, with areas of great deprivation, and this building will be a centralised hub that will provide accessibility to everybody," says Steve. It will also serve to support the university's wider commitment to increase student numbers to fill workplace needs and provide an education with real-world industry experience.

"We want to engage our community and welcome them to our campus, using the power of participation to combat health inequality," says Gill. "We know that football has the ability to change people's lives and outcomes, and we can support footballers into fulfilling and successful careers."

Pitch perfect

SPORTS CLUBS THROUGHOUT THE UK USE ARTIFICIAL SURFACES MAINTAINED BY REPLAY, FOR WHOM AUTHENTICITY IS THE NAME OF THE GAME

www.replaymaintenance.co.uk

For fans and players of a certain age, the plastic football pitches used in the 1980s by clubs such as QPR and Luton still raise a rueful smile. But synthetic sports pitches have come a long way since the burn-inducing, bounce-producing plastic pitches of yore; now 3G pitches deliver an exceptional all-weather experience that replicates a traditional grass pitch when correctly maintained. That crucial job of maintenance often falls to Replay Maintenance, a company that has spent 20 years looking after artificial surfaces all over the UK, including those used at many football academies and training grounds.

"These surfaces are exceptional and can offer great usage levels, but if people want a return on their investment they need to look after them," says Managing Director Nick Harris. "We provide our clients with a maintenance package to ensure the player and ball interaction with the surface is consistent and replicates the playing characteristics of natural grass. We are providing these top-quality surfaces so the players of the future can be developed."

Replay Maintenance has around 1,500 clients and maintains as many as 200 pitches each week. These can be used for a variety of sports, including football, hockey, rugby, tennis and athletics. The company maintained the athletic tracks used in the 2012 Olympics and the Commonwealth Games, and the work takes them to a wide range of places, from schools, universities and sports clubs to prisons and military bases. Because of Replay's unique expertise in these surfaces, it has been able to produce a range of innovative maintenance techniques and solutions, all designed to extend the life of the surface and ensure it continues to deliver the best experience. The company has even developed its own software program to support the maintenance schedule, something it has been able to sell to peers around the world.

As well as helping to produce a new generation of footballers, Replay's experts are developing another generation of surfaces. These are not so much 4G as an improvement on existing 3G technology, replacing the shredded rubber used in pitches with something more environmentally friendly such as cork and other organic infills. Replay's commitment to recycling is also addressing the issue of sustainability. Previously, old pitches were typically reused for cattle and golf course pathways, but now Replay can separate a pitch into its component parts. Sand and rubber are recycled within the industry, while the surface itself is shredded and reused in the plastics industry.

While synthetic surfaces are unlikely to ever be used at the very highest level, they will continue to play a vital role within the wider football environment. Artificial pitches are in use in parts of the world where the conditions make it hard to maintain grass; in non-league, they allow smaller clubs to get more use out of their grounds; and they are widely employed for training and academies.

"We maintain these surfaces to the highest standards to ensure the player experience is every bit as good as it would be with grass," says Garry Martin, Replay Maintenance CEO. "We are providing and preparing the best playing surface for future generations so they can develop as players and then transition to grass. Our goal is to make the surface so authentic that they don't even realise the difference. That's how we use our knowledge and our maintenance processes, and that's how we get the continued trust of our customers."

The sounds of music

ABSOLUTE SOUNDS' EXPERTLY CURATED HIGH-END AUDIO EQUIPMENT BRINGS THE AMBIENCE OF A LIVE EVENT INTO THE HOME

www.absolutesounds.com

"I wanted my sound systems to be objects of desire, just like Enzo Ferrari's cars, that people would buy as a reward for their hard work," says Ricardo Franassovici, founder and Managing Director of Absolute Sounds. "I felt there was no reason why a good audio system built by artisans should not be as aspirational as a Ferrari car."

The love of music stemmed from Ricardo's career as a rock promoter; he also managed a jazz club and worked in PR for record labels Warner and RCA. He appreciated 1960s jazz, the golden age of recording and the immersive, emotional pleasures of the live experience, be it rock or classical. In 1977, Ricardo found the endless demands of a showbusiness timetable and marriage did not mix, but he could not give up his love and need for music. So, he set up Absolute Sounds, curating high-performance sound systems dedicated to replicating the detail, ambience and sheer impact of great live music in the home.

Ricardo is no ordinary purveyor of sound systems. "I don't consider myself a hi-fi man or an audiophile," he says. He compares himself, rather, to a master chef, putting together the various "ingredients" for the perfect system, drawn from a diverse array of manufacturers. "I travel the world, find components designed not just by engineers, but by music lovers. The engineers who only look at facts and figures, distortion and specification mostly don't deliver 'instruments' – objects of desire – that make music. And so, I might create a system mixing the finest electronics from Japan and England, and maybe speakers from America, to create a thrilling musical experience – all designed by people passionate about music."

He believes in the wellbeing that comes from exposure to a great sound system, which he wishes everyone could share. He describes himself as an "audio addict", a "pusher of endorphins", who cannot go long without his ritual of sipping on a fine cognac and listening to, say, a Miles Davis album so faithfully rendered it was as if the jazzman were in the room.

"Typically, you used to buy your sound system from a shop on Edgware Road on the same floor as fridges and washing machines," says Ricardo with a shudder. "I've tried to elevate the whole thing. After four decades, I'm regarded as the Karl Lagerfeld of audio."

Full of energy

REFRESHING, LIGHT AND MADE WITHOUT ARTIFICIAL INGREDIENTS, GOAT DRINKS OFFERS AN ALTERNATIVE BOOST TO BOTH TRADITIONAL ENERGY DRINKS AND TRADITIONAL HEALTH DRINKS

www.goatdrinks.com | www.mythdrinks.com

"I wanted to make a drink that was healthier, had more personality and, most importantly, tasted better than other energy drinks," says Colette Safhill, founder of Goat Drinks. "In our original drink, Horny Goat, we have zinc, B vitamins, natural caffeine and the amazing natural flavours of mango and pomelo."

Colette believes her energy drinks have considerable potential benefits for athletes, gamers and clubbers alike, supporting "energy yield and blood flow". Goat Drinks – named after Colette's star sign, Capricorn – has also just launched a sugar-free version, Funky Goat, which again uses entirely natural ingredients. It is sweetened with plant-based stevia, so it contains no carbs, calories or sugar, and has a tangy sour cherry flavour.

"These taste completely different from other energy drinks – they aren't at all sweet and sickly, and they aren't too fizzy either. Lots of people say they don't like energy drinks, but our drinks don't actually taste like any other energy drink. They're for the many people out there who are looking for something new."

Based in North Yorkshire, Colette originally entered the drinks market in 2022 with Myth Drinks, motivated by a desire to create a drink that she – a non-drinker for 20 years – could enjoy herself. She developed two alcohol-free spirits: Myth Coconut, which is coconut flavoured and light rum-inspired, and Myth Dark Spiced, which is spicy and dark rum-inspired. Myth Coconut won the 2022 International Wine and Spirits Competition for the best non-alcohol drink available. Vegan-friendly and gluten-free, the drinks are now widely stocked in zero-alcohol bars and off-licences in North America and are making inroads in the growing alcohol-free drinks sector in the UK.

Goat Drinks – the original Horny Goat and its sugar-free companion Funky Goat – is headed for similar success. "Our next step is to launch a caffeine-free version that's also isotonic," says Colette, "while with Myth Drinks I intend to create a small, exclusive range of canned ready-to-drink cocktails, making things like piña coladas. Everything is made in the UK, which we're very proud of. Our aim is simple across both brands: we want to offer exciting, great-tasting drinks that challenge the traditional unhealthy offerings of the energy drink and alcohol sectors."

Chapter Five

2013|14 – 2021|22

In 2021, Gordon Taylor stood down after 40 years as Chief Executive of the PFA, passing the baton on to the current office holder, Maheta Molango. In that time, football in England and Wales had grown to become one of our most popular pastimes and the country's most lucrative cultural exports.

In 1981, the sport was played predominantly by male, homegrown footballers, who earned relatively modest wages, had weak employment rights and often had few post-playing career opportunities. By the 2020s, the PFA's work has contributed to a sport played by men and women from around the world in state-of-the-art stadiums and watched by millions across the globe, with far greater employment protection and a plethora of opportunities to pursue vocational prospects, in and out of football. Put simply, the professional game had been transformed.

The increasingly global nature of English football was underlined when Liverpool's Luis Suárez was named PFA Players' Player in 2014. The Uruguayan was the first non-European to win the award, while Manchester City's Manuel Pellegrini became the first South American coach to claim the Premier League that same season. Players and managers now come to England from far and wide to test their skills in what has become the world's most competitive competition.

Proof of that competitiveness would come in 2015/16 in the shape of the longest of title longshots. Playing in the top flight for the first time in ten years, Leicester City were promoted to the Premier League in 2014. One season's survival and managerial change later, incoming boss Claudio Ranieri's outfit was given odds of 5,000/1 to win the Premier League by the bookies. The press and even boyhood Leicester fan Gary Lineker were sceptical of the new appointment.

Just over a year later, Lineker found himself presenting *Match of the Day* in nothing but a pair of shorts, having promised to do so in December 2015 if Leicester somehow won the league. Two of the squad who steered the Foxes to their glorious title went on to be recognised by their peers as PFA Players' Player of the Year: Riyad Mahrez took the prize that season, becoming the first African player to do so, and his teammate N'Golo Kanté, signed by Chelsea the following summer, went on to win it in 2016/17.

Perhaps the most significant rule change during this period was the introduction of Video Assistant Referee or VAR. In November 2018, Premier League clubs voted unanimously to introduce VAR for the following season, with the system having been trialled for the first time in England in January of that year in the FA Cup match between Brighton and Crystal Palace.

This most recent decade in PFA Awards history has been one of transition for several of the Premier League's most established clubs. As Pep Guardiola and Jürgen Klopp settled into management roles at Manchester City and Liverpool, respectively, something of an arms race developed, with each driving the other on to record-breaking heights and points tallies. The dominance of these two teams is reflected in the PFA Players' Player of the Year of the past five years: three for Liverpool, two for Manchester City. Egyptian Mohamed Salah and Belgian Kevin De Bruyne have both won the award twice – recognition of the world-beating quality of two masters of the sport, and the globe-spanning breadth of the English game.

7

AIA

11
AXA
2022

Emirates

AIRWAYS

WOMEN'S PLAYERS' PLAYER OF THE YEAR

Lucy Bronze

HAVING HELPED LIVERPOOL TO THEIR FIRST TOP-FLIGHT TITLE IN 2013, THE ONLY PERSON SURPRISED AT HER PFA AWARD WIN WAS THE STAR DEFENDER HERSELF

Above | Bronze with the Women's Players' Player of the Year award, 2014

Opposite | On the ball for Liverpool in an outing against Chelsea, 2014

PFA: You're a seasoned pro now, but looking back to the early stages of your career, what was it like trying to make a living in the women's game back then?
Lucy Bronze: Yeah, I wasn't really making a living in football. I actually think the first time I won the PFA award, I was still studying. The famous story is that I was working in Domino's as well. But we didn't start playing football just to be a footballer, we played because we loved it. It wasn't, "Oh, this is going to be our job." We didn't know that existed, but obviously we're very fortunate that women's football has been on the rise for the last 15 years and we've all been lucky enough to have these amazing careers.
PFA: Obviously, you're in a completely different place now, playing for Barcelona. Do you ever reflect on how far you've come in your career?
LB: A little. It's nice to look back and reminisce about the good old days. Sometimes those days were the best days, when you were just making do sleeping on a sofa and stuff like that. Things are very different now and very professional, it's amazing. But I quite like the journey that I've been on. I've been, you know, right at the bottom. I remember playing in the FA Cup final in 2009. We had to pack the bags in one of the supermarkets to raise money for the bus for us as a team to get to the final.
PFA: To go from that to winning Euro 2022 with England, does it make you appreciate success all the more?
LB: Yeah, exactly. From nothing to now European champions and we play at Wembley and have all these fans. The ceiling has just been completely blown off.
PFA: Going back to the year you won the award for the first time at Liverpool, do you remember much from that season?
LB: I do. Previously I'd had numerous knee surgeries and never really got going, and then I signed for Liverpool who were bottom of the league and we won back-to-back leagues. It was incredible. I played with some really special players and I remember winning the award and, I know everyone says they're surprised when they win an award, but it really was like, "I'm a right back." I mean, you look at all these players, they're all goalscorers… I think I maybe scored two or three goals in the season.
PFA: Does the fact that it's voted for by the players make it all the more special?

"I signed for Liverpool
who were bottom of
the league and we won
back-to-back leagues.
It was incredible"
Standard

Left | The Reds right back clears the ball under pressure from Chelsea's Yuki Nagasato, 2014

"I never settle for anything. Even with these awards, it's like, what's the next thing? I can't sit still"

LB: One hundred per cent. Even now, no matter what award it is you win or you get nominated for, the ones that are voted for by the players – they're the ones that know. You can watch the TV and think "they look fast" or "they look good", but when it's player nominated, it's "that person found it hard to play against me so they've put my name forward."

PFA: By the time you won the second PFA award in 2017 you were well established. Did it still mean as much?

LB: Yeah, it was just as much of a surprise. It's so difficult when some people already have an expectation of what your level is. You have to outdo yourself – you're not only having to compete against other players, you're also competing against your own previous performances. So then to do it again, it's like that sense of achievement – you're improving and you get better because you have to compete with your own self and people's expectation of what you are as a player.

PFA: That's something you've done throughout your career, in England, in France and now in Spain. What motivates you to keep challenging yourself?

LB: I don't know. I just feel like I never settle for anything. Even with these awards, it's like, okay, put that aside, what's the next thing? It's a good and a bad thing. Sometimes people say, "Why don't you enjoy these things in the moment?" and I do, but I think when I finish my career, I'll sit back and be like, "Wow, that was amazing." But I'm constantly looking for the next thing. My attention, my focus is constantly going forward and forward. That's probably why I've changed teams a lot, because it's like I'm looking for another thing to do and another thing to do. I can't sit still.

MEN'S PLAYERS' PLAYER OF THE YEAR

Luis Suárez

THE URUGUAYAN DELIVERED 31 GOALS AND 12 ASSISTS IN WHAT WOULD PROVE TO BE HIS FINAL SEASON AT ANFIELD

Norwich City goalkeeper John Ruddy had a front-row seat to what felt like his own funeral.

"The speed of thought he has," said a shellshocked Ruddy after Luis Suárez plundered four goals in a 5–1 Liverpool win in December 2013. "He's taking shots that people wouldn't take in a million years and he's pulling them off, making people look stupid. You sort of stand there and think: 'What's just happened?'"

An insatiable centre forward at the peak of his powers, that's what. Beginning with a 35-yard lob and featuring a twisting run and rasping half-volley, Luis Suárez's Canaries gluttony was a one-man goal-of-the-season application and summed up an animalistic authority to subjugate any player unfortunate enough to find themselves in front of him. The Uruguayan's 31 goals in 33 games came at a top-flight rate not bettered since Jimmy Greaves' 41 goals in 40 1960/61 appearances. More impressive still, none were penalties.

"He has everything. He's in your face, he's arrogant in a good way," said Arsenal's Thierry Henry. "He has that vicious side to his game."

Embodying the Uruguayan *garra charrúa* spirit of the street, Suárez was a professional irritant, his excellence to be celebrated, even if talk of "rehabilitation" went a little far. Two seasons on from the Patrice Evra incident, he had missed the first five games of 2013/14 for biting Chelsea's Branislav Ivanović.

Though he couldn't maintain the staggering goalscoring form that yielded 19 goals in 12 Premier League games before Christmas – despite a March hat-trick at Cardiff – Suárez became a 12-assist machine as strike partner Daniel Sturridge kept the Reds' title hopes alive. That was until Steven Gerrard's infamous slip at home to Chelsea and draw at Crystal Palace reduced Suárez to tears. The 27-year-old had to make do with becoming the first non-European winner of the Men's Players' Player of the Year award, plus taking the Football Writers' Association honour.

"In the last year he's been near-unplayable," said Liverpool boss Brendan Rodgers. "He on his own can occupy a back four with his movement and his cleverness."

Suárez celebrates his third goal during the Premier League match against Fulham at Anfield, 2013

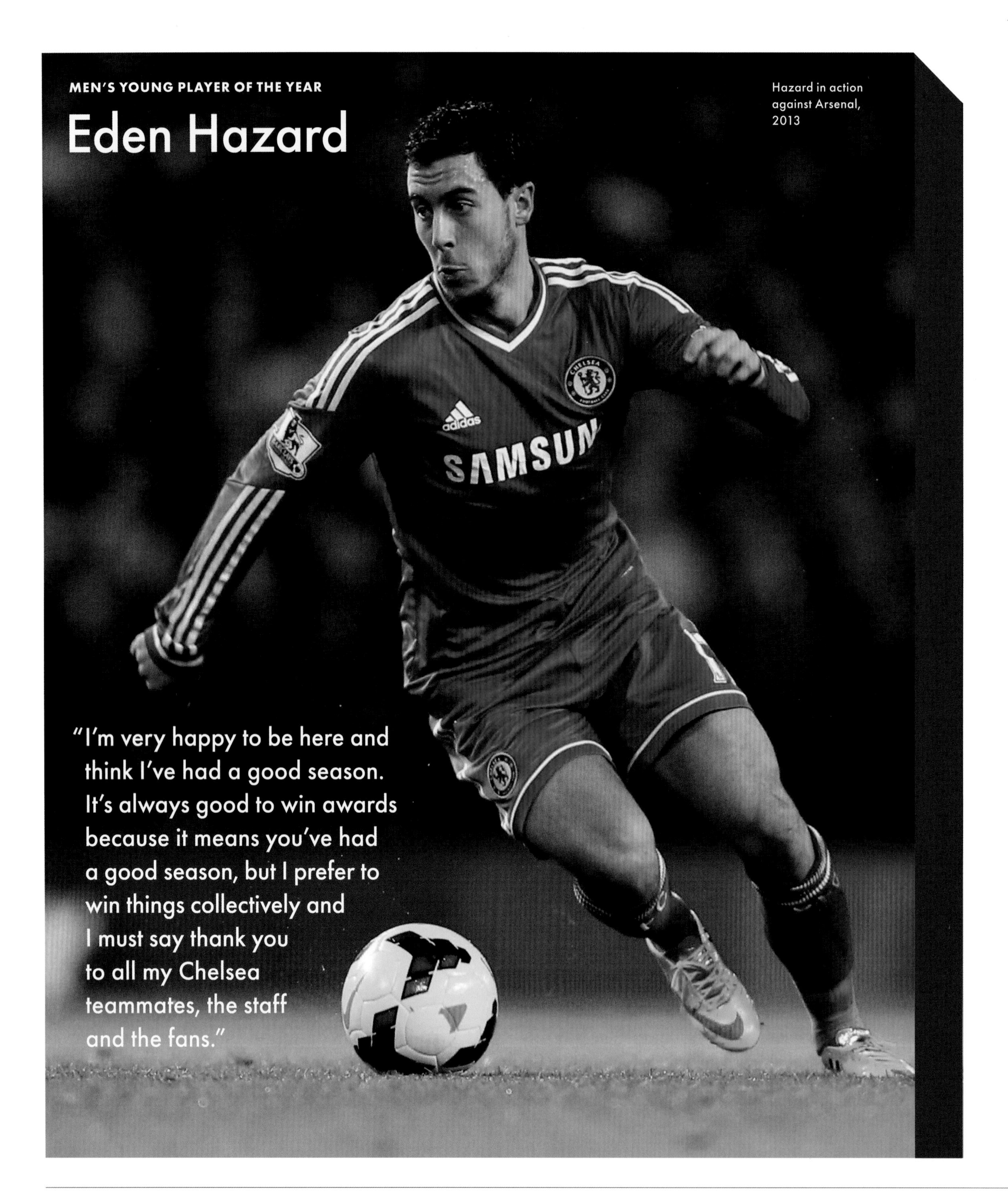

MEN'S YOUNG PLAYER OF THE YEAR

Eden Hazard

Hazard in action against Arsenal, 2013

"I'm very happy to be here and think I've had a good season. It's always good to win awards because it means you've had a good season, but I prefer to win things collectively and I must say thank you to all my Chelsea teammates, the staff and the fans."

WOMEN'S YOUNG PLAYER OF THE YEAR

Martha Harris

Liverpool were never going to stand still after ending a 24-year wait for a first women's top-flight title when they won the 2013 WSL. Desperate to improve from a position of strength, the Reds bought full back Martha Harris, whose consistency for Notts County (formerly Lincoln Ladies) had just delivered the top flight's second-best defensive record.

"Martha is a very talented and versatile player who will add an extra dimension to the squad," Liverpool boss Matt Beard said in making Harris his first signing in December 2013.

A model of defensive diligence and attacking brio, the 19-year-old's vision, touch and tenacious tackling were the central tenets of a back four that conceded just 15 times in 14 WSL games – four fewer than the title winners she was joining – and had impressed in reaching the 2013 UEFA Women's Under-19 Championship final with England.

It was no surprise when Harris became the inaugural winner of the PFA Women's Young Player of the Year Award.

Above | Harris with the PFA Women's Young Player of the Year award, 2014

MERIT AWARD

Donald Bell

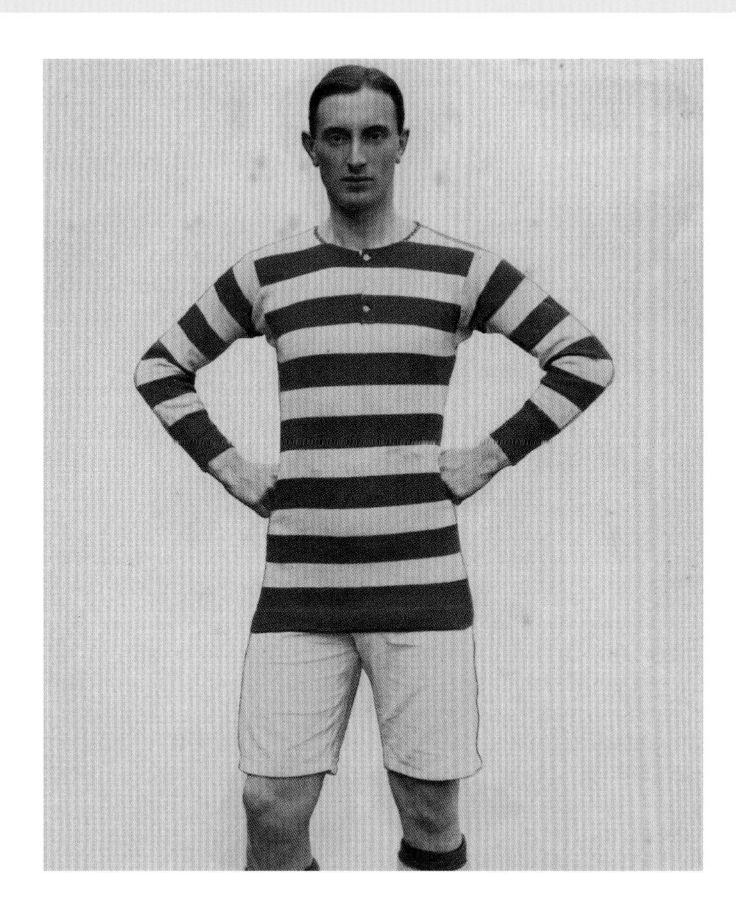

Right | Bell, the first footballer to have won the Victoria Cross

Football heroes don't come any more worthy of recognition than Donald Bell.

A skilful Bradford Park Avenue player when the First World War began in 1914, Bell was driven by a compulsion to serve his country and soon became the first professional footballer to join the British Army.

On 5 July 1916, the fifth day of the Battle of the Somme, Bell attacked an enemy machine-gun post at Horseshoe Trench, killing the gunner and securing the position for his company with a well-thrown bomb. His act, for which he received a posthumous Victoria Cross, saved the lives of many of his fellow soldiers.

Bell's heroism was eclipsed only by his modesty. "It was the biggest fluke alive and I did nothing," he wrote home to his parents.

Five days later, aged 25, Bell was killed on a similar manoeuvre at Contalmaison. To mark the 100th anniversary of the beginning of the Great War, his memory was honoured with the PFA Merit Award in recognition of Bell and the hundreds of other footballers who lost their lives during the conflict.

"He knows that he is one of the three best players in the world, and he is coping with that responsibility"
José Mourinho

MEN'S PLAYERS' PLAYER OF THE YEAR

Eden Hazard

THE MERCURIAL BELGIAN WON A RAFT OF AWARDS FOR HIS PERFORMANCES IN 2014/15, AS CHELSEA WON A LEAGUE AND LEAGUE CUP DOUBLE

Above | Hazard scores Chelsea's second goal of the game against Spurs at White Hart Lane, 2015

There's irresistible and then there's a 24-year-old Eden Hazard in 2014/15.

Fourteen Premier League goals, 9 assists, most chances created, most dribbles completed, most fouls received and more than 150 more completed passes in the final third than his nearest rival, Manchester City's David Silva. He even scored what was just a second header of his career in a 2–0 win over Hull. "I was surprised," winked Blues boss José Mourinho. "Normally, he closes his eyes."

What really stood out was his consistency. Whereas centre forward Diego Costa and midfield playmaker Cesc Fàbregas couldn't maintain their early-season form, on only one occasion all season did Hazard go more than three games without contributing a goal or an assist, and even that blank featured a ten-minute cameo in an already-won League Cup tie.

"He's the guy who, when you pass him the ball you just have to leave him to it," Chelsea teammate Branislav Ivanović said. "He'll do everything. He's something different."

Better still, following spring's League Cup success, Hazard delivered when it mattered most. In successive games in April, his 88th-minute run and measured cutback for Fàbregas beat a resolute QPR, before the brilliant Belgian's winner took Chelsea ten points clear at the Premier League summit a week later against Manchester United.

"He knows that he is one of the three best players in the world, and he is coping with that responsibility," Mourinho said in comparing his charge to Lionel Messi and Cristiano Ronaldo. "If people are fair, then he gets the [Player of the Year] award, but the first thing I want him to win is the Premier League."

The Special One would be satisfied within a fortnight. Hazard's rebound from his own penalty against Crystal Palace sealed a first Blues title since 2010 a week after he romped home to win the PFA Men's Players' Player of the Year award.

"It's better to be voted by the players, they know everything about football," said Hazard, who had just missed out for the PFA award to Luis Suárez the season before. "I've been there in the big games and scored a lot of important goals, this is why I'm better this season."

WOMEN'S PLAYERS' PLAYER OF THE YEAR

Ji So-yun

IN HER DEBUT WSL SEASON, THE KOREAN TRICKSTER LIFTED CHELSEA TO THE BEST LEAGUE FINISH IN THE CLUB'S HISTORY

Nowhere in English football were diminutive, 24-year-old playmakers blessed with the smoothest of techniques more de rigueur than at Chelsea in 2014/15. On the same night that Eden Hazard scooped his individual honour, Ji So-yun matched her Blues teammate by winning the Women's Players' Player of the Year award.

Chelsea manager Emma Hayes had promised "our fans will love her" when Ji made the move from Japanese side INAC Kobe Leonessa ahead of the 2014 WSL season. But not even the most ardent Blues followers could have anticipated the number ten's rapid acclimatisation to English football.

"I was worried about the difference in culture and language," she said. "But everyone helped me to settle in."

Though runners-up Chelsea were overhauled by Liverpool on the final day of the 2014 WSL season after a heartbreaking 2–1 loss to Manchester City, there was no doubting Ji's galvanising effect on a team that had never finished higher than sixth in three WSL campaigns. Fellow midfield arrivals Katie Chapman and Gilly Flaherty helped, but it was the so-called South Korean Messi, who made her international debut aged just 15, that provided the impish stardust, scoring nine goals in 19 games in all competitions and registering a joint-high WSL assist tally.

"She has only just scratched the surface and is a fantastic young playmaker who controls a game," said Blues boss Hayes. "Like all good players she finds a way to solve problems on the pitch. Ji will kick on and the world stage will see what a player she is."

Ji proved the catalyst of a WSL-winning machine that lifted six of the following eight top-flight titles. Far from Ji adapting to England, it was England that had to adapt to her luscious touch and bright movement.

"It's a big honour to receive this award," said Ji about the honour that began it all in 2015. "I'm really, really happy to be nominated alongside Hazard, I'm really proud of myself and Chelsea."

Ji on the ball against Everton at Wheatsheaf Park, 2014

WOMEN'S YOUNG PLAYER OF THE YEAR

Leah Williamson

Leah Williamson was faced with a serious choice in 2012. Captivated by the London Olympics, the 15-year-old Arsenal youngster considered switching to a career in athletics when Greg Rutherford – a fellow Milton Keynes native – took gold on Super Saturday. Less than three years later, football having won, Williamson's peers voted her the best young player in the country.

"I'm overwhelmed," said the 18-year-old. "It's amazing to be recognised by fellow players so I'm just very humbled. It's taken a lot of work since the moment I started playing football, but this is my first full season with the first team so you have to try to make an impact, make yourself known and give it everything you've got."

Had she ever. The day after she turned 17, Williamson made her senior debut for the club she'd joined as a nine-year-old, as Arsenal fell to a quarter-final Champions League defeat to Birmingham City in March 2014. A smooth, versatile operator whose graceful movement would make Margot Fonteyn blush, she became an instant regular as a defensive midfielder of rare game-reading ability, soon winning the FA Cup.

Williamson missed just one 2014 WSL fixture as Arsenal finished fourth, but it was in the League Cup that the teenager most impressed. Deployed as a midfield anchor, forward-thinking left back and the centre back role she has since gravitated towards, Williamson appeared in every minute of the tournament – scoring against Millwall in the group stage – as only Izzy Christiansen's second-half header for Manchester City prevented a second trophy. Instead, Williamson received the Player of the Tournament, the England Women's Youth Player of the Year and the PFA Women's Young Player of the Year awards.

A fortnight before picking up the latter in April 2015, the number fourteen proved why she was held in such high regard. In a vital qualifier for the summer's UEFA U19 Championship finals, England trailed Norway when they were awarded an injury-time penalty. Captain Williamson stepped up and scored, only for the goal to be incorrectly ruled out by the match officials with no re-take awarded. Five days later, following an appeal, the game's final 16 seconds were to be replayed from the moment of the penalty.

Williamson playing for Arsenal against Liverpool at Meadow Park, 2014

An impossibly cool Williamson dispatched the spot-kick to qualify England for the upcoming finals in Israel.

"Leah was earmarked for success at an early age," said Arsenal legend and former England captain Faye White. "She showed so much confidence and composure in her first season at the top level, never more so than when she took that penalty having had a whole day to think about it. It took a lot of nerve."

Williamson's nerve would also lead the senior side to unprecedented Euro 2022 glory seven years later, again as captain. Thank god she chose football.

MEN'S YOUNG PLAYER OF THE YEAR

Harry Kane

Mauricio Pochettino was desperate. The Argentinian had won just three of his first nine league games as Tottenham Hotspur manager and was 1–0 down to Aston Villa with half an hour left of his tenth. Fearing for his job, he sent on a 21-year-old with no 2014/15 top-flight starts to his name.

Harry Kane had scored six goals in five Europa League outings but this was different, no matter how much Spurs sang "he's one of our own". Having previously played out on loan at Leyton Orient, Millwall and Leicester City, the striker scored an injury-time winner, the first of 21 league goals in a breakthrough campaign.

Kane became the first Spurs player since Gary Lineker 23 seasons earlier to score more than 30 in all competitions as the Lilywhites reached the League Cup final, and scored 79 seconds into his senior international career. The Men's Young Player of the Year award was a formality. In less than a decade, he was England's record goalscorer.

"That Villa goal was a statement," Kane later recalled. "I was ready." Was he ever.

Kane celebrates his hat-trick against Asteras Tripolis in the Europa League group tie at White Hart Lane, 2014

Gerrard and Lampard vie for the ball during the Champions League semi-final first leg at Anfield, 2007

MERIT AWARD

Steven Gerrard and Frank Lampard

It was somehow fitting that Steven Gerrard and Frank Lampard jointly received the 2015 PFA Merit Award. In inextricably linked careers that began just three years apart in the late-'90s, the standout English midfielders of their generation shared 22 major club honours, appeared in more than 1,600 games in all competitions and each won a century of caps for their country.

At their mid-noughties peak, as Chelsea ruled the domestic roost under José Mourinho, Gerrard's Liverpool and Lampard's Blues met in five successive Champions League seasons from 2004/05 as familiarity bred a form of contempt. It finished two Gerrard knockouts, two for Lampard and one group stage stalemate.

Like boxing judges who score the same fight differently, contemporaries' preference depended on what they liked from a barnstorming number eight. Lampard scored more club goals – 274, including a Chelsea record 211, to Gerrard's 190 – and won more trophies, but Gerrard was more versatile.

"He gives the players around him confidence and belief," said Zinedine Zidane in putting Gerrard on a par with Lionel Messi and Cristiano Ronaldo in 2009. "Players like him are just born with that presence."

Mourinho preferred his charge's consistency. "For me he was the best, for ten years," said the Special One. "I don't see another one."

As the pair prepared to depart for an American adventure in MLS, Gerrard with LA Galaxy and Lampard at New York City, the joint PFA Merit Award was a justified celebration of co-existing domination.

"Frank is an unbelievable, world-class player and I couldn't ask for anyone better to share it with," said Gerrard, on-stage with his co-winner. Lampard agreed: "I'm proud to stand alongside a good friend. For the two of us to get it is a nice send-off."

MEN'S PLAYERS' PLAYER OF THE YEAR

Riyad Mahrez

THE ATTACKING VERVE OF THE FIRST AFRICAN TO BE NAMED PLAYERS' PLAYER OF THE YEAR HELPED LEICESTER CITY DEFY THE ODDS IN A TITLE-WINNING SEASON

In February 2016, just after he had scored one and created another as Leicester City beat Manchester City 3–1 to go five points clear at the Premier League's summit, Riyad Mahrez was asked if the Foxes could achieve the impossible.

"I still don't think we can win the league," he said. Why not? The Algerian winger smiled. "Because if maybe I keep saying that, we'll stay top."

Not only did the ramshackle group of 5,000/1 odd-jobber outsiders do just that, never to relinquish top spot, the ultimate underdogs doubled their advantage to ten points, with the rakish Mahrez voted the Men's Players' Player of the Year – the award's first African winner.

Mahrez had never played a minute of top-flight football before arriving to the square root of no fanfare at the second-tier Foxes in January 2014 from Ligue 2 side Le Havre.

"I thought Leicester were a rugby club," he recalled. His own lack of pretension and non-academy background helped him settle. "Sometimes you see me on the pitch and you think I'm playing on the street. That brings something different to the team."

Incoming manager Claudio Ranieri indulged that instinct in 2015/16. "In the last 30 metres, I told him: 'You can do what you want. You are a fantasy player'," recalled the Italian.

Mahrez began with four goals in his first three games, cutting inside from the right wing to curl a magnificent left footed strike against Tottenham Hotspur to set the blueprint for much of what followed. When the sinuous attacker's solo run helped best City to make title-winning dreams a reality in February he surpassed reigning PFA winner Eden Hazard's 2014/15 tally of 14 goals and nine assists with three months to play. Only Jamie Vardy, who went on a Premier League record 11-game scoring run and took the Football Writers' Association gong, scored more for Leicester than Mahrez's final league tally of 17.

"It's a big honour to be the first, if not the best, African to win this award," beamed the modest Mahrez after receiving the PFA award.

Mahrez lifts the Premier League trophy, 2016

WOMEN'S PLAYERS' PLAYER OF THE YEAR

Izzy Christiansen

MANCHESTER CITY'S MIDFIELD DYNAMO SCOOPED THE PLAYERS' PLAYER AWARD AS THE BLUES FINISHED IN THE TOP TWO WITH A PLACE IN EUROPE

Delivering when it matters is what separates the elite from the merely excellent. Izzy Christiansen's steadfast refusal to accept a limp denouement to the 2015 WSL season for Manchester City was testament to the marauding midfielder's nerveless ability to reproduce her best form when it mattered most.

When the top-flight season paused for England's third-place finish at the 2015 World Cup, City had picked up just five points in five games, midtable mediocrity seemingly certain. Steph Houghton, Lucy Bronze, Jill Scott and Toni Duggan returned from Canada full of rejuvenated confidence to spark a run of eight wins in nine games taking a title challenge to the final day yet, for all that quartet's experience, it was Christiansen who shone brightest. The 24-year-old scored six goals in City's final six fixtures, including two in a 6–0 thumping of Bristol Academy plus winners against Sunderland and Notts County, the latter to secure Champions League football for the first time in the club's history.

That goal against the Magpies, a month after she'd scored on her senior England debut against Estonia, was Christiansen in microcosm. Ghosting into the box as City poured forward in search of the lead just before half time, the all-action former Birmingham City playmaker met Natasha Harding's right-wing cross with a savage half-volley that flew into the top corner. Athleticism, appreciation of space and sublime technique, all delivered at a moment of maximum pressure.

Nor was it the first time. Part of the Birmingham squad as a teenager that had won the 2012 FA Cup, the multi-functional Christiansen's deadly 73rd-minute header secured City's first major trophy to win the League Cup in October 2014. Six months earlier, she'd been nominated for the PFA Women's Young Player of the Year.

"Izzy is an exceptional player who forms an integral part of our midfield. She's a fantastic role model," said City head coach Nick Cushing. "She's a team player who knows it takes hard work and determination to be successful on the pitch and more importantly she's a good person whose passion for the game is second to none."

Though Chelsea won the 2015 WSL title, Christiansen's barnstorming performances ensured she received the Women's Players' Player of the Year award.

"There's no better accolade than being recognised by your teammates and this is the icing on top of the cake. I'm so honoured to win this award in such a fantastic era for women's football," she said. "I want to thank everyone who's helped me get to where I am today. It's just the start."

Christiansen was right. Convalescing from an ankle injury, she would soon return to fitness and guide City to a first WSL title later that September, winning the league unbeaten. She would also go on to win a treble with French giants Lyon, including the Champions League, but it was in 2015/16 that Christiansen ascended to the elite.

Left | Christiansen holds the Players' Player of the Year award, 2016

Right | The midfielder sprints away from Liverpool's Kate Longhurst, 2015

ETIHAD
AIRWAYS
Standard
Chartered
LFC
7

WOMEN'S YOUNG PLAYER OF THE YEAR

Beth Mead

The 2015 WSL season wasn't even half an hour old when Beth Mead proved her goalscoring prowess for newly promoted Sunderland. The 19-year-old forward had scored 13 in 15 WSL 2 fixtures the previous campaign to return the Black Cats to the top flight, her towering 28th-minute header preceding a hard-won penalty to secure an opening day 2–1 win at defending champions Liverpool.

By season's end, Mead would add another 11 league goals, but it was her July hat-trick in a 4–0 victory against Chelsea – one of only two defeats the eventual champions would suffer – that most made headlines. Two days earlier, the number nine had miraculously escaped with cuts and bruises after rolling her car three times in trying to avoid hitting a deer near the family home in Hinderwell, a tiny fishing village near Whitby.

"I was in a state of panic and just thought the worst was about to happen. I don't think anybody gave me a chance to play," she said, her attention soon returning to Sunderland. "People look at us as an average team and I think we've shown today that we are one of the best at the moment."

No one who witnessed that display of express pace, clever movement and a deadly eye for goal would have thought Mead was anything close to average, especially after her death-defying experience. A fierce competitor who channelled her childhood hyperactivity into football, she had been a first-team regular since joining the club aged 16 in 2011, a seven-minute hat-trick for Middlesbrough three years earlier first alerting the Black Cats to her manifold talents. By the time she joined Arsenal in January 2017, Mead had scored 77 goals in 78 Sunderland games in all competitions.

"She was a proper goalscorer, with either foot, from anywhere," said Sunderland manager Mick Mulhern, present for that early triple. "When you think of someone at such a young, tender age, that I was so determined to sign her, it tells you what I thought of her then and what I knew she would become."

Swapping notes with Sunderland men's forward Jermain Defoe in the players' canteen – "I've never scored one like that before, what were you thinking when you did that?" Defoe once asked – Mead became the WSL's youngest Golden Boot winner as the Black Cats finished fourth. Voted the 2015 WSL Players' Player of the Year, she was a shoo-in for the PFA Women's Young Player of the Year award.

"I can't believe I've won," she said. "It's a huge honour to be recognised by your peers. It caps a really great year but I couldn't have achieved any of this without my teammates and everybody at the club who have supported me and believed in me."

Mead controls the ball against Liverpool at The Hetton Centre, 2015

MEN'S YOUNG PLAYER OF THE YEAR

Dele Alli

What Dele Alli had done to Yeovil Town and Rochdale in 2014/15 for MK Dons, he did to Manchester United and Arsenal in his first Premier League season for Tottenham Hotspur 12 months later. The deftness of touch, ability to find space and dismissive finishing were identical.

"In the box, he looks like a striker, and outside the box, he plays like a midfielder," said Spurs boss Mauricio Pochettino.

Dele's ten goals in 33 league games and abundance of skill earned an England debut, but it was his ball-juggling volley against Crystal Palace in January 2016 that most slackened jaws.

"I doubt whether I'll see a goal scored with such individual flair, and by a 19-year-old," said former Spurs forward Garth Crooks.

Though Spurs's title challenge would implode in the Battle of Stamford Bridge at Chelsea, the teenager was comfortably the country's most promising youngster and the obvious choice for Men's Young Player of the Year, an award he'd retain 12 months later.

Above | Dele (left) receives his PFA award from ex-Spurs forward Paul Allen, 2016

MERIT AWARD

Ryan Giggs

Right | Giggs is all smiles at the final whistle in the FA Cup final against Newcastle United, 1999

The most decorated player in English football history, Ryan Giggs became the first individual to receive the PFA's three main honours when adding the 2016 Merit Award to his Men's Young Player and Players' Player of the Year trophies.

A quarter of a century on from his first-team debut in March 1991, Manchester United's record appearance holder won 36 major honours, including 13 Premier Leagues and two Champions Leagues, as the defining player of Sir Alex Ferguson's Manchester United winning steamroller.

"I'm chuffed to have won all three awards. The Young Player was a long time ago and then the Players' Player award was a big surprise," the 64-cap Welshman said, receiving the award from PFA Chairman Ritchie Humphreys and Chief Executive Gordon Taylor. "You look down the trophy and you see the players who have won it before and you realise what a great accolade it is. This is the same. I've been here on the nights when people have won it and it's legends of the game."

MEN'S PLAYERS' PLAYER OF THE YEAR

N'Golo Kanté

ONE OF THE FINEST DEFENSIVE MIDFIELDERS OF HIS ERA, THE FRENCHMAN BAGGED THE PLAYERS' PLAYER OF THE YEAR AWARD IN HIS SECOND CONSECUTIVE TITLE-WINNING SEASON

Two players since 1888/89 have appeared in successive title-winning English top flight seasons with different clubs. Eric Cantona spent most of his Leeds United half-season on the bench in 1991/92 before completing the inaugural feat with Manchester United, but Chelsea's 2016/17 Premier League triumph a season after Leicester City's odds-shattering crown were wholly predicated on the transformative N'Golo Kanté.

A one-man midfield – "we play Danny Drinkwater in the middle with Kanté either side," Leicester's head of recruitment Steve Walsh once laughed – the Frenchman was everywhere and evolving. In his two previous seasons at Caen and the Foxes, Kanté had made more tackles than any player in Europe's top five leagues but in a Chelsea side that dominated possession, creation and destruction had to co-exist.

Following a 3–0 defeat to Arsenal in late-September, Antonio Conte switched to a 3-4-3 formation, knowing the system could only function with Kanté's notorious dynamism – Chelsea fans joked that "70 per cent of the earth's surface is covered by water, the rest is covered by N'Golo Kanté" – peerless intelligence and tactical awareness. Chelsea won 13 games in a row.

"N'Golo's a complete midfielder, not only a defensive midfielder," Conte said after Kanté's slaloming run and finish put the seal on a 4–0 October defeat of Manchester United. "He's a player that always arrives in the box and he has fantastic stamina, good technique and also good positioning and personality."

Kanté's all-round contribution earned him the PFA Men's Players' Player of the Year and Football Writers' Association Awards.

"This means a lot," the softly spoken 25-year-old said in picking up his PFA award from David Beckham. "It's been two beautiful seasons, one with Leicester, and we are in good form with Chelsea."

Three weeks later, the Blues wrapped up the league with two games to spare thanks to a 1–0 win at West Bromwich Albion. At the final whistle, Kanté's teammates threw the midfielder high into the Black Country air for some victory bumps. It was the only time he'd not been in control of a situation all season.

Kanté playing against Southampton at Stamford Bridge, 2017

WOMEN'S PLAYERS' PLAYER OF THE YEAR

Lucy Bronze

"It's not really sunk in that I've won the award, but it's a huge honour and I'm so grateful. The fact that I've won the award is credit to the players around me. Those relationships are really important to the success of both club and country"

The Women's Players' Player at City Academy, 2016

MEN'S YOUNG PLAYER OF THE YEAR

Dele Alli

"The big thing for me, after last season, is I wanted to put my chances away more. I got a lot of chances last season that I wasn't putting away. I wasn't as clinical. I've still got to improve on that, still had a few chances that I've missed, so I'll keep working on that. But there's a lot of little bits that need improving."

Above | Dele scores Tottenham's third goal against Watford at Vicarage Road, 2017

WOMEN'S YOUNG PLAYER OF THE YEAR

Jess Carter

It takes a special sort of character to make your senior debut in a Champions League quarter-final. To do so as a 16-year-old against former winners Arsenal and win Player of the Match takes superhuman mental strength and special football ability. Jess Carter made it look normal.

Three years on from that memorable March 2014 entrance, the Birmingham City star was voted PFA Women's Young Player of the Year. Carter missed only 31 minutes of the 2016 WSL season, but it was the quality of her displays as much as their abundance that impressed most.

Appearing as a full back, centre back, wide midfielder and a defensive midfield anchor, the 19-year-old's versatility was the glue as the Blues finished fourth, reached the 2016 League Cup final and went on a club-record 12-game unbeaten run in all competitions. Indicative of her maturity and smooth technical elan, Carter also won four of Birmingham's end of season awards, as well as her PFA honour.

"The fact it's voted for by players I play with day in, day out is special," said Carter. "It's a massive privilege to accept this award."

Above | Carter playing for Birmingham against Sunderland, 2016

Beckham celebrates scoring arguably his most famous goal, a last-gasp free-kick equaliser against Greece, 2001

MERIT AWARD

David Beckham

A lot had changed for David Beckham between winning the 1996/97 Young Player of the Year award and the Merit Award two decades later. The skinny 21-year-old with a nervous smile now transcended his sport.

Nineteen major honours for Manchester United, Real Madrid, LA Galaxy, AC Milan and Paris Saint-Germain was a fine haul, but Becks's story was a triumph of everyman graft. His succession to the United first team was far from pre-ordained, the nonpareil crosses and inch-perfect set-pieces – two of which set up United's stunning 1999 Champions League final comeback against Bayern Munich – central to his aptitude for self-improvement learned from his hairdresser mother and kitchen fitter father.

"David Beckham is Britain's finest striker of a football not because of god-given talent," his United boss Sir Alex Ferguson once said, "but because he practises with a relentless application that the vast majority of less gifted players wouldn't contemplate."

Beckham's 115 England caps – an outfield record when he retired in 2013 – each reeked of the passion and pride he felt at representing his country. He went from pariah in France '98 to delivering one of the great individual performances against Greece in a 2–2 result that ensured the Three Lions' qualification for the next World Cup.

"The PFA's such an important part of the game, to be awarded this is special," said Beckham after receiving his Merit Award. "I feel very blessed."

MEN'S PLAYERS' PLAYER OF THE YEAR

Mohamed Salah

THE EGYPTIAN KING WON THE PLAYER OF THE YEAR AWARD IN A RECORD-BREAKING DEBUT SEASON FOR LIVERPOOL

"He remains unproven at the highest level," wrote the *Liverpool Echo* when Mohamed Salah arrived on Merseyside in the summer of 2017 for a club-record £37 million from AS Roma. "It's a big outlay – and risk – for a player of his kind."

To an extent, such reservations were well founded for a 25-year-old wide forward yet to pass 20 goals in a single season. Memories of the Egyptian's 13 Premier League outings in 18 unhappy months under José Mourinho at Chelsea from January 2014 – one coming at Anfield in that April's 2–0 win in which Steven Gerrard slipped to cost the Reds the title – weighed heavily. Even more so than the 29 Serie A goals Salah had struck in 65 appearances in two-and-a-half vibrant Italian top-flight seasons for Fiorentina and the giallorossi. Liverpool boss Jürgen Klopp, however, knew what he was signing.

"Mohamed has the perfect mix of experience and potential," said the German coach. "His pace is incredible, he gives us more attacking threat. Most important, though, is that he is hungry, willing and eager to be even better."

By the end of his first Liverpool season, Salah had plundered 44 goals in all competitions. He'd broken the Premier League goalscoring record for a 38-game season, jointly held by Luis Suárez, Cristiano Ronaldo and Alan Shearer. Only Ian Rush's 47 in 1983/84 was a better single-season tally for the Reds. Perhaps more incredible still, Salah expected it of himself.

"I don't want to sound arrogant but, yeah," he laughed just halfway through the season. "Come on, I know I'm good! I was comfortable at Roma, I had two great seasons and I was happy, but I've always put myself under pressure. Klopp changed something in me. Now I play closer to the goal than in any club before."

At the heart of an expansive side in a more open and attacking league, Salah's season was remarkable for the speed at which he dovetailed with Roberto Firmino and Sadio Mané, and began with a poacher's finish on the opening day against Watford. Given the freedom to drift infield from a right-wing starting position onto his stronger left foot, Salah's every swivel of his hips seemed premeditated, a subtly disguised act to obfuscate and deceive opposition defenders.

By late December when Leicester City visited Anfield and went 1–0 up, he'd scored calm one-on-ones (Arsenal), delicious curlers (Everton) and stinging volleys (Stoke City) . If Salah's equaliser played to type, evading two tackles to fire unerringly past Kasper Schmeichel, the Egyptian's winner couldn't have been more uncharacteristic. Harry Maguire was tight to his man as the ball reached Salah's feet. His back to goal, the Liverpool man controlled, turned and palmed off the hulking England centre back before rifling into the bottom corner.

Such strength was a new addition to the Salah armoury. The busy, bustling gait that had always drawn comparisons to Lionel Messi was now allied with a square-shouldered, stockier frame than that which had struggled at Chelsea.

"I'd like to show you all the scouting footage we had," said Klopp after that Leicester game. "A goal like this was not involved. He is so physically strong."

The Liverpool boss was so impressed, he didn't blink when La Liga giants Barcelona offered £142 million for playmaker Philippe Coutinho barely a week later. The Brazilian's replacement was already at the club and firing, Klopp using half the money to bolster his defence with the transformative Virgil van Dijk.

Salah didn't let up, his economy of movement was such that he never seemed to tire – no Liverpool player started more games in 2017/18 – conserving his energy to settle a match when it mattered most. He began 2018 with a goal and an assist in a thrilling 4–3 defeat of table-topping Manchester City, and struck 14 goals in his first 12 Premier League games of the new year, including March's four-goal haul against Watford.

Former Liverpool captain Steven Gerrard said, "we are witnessing the start of

Salah after scoring the last of Liverpool's seven goals against Spartak Moscow in a Champions League group match at Anfield, 2017

"We are witnessing the start of greatness"

Steven Gerrard

greatness," while ex-Manchester United captain Gary Neville called Salah "an absolute killer".

Though too many draws meant Liverpool finished the season fourth, the Reds' scuttling matchwinner ensured progress in the Champions League. Of his 11 goals in 14 outings as the Merseysiders reached the final, two stood out.

"The one that will always have so much emotion on it was Manchester City away," he recalled, "closely followed by Roma at home."

Salah's semi-final first leg brace against his former club – featuring a spellbinding edge-of-the-box smash – helped Liverpool to the final, but it's not hard to understand why the defeat of a domestic rival in the previous round meant more. The 3–0 first-leg victory at Anfield contained an intensity that superseded anything yet witnessed in Klopp's era, while the Reds' 2–1 win at the Etihad included a dinked Salah finish so calm it came with its own pipe and slippers.

A fortnight later, the Kop's new star received the PFA Men's Players' Player of the Year award, and would later pick up the Football Writers' Association and Premier League Golden Boot for his record 32 league goals.

"It's an honour and especially as it's voted by the players," Salah said at the PFA event, before turning his attention to his past. "I didn't have my chance at Chelsea. It was clear I would return and show everyone my football. I think I left and came back a different person, man and player.

"I have a room at home with a trophy cabinet. And I make sure that I have a lot of space for more. I always keep space for something new... the Golden Boot is the same. I'm always keeping a space and just try to imagine that the trophies come there."

Individual awards would prove to be the extent of the silverware in Salah's annus mirabilis, as Sergio Ramos's arm lock dislocated the Egyptian's shoulder in the Champions League final – without their talisman Liverpool laboured to a 3–1 defeat against Real Madrid. Yet a trophy deluge was in the post. From the Champions League (2018/19) and Premier League (2019/20) to a domestic cup double and another PFA crown (2021/22), Salah would soon need all the space in his trophy cabinet he could spare.

The Liverpool man with his PFA Players' Player of the Year award, 2018

WOMEN'S PLAYERS' PLAYER OF THE YEAR

Fran Kirby

THE ATTACKING MIDFIELDER'S INSATIABLE GOALSCORING APPETITE PAVED CHELSEA'S ROAD TO THE LEAGUE TITLE

Fran Kirby's dexterity of touch, deftness of movement and coolness of mind had already yielded two WSL titles, an FA Cup and third place with England at the 2015 World Cup but there was something different to the Chelsea forward before the 2017/18 season. Aged 24, Kirby was imbued with a determination like never before.

The Blues' number fourteen had missed nearly 11 months from May 2016 after playing on through a fractured knee, bruising the bone so badly she could barely walk. Sure, she had recovered in time for a Euro 2017 semi-final but the lack of match sharpness for someone whose game revolves around speed of thought and subtle changes of pace was to deprive the Lionesses' goalscoring engine of fuel.

Now back to full fitness, Kirby was insatiable. Up and running 40 minutes into the season with a cool finish against Bristol City, the former Reading star was at her effervescent best all campaign long. It was Kirby who found the top corner to knock Bayern Munich out of the Champions League last 32, scored spectacularly from distance to all but secure the WSL against Birmingham City in May 2018 and fired a fine brace against Manchester City in the FA Cup semi-final. There was also the small matter of a trademark curler in the 3–1 final defeat of Arsenal to secure the double for Chelsea.

Blessed with a low centre of gravity, supreme lower-body strength and the instinctive knack of knowing where chances will fall, Kirby scored 25 times in 36 games in all competitions.

"She's a generational talent," Chelsea boss Emma Hayes has said of the Blues' all-time top goalscorer. "Rarely have I seen a football player that can do what she does in the way that she finds space, makes decisions and plays with selfless attributes in possession. She's got eyes in the back of her head.

"She's a winner, every day she wants to be on a winning team. Trust me, she's a grumpy one when it isn't going well, she'll openly acknowledge that because she wants to win so badly."

"It's humbling," said Kirby in receiving the PFA award. "In every game I play, I try to do something that I'll remember afterwards. It's been such a whirlwind and, having come off an injury last season, the highlight has been being able to play week in, week out."

Above | Kirby makes it 1–0 in the Champions League quarter-final between Chelsea and Montpellier at Kingsmeadow, 2018

Hemp proudly shows off her Women's Young Player of the Year award, 2018

WOMEN'S YOUNG PLAYER OF THE YEAR

Lauren Hemp

Lauren Hemp admitted to feeling a little "overwhelmed" when she won the Women's Young Player of the Year award. Of the occasion, perhaps, but everything the 17-year-old Bristol City star produced in her first full WSL campaign – the seven goals, the displays of elite forward play – proved beyond any doubt that Hemp's nascent virtuosity belonged.

"She is probably the quickest player in the league," said Robins boss Willie Kirk. "She's become a real focal point of our team. The way other teams line up against us now is to try to nullify Lauren. She is great to work with and desperate to learn every day."

A talented top order batter who represented Norfolk in age-group cricket, the 16-year-old Hemp eventually chose football as her full-time sport when joining Bristol City in 2016, 12 months after Norwich City's Centre of Excellence had shut. Passion burned deeply, having selected "the sport I enjoyed the most, I don't class football as a job".

It proved an inspired decision. While also studying for a BTEC in Sport at a local college, Hemp's precocious talent couldn't be contained in the academy and she soon made her senior debut as the Robins won promotion into the top flight. By September 2017, she was voted England Young Player of the Year.

Hemp didn't miss a minute of the 2017/18 season. Whether deployed on the right, left or through the middle of boss Kirk's front three, her superb balance, tenacious strength and ability to manoeuvre the ball shone brightly even as City finished third bottom. Of her nine goals in all competitions, Hemp's first WSL strike in October's 1–1 draw at Arsenal stood out. A Goal of the Season contender, she cut inside from the left at ferocious speed and unleashed a superb curler into the top corner.

"I'm quite fearless and my strength is taking on people," Hemp said. "I'm still not the finished article, there are things I need to work on. I try not to set a limit on myself because you can do things you never thought possible."

The PFA honour secured, a move to a WSL giant seemed inevitable.

"We're not naive about it. Lauren will have an offer from every club in the league, probably, come her 18th birthday," added Kirk. "We don't want her to be at Bristol City for the long term because if she is, somebody's not done their job."

Kirk soon got his wish. By the end of May, Hemp was a Manchester City player, her journey to FA Cup successes and senior England honours well underway. PFA records would be broken, too...

MEN'S YOUNG PLAYER OF THE YEAR

Leroy Sané

To truly appreciate Leroy Sané's jet-heeled 2017/18 form, you just need to look at his main PFA Men's Young Player of the Year challenger. Harry Kane scored more than 40 goals in all competitions for the first, and so far only, time in his career, yet the electric 22-year-old German winger still beat the Tottenham Hotspur striker to the prestigious individual award.

October's Premier League Player of the Month for registering a goal and an assist in each of his three appearances, Sané was a City love child combining Dennis Tueart's pacy directness with Georgi Kinkladze's talent for extricating himself from tight spaces. Only Kevin De Bruyne registered more than Sané's 15 Premier League assists as City swept to the title with 100 points and scoring more than a century of goals, the German providing ten of them.

"Leroy is playing at a high, high level," said City boss Pep Guardiola. "He has a lot of qualities, he's so fast and runs in behind like few players in the world."

Above | Sané beats Liverpool's Trent Alexander-Arnold to make a cross, 2018

MERIT AWARD

Cyrille Regis

Cyrille Regis won the FA Cup with Coventry City, played for England and scored a Goal of the Season so good, his chest, turn and top-corner 1982 screamer against Norwich City still quickens the pulse four decades on. Off the pitch, he was a gentle, inspirational colossus.

Described by Ian Wright as "football's Martin Luther King", Regis's ability to turn the other cheek in an era of rampant racism as part of West Bromwich Albion's supreme Three Degrees alongside Brendon Batson and Laurie Cunningham from 1977 to 1984 showed a new generation of black footballers that change was possible.

"He was a great footballer, a true gentleman and a role model and mentor for black players," said PFA Chief Executive Gordon Taylor in presenting the 2018 PFA Merit Award to Regis's surviving family members four months after the former striker's death, aged 59.

"Cyrille was more than just a footballer, he blazed a trail for every black player who followed him," said Wright's former Crystal Palace teammate Mark Bright. A legacy like no other.

Above | Regis playing for West Brom

Van Dijk on goalscoring duty against Wolves at Molineux, 2018

MEN'S PLAYERS' PLAYER OF THE YEAR

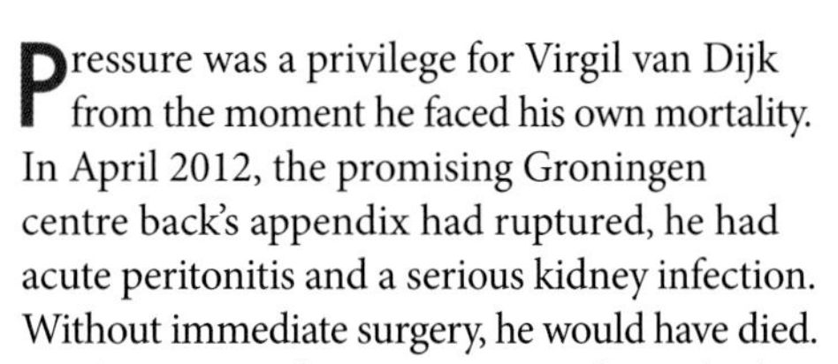

Virgil van Dijk

IN HIS FIRST FULL SEASON AT LIVERPOOL, THE IMPOSING CENTRE BACK PROVIDED THE FOUNDATIONS FOR THE CLUB'S CHAMPIONS LEAGUE GLORY

Pressure was a privilege for Virgil van Dijk from the moment he faced his own mortality. In April 2012, the promising Groningen centre back's appendix had ruptured, he had acute peritonitis and a serious kidney infection. Without immediate surgery, he would have died.

Seven years later, as Liverpool matched the defending Premier League champions Manchester City win for win in the title race, he retained that pressure-loving outlook.

"Honestly, I like being a part of it," the Reds' number four said in March 2019. "I understand our fans would rather be seven points clear, but this is the situation we're in, you know? I like to remind myself to enjoy it."

Liverpool would lose just once in the league all season, winning their last nine games, but still missed out to a relentless City by a point. Fourth the season before, the Reds had never come closer to ending their 29-year wait for the title. It was no coincidence that such an improvement came in the composed, record £75 million man's first full season at Anfield.

"He's the daddy," laughed former Liverpool defender Jamie Carragher. "He makes everyone else play better. Tony Adams did the same in that Arsenal backline."

Van Dijk missed just 35 Premier League minutes in a 2018/19 defence that conceded fewer goals (22) and kept more clean sheets (21) than anyone else. He was as immaculate at the back as the front three of Mohamed Salah, Sadio Mané and Roberto Firmino were in attack.

"In my position, you have to lead, organise players and be an example," the former Celtic and Southampton defender said. "We see games out now, controlling them better than we used to. I've never been a quiet guy. If I think about something, I'll always open my mouth and tell you."

Not only that, his teammates appreciated the help. "It's nice playing with him behind me because he's always coaching," said Liverpool and fellow Netherlands midfielder Gini Wijnaldum. "He keeps talking."

In a Premier League season of aerial dominance and laser-guided passing range, two contrasting moments stood out. In December, fresh from scoring his first league goal for the Reds with a coolly taken left-footed volley, Van Dijk made up a five-yard gap to speed past and outmuscle Wolverhampton Wanderers' flying winger Adama Traoré.

Brains followed brawn when Tottenham Hotspur visited Anfield in March. The score locked at 1–1 with five minutes to go, Moussa Sissoko and Son Heung-min had a two-on-one with only Van Dijk for company. Between Scylla and Charybdis, the Dutchman surmised that under no circumstances could the deadly South Korea forward receive the ball and instead blocked a passing pathway to leave Sissoko a shot at goal on his left foot before applying late pressure. The Frenchman's effort flew over the crossbar. As the clock ticked past the 90th minute, Liverpool forced a winner, impossible without their defensive colossus.

"He's the best centre half of all time," said Michael Owen. "He's bigger, faster and stronger than everyone. He's brilliant on the ball, he scores goals. I've never seen anything like it. As a one-off, I look at him and think: how can you get any better than that?"

In the Champions League, he was. In the last 16 second leg at Bayern Munich, Van Dijk's superb pass set up Mané's opener, before he added the third in a 3–1 win with a towering header. Three-nil down to Barcelona from the semi-final first leg at the Camp Nou, a depleted Liverpool needed their leader more than ever for the Anfield return. Constantly cajoling alongside captain Jordan Henderson, the defender made his side believe the impossible to be possible as the Reds swept to a 4–0 win.

In the final against Spurs, Van Dijk dropped another masterclass in a 2–0 win that exorcised the previous season's ghosts, neutralising Harry Kane with a player-of-the-match display. Proof, were it needed, that the man voted PFA Men's Players' Player of Year a month earlier fully deserved the honour.

"This season with Liverpool ended today, we got the Champions League," said the Ballon d'Or runner-up, immediately turning his attention to the following campaign and ending Liverpool's three-decade wait for the trophy that really mattered. "Winning the Premier League puts you in the history books forever and makes you a legend. That's why you play football, you want to be a legend."

WOMEN'S PLAYERS' PLAYER OF THE YEAR

Vivianne Miedema

THE FORWARD'S TIRELESS PURSUIT OF GOALS AND ASSISTS MADE HER ONE OF A DUO OF DUTCH PFA AWARD WINNERS IN 2018/19

Above | Miedema playing for the Netherlands against the US in the 2019 Women's World Cup final

Opposite | The Arsenal striker in action against Chelsea, 2018

The numbers were staggering enough. Vivianne Miedema fired 31 goals, plus 14 assists, from 28 appearances in all competitions for Arsenal in 2018/19 as the Gunners surged to the title by seven points. The Dutchwoman's 22 WSL goals were six more than anyone had ever managed in a single season in tournament history. She had done all this before turning 23 yet, most incredibly of all, Miedema didn't particularly enjoy being a goalscorer.

"I play more like a number ten," she said a few weeks after winning the PFA Women's Players' Player of the Year award. "I know I have my goalscoring qualities, but I like setting people up. I like to drop and pick up the ball and see if I can send someone through on goal."

Most forwards would go way beyond traditional Faustian pacts for a record even half as good, yet the Dutchwoman worried about being pigeonholed. Nothing could be further from the truth.

"Viv should be spoken about as one of the greatest, that's what her talent deserves," said Gunners icon Ian Wright. "She's the best number nine in the world and the best number ten at the same time. There's not many players that can do that."

A childhood Feyenoord fan who grew up idolising Robin van Persie, another Dutch playmaker-cum-striker, Miedema began 2018/19 with a hat-trick against Liverpool to prove no defence was safe from the 5ft 9in Miedema's rangy frame and sure technique with either foot. A brace in October's 5–0 thumping of defending champions Chelsea – featuring a deadly left-footed finish after a first touch so deft it deserved a place in a museum – served notice that Arsenal were the team to beat after a seven-year WSL drought.

"She is just the complete striker," said Gunners great Kelly Smith. "She's always a threat no matter what minute of the game it is. Her movement is very clever, and her finishing ability is phenomenal."

Two defeats in three games around the turn of the year tested Arsenal's resilience to scratch their title itch. A back-to-back Bundesliga winner with Bayern Munich in 2015 and 2016, the totemic Miedema stepped up to score seven times as Arsenal won eight in a row to clinch the title. Her PFA honour was a fait accompli.

"I'm obviously really proud to represent my team here, we've had an amazing year," she said, before focusing on the Dutch clean sweep of the PFA's two top honours with Virgil van Dijk. "It'll be quite a big thing back home – two Dutch players winning it makes it even bigger than it probably was for me and for him."

Miedema was far from satiated. By the end of 2019, she'd struck 53 goals in the calendar year for club and country, become the Netherlands' all-time leading scorer, played in a World Cup final and set a WSL record for scoring six and assisting four in Arsenal's 11–1 demolition of Bristol City.

Just don't call her a goalscorer. Vivianne Miedema is so much more.

"She's always a threat no matter what minute of the game it is. Her movement is very clever, and her finishing ability is phenomenal"

Kelly Smith

MEN'S YOUNG PLAYER OF THE YEAR

Raheem Sterling

Doubts, whispers and criticism had followed Raheem Sterling for years. They'd even persisted at the start of the 2018/19 season, despite the Manchester City winger having just smashed a career-best 23-goal season to win the Premier League. A one-off, dismissed the naysayers, he won't back it up.

They were right, too. He bettered it. Not only did the 24-year-old register 25 goals and 17 assists as City won a domestic treble, but also the shuffling Sterling established himself as the go-to player. It was his penalty that won the League Cup final shootout against Chelsea, his brace that set up a 6–0 walloping of Watford in the FA Cup final and his season-defining goals that helped beat Arsenal, Chelsea and Everton and win the Sky Blues' last 14 games to win the title. What had changed?

"His head," said coach Pep Guardiola. "He was scared, looking at where to pass to. Now he's in incredible form, he's sharp, fast, clever, fighting, decisive."

"People understand me now," Sterling said after speaking publicly in December 2018 as the racist abuse to which he was constantly subjected forced a reappraisal of his undeserved tabloid-target image. "They can see the truth and ignore what they have heard about me."

The truth was that Sterling was the country's best young player.

Sterling during the 2019 FA Cup final against Watford at Wembley

MERIT AWARD

Steph Houghton

Women's football would be unrecognisable without Steph Houghton. The 30-year-old centre back had won every domestic honour more than once during her time at Arsenal and Manchester City, reached a century of England caps and was about to lead her country into her third World Cup, but the reasons for Houghton becoming the first woman to receive the 2019 PFA Merit Award extended far beyond her vertiginous on-field successes.

One of the first 17 players to earn an FA central contract in 2009, she spent much of the intervening decade spearheading the women's game's professional metamorphosis into the WSL era. Houghton campaigned tirelessly for parity and joined the PFA's management committee to better represent the women's game.

"She's a motivator and an incredible professional," said City manager Nick Cushing. "Without her we simply wouldn't be where we are."

"I'm very honoured. There are so many fantastic people who have won this award before me, so to be recognised by such a wonderful organisation as the PFA is a special moment," said Houghton. "I want to represent women's football, to have a voice."

Above | Houghton celebrates England's 3–0 defeat of Norway in the quarter-final of the 2019 Women's World Cup

WOMEN'S YOUNG PLAYER OF THE YEAR

Georgia Stanway

Born into a football-mad household in Barrow-in-Furness with three brothers, Georgia Stanway got used to confounding expectations from an early age.

"Once you put the ball through someone's legs and score a goal," she later laughed of playing against boys' teams, "they have so much respect for you."

Stanway's breakthrough Manchester City season featured that same youthful impudence, as the versatile attacking midfielder scored 15 goals in 30 appearances that delivered an FA and League Cup double. Cutting from out to in and finishing across the goalkeeper became a 2018/19 trademark – Stanway scored mirror-image goals in the FA Cup final defeat of West Ham United and a bravura display in beating eventual WSL champions Arsenal 2–0.

"The sky is the limit in terms of her ability," said City boss Nick Cushing.

"It's hard to put into words, really," said the 20-year-old, who picked up the PFA Women's Young Player of the Year award ahead of her City teammate Keira Walsh. "My family have been through the ups and downs, but they can share in this special moment with me."

Above | Stanway on the ball against Birmingham City, 2018

MEN'S PLAYERS' PLAYER OF THE YEAR

Kevin De Bruyne

THE BELGIAN'S 16 GOALS AND 23 ASSISTS IN ALL COMPETITIONS CEMENTED HIS REPUTATION AS ONE OF THE FINEST PLAYERS TO HAVE GRACED THE ENGLISH GAME

In a season of unprecedented upheaval because of the pandemic, there remained one reassuring constant, something upon which the public could rely even in the darkest depths of lockdown: Kevin De Bruyne laying goals on a plate for grateful Manchester City attackers.

Even then, his tally of 20 Premier League assists to equal Thierry Henry's 17-year-old record was extraordinary. The Belgian also scored 13 league goals and created 104 chances from open play, the most for a player in any of Europe's top five leagues since 2006.

Though the 28-year-old's previous season had been destroyed by ligament injuries, the two campaigns before that yielded 18 and 16 assists respectively. Now, he had another 20. De Bruyne's blue period featured a creative outpouring every bit as sustained as Claude Monet's.

"Kevin does everything. Without the ball he is the first fighter, and with the ball he is clear – he sees absolutely everything," said Guardiola. "He is a masterclass player, one of the best players I have ever trained in my life. Right now, he is the best midfielder in the world."

He certainly began the season like it. De Bruyne registered eight assists in his first seven Premier League outings, each one better than the last. On three separate occasions – against Tottenham Hotspur, Watford and Everton – the footballing chorister's delicious crosses from the inside right channel arced into the space between the opponents' defensive line and goalkeeper for easy first-time finishes. Effortless, efficient and precise.

Though City couldn't keep pace with Liverpool's heavy metal beat, De Bruyne refused to go through the motions. Many felt he was unlucky to lose out to Mohamed Salah in the 2017/18 PFA Men's Players' Player of the Year voting; two seasons on he redoubled his efforts to ensure an individual prize if a third successive Premier League title was beyond even his prodigious skill.

Having his manager's support also helped. At Chelsea half a decade earlier, an inexperienced De Bruyne had fallen foul of José Mourinho's distaste for ingenuity, but Guardiola indulged his playmaker's uniqueness.

"He gives me a lot of freedom," said De Bruyne. "He knows in one way I will always put the team first and then obviously if I can help myself, I'm going to do that."

In the clinical confines of locked down stadia post-June, De Bruyne continued to shine. He scored one and made one in a 4–0 defeat of champions-elect Liverpool, then bagged a brace, including a magnificent curler, in a 5–0 final-day drubbing of Norwich City – the second time that season he'd won the division's Goal of the Month prize.

"It's the ultimate honour to be nominated by fellow professionals because you compete against them, they want to win the trophies, they want to be the best," said the first City player to win the main PFA award.

We need to talk about Kevin. He might just be the best player in Premier League history.

Above | De Bruyne holds the Players' Player award

Opposite | Playing against Crystal Palace at the Etihad, 2020

"He is a masterclass player, one of the best players I have ever trained in my life. Right now, he is the best midfielder in the world"

Pep Guardiola

WOMEN'S PLAYERS' PLAYER OF THE YEAR

Bethany England

TWO PLAYER OF THE MONTH AWARDS AND 14 GOALS IN 15 LEAGUE APPEARANCES HERALDED A BREAKTHROUGH SEASON FOR CHELSEA'S TIRELESS FORWARD

Above | England and her teammates, after the striker scored the equalising goal against Arsenal at Kingsmeadow Stadium, 2019

The only thing that could stop Bethany England in 2019/20 was a once-in-a-generation pandemic. Less easily contained than your average forest fire, the 25-year-old Chelsea centre forward scored 21 goals in a ravenous campaign, one prematurely curtailed just after her injury-time winner in the League Cup final against Arsenal at the end of February.

"She's the best English number nine in the country," said Chelsea manager Emma Hayes.

Yet England's crowning season was anything but inevitable. Five years earlier, she was working in a chip shop in hometown Barnsley to top up her income at second-tier Doncaster Belles. Three years after that in 2017, she was toiling as an occasional, unconvincing wing-back having joined Hayes' west London giants. What changed?

A confidence-boosting 2017/18 loan at Liverpool helped, but England's indefatigable work rate and determination to improve were instructive. Only Vivianne Miedema and Nikita Parris had found the net more often in 2018/19 as England forced her way into Hayes's first-team reckoning, her devastating power and cool finishing proof of her hard work.

"I have always been a grafter," England said. "And Emma is starting to, especially this season, really show her faith in me leading that front line as a number nine."

A sumptuous left-footed strike from distance against Tottenham Hotspur at Stamford Bridge to begin 2019/20 showcased a complete forward who caused havoc whether with her back to goal or rampaging into space. A first Lionesses goal, against Brazil in October, soon followed.

"There's nothing more joyful than when a player who you don't really know if they are going to be able to cut it at the top level gets their head down and puts everything into their career," said Chelsea boss Hayes. "The talent was always there."

The unstoppable England won the WSL Player of the Month for January and February before the pandemic ended the season early. When the unbeaten Blues were awarded the WSL title on a points-per-game basis, she was the standout choice for the PFA Women's Players' Player of the Year.

"It's a huge honour to be voted for by your fellow peers," said England.

Manchester City's star forward proudly displays her Women's Young Player of the Year award

WOMEN'S YOUNG PLAYER OF THE YEAR

Lauren Hemp

"The future is bright for Lauren. She's been exceptional this season; she's really shown her offensive ability and she will get better. She knows she can be so much better. She has so much potential and we have to keep playing her and keep pushing, and we'll both benefit from that. Her attitude is exceptional and her drive to improve is brilliant. We know how dangerous she can be when she's running at full backs, creating chances."

Nick Cushing

MEN'S YOUNG PLAYER OF THE YEAR

Trent Alexander-Arnold

Defenders just shouldn't be able to do what Trent Alexander-Arnold did in 2019/20. A season after breaking the Premier League assist record for a defender, the 21-year-old Liverpool right back went one better to lay on 13 goals for his teammates.

"In the best team in Europe, the best playmaker is a right back from [Liverpool inner-city district] West Derby. It's mad," said former Reds defender Jamie Carragher. "I have never seen a full back have such an influence on a team before."

The Premier League Player of the Month for December, Alexander-Arnold was the outlet through which Jürgen Klopp's side could counter-press to a first league title in three decades. On the night Liverpool lifted the trophy, it was appropriate that TAA was at the heart of the 5–3 victory, his laser-guided free-kick a fourth goal of the campaign before a signature right-wing cross found Roberto Firmino's head to break that assist record.

"He's David Beckham and Kevin De Bruyne at right back," cooed former Manchester United defender Gary Neville. "Breath-taking."

Above | Alexander-Arnold controls the ball during the Champions League away tie against Napoli at Stadio San Paolo, 2019

Rashford is made a Member of the Most Excellent Order of the British Empire by Prince William at Windsor Castle, 2021

MERIT AWARD

Marcus Rashford

Stick to your football, they said. Donate to a food poverty charity, sure, but stay in your lane and don't rock the establishment too much.

Marcus Rashford, however, wanted meaningful change. Having experienced food poverty as a child, he teamed up with FareShare to ensure Greater Manchester families who relied on free school meals continued to receive them despite the pandemic.

It wasn't just that his involvement raised £20 million, went nationwide and helped 1.3 million families across the country, the 22-year-old stood up for what he knew to be right and even forced the UK government into extending free school meals for children during the 2020 summer holidays. Inspired to act, he has changed government policy on multiple occasions.

"It's a huge honour and I hope it encourages other players to do things to help communities," said Rashford after receiving the Merit Award. "I would be doing myself, my family and my community an injustice if I didn't stand here with my voice and my platform and ask you for help."

The Manchester United forward has continued to fight injustice and counts former US president Barack Obama as a fan. Perhaps most impressively of all, however, is his universal adoration in football. Few are the United players to have their names sung on Liverpool's Kop or Everton's Gwladys Street. There's only one Marcus Rashford.

MEN'S PLAYERS' PLAYER OF THE YEAR

Kevin De Bruyne

"The fact that players chose me for this award means that I've done really well. You want to win all the trophies with the team, and this is probably the most important one as an individual trophy in the league. To be voted by your competitors, by players who you compete with every game – to choose you, that says a lot. They're the people in my view who know the most about the game. When you have these things, you can show your kids and say, 'Look! This is what Daddy did when he was younger'."

De Bruyne in action against Leicester City at the King Power Stadium, 2021

WOMEN'S PLAYERS' PLAYER OF THE YEAR

Fran Kirby

CHELSEA'S ALL-TIME LEADING GOALSCORER BEAT THE COMPETITION TO WIN HER SECOND WOMEN'S PLAYERS' PLAYER OF THE YEAR AWARD

Above | Kirby with her second Players' Player award, 2021

PFA: You're one of only two players to be named Women's Players' Player twice. What did winning it mean for you?
Fran Kirby: I was really shocked when I won it. It's probably one of the highest accolades you can win in terms of, you know, your opposition are the ones who are voting for you. For them to pick you, it's really special. It just shows that you did something good throughout the whole season and the people, even though maybe it wasn't always the best experience for them, they appreciate the work that you put in and the performances.
PFA: How did it feel to win the award for a second time?
FK: It was a bit weird because that was the Covid year, but it was the same kind of feeling. I'm really lucky at Chelsea that I get to play with some amazing players. That year I came back from illness, so to win the award, that was a really proud moment for me because I'd worked so hard to be able to get myself back into a position where I was able to play week in, week out.
PFA: When did you find out that you'd won it? How did you receive the news?
FK: Emma [Hayes] came down into the changing room. I was getting some treatment and she said so casually, "I'll just let you know, you've won PFA Player of the Year." Obviously, it was a nice moment and my teammates were super happy for me.
PFA: Chelsea is a team that, even if you're not playing at your best, you always seem to get results. Where do you think that comes from?
FK: We just have so many players that can provide an individual moment of brilliance. Someone can step up and grab the game and go, "We're going to go for this now." That's the kind of the mentality we have in the team, we never give up. I remember speaking to some of the players we play against, and they're like, "You're so frustrating to play against because you won't be playing well, but you'll still manage to win." We want to play well, but we know how to graft out results.
PFA: With all your team success and individual accolades, is there one moment you look back on as your favourite?
FK: It has to be Euro 2022 with England, winning that at Wembley in front of your friends, your family. For me growing up, I didn't even know if I was going to make it to where I am now, and to look back and go, wow, you're a Euros winner...

WOMEN'S YOUNG PLAYER OF THE YEAR

Lauren Hemp

"We're so proud of Lauren for winning this award – she's an unbelievable talent and we feel very lucky to have her here at Manchester City. The fact that she's now won it three times speaks volumes about what the footballing world thinks of her and the fact that she's only 20 years old is incredible – she is only just getting started. She has such potential."

Gareth Taylor

Above | Hemp holds off West Ham's Hawa Cissoko, 2021

Foden whips a ball in against Olympiacos in the Champions League group match at the Etihad, 2020

MEN'S YOUNG PLAYER OF THE YEAR

Phil Foden

The first time Pep Guardiola saw Phil Foden, he knew he had something exceptional. Slight of frame but with manifold technical gifts, the Manchester City academy graduate just took so quickly to the first team from his 2017 debut.

"I didn't meet Leo Messi at 17 like I met Phil, but at that age, I've never seen a player with this potential," said the former Barcelona manager. "His problem is sometimes his manager doesn't put him in the starting XI."

In 2020/21, Guardiola did just that, Foden responding with 16 goals and ten assists as City won the Premier League, League Cup and reached the Champions League final. Off either wing, as a roving midfielder or even his own interpretation of a false nine in February's 4–1 defeat of Liverpool in which he scored one and had a hand in another two, the 20-year-old confirmed himself as English football's most natural, free-form talent since Paul Gascoigne.

"He has everything to become something unique and special," said the Spanish coach as Foden won the first of successive Men's Young Player of the Year awards.

MERIT AWARD

Gordon Taylor

Gordon Taylor was the longest-serving trade union boss in the world when he announced he would step down as PFA Chief Executive in July 2021 after 40 years at the helm. Taylor had served the sport he loved, growing the support provided by the PFA to include services such as education and coaching funding, hardship grants and counselling services for both current and former members.

The former Bolton Wanderers, Birmingham City, Blackburn Rovers and Bury winger was already the PFA chairman when his 18-year playing career ended in 1980, then replaced Cliff Lloyd in the top job a year later. A driving force behind the establishment of the first YTS programmes and football's increasing awareness of its responsibilities in the community from the 1980s, Taylor also helped to negotiate funding deals with the football authorities on behalf of, and for the benefit of, PFA members.

The recipient of an OBE for services to football in 2008, the 76-year-old was honoured with the Merit Award as he stepped aside to be replaced by Maheta Molango.

"It's been a long journey, a rollercoaster. I never thought I would be here four decades later but it's been a real privilege," said Taylor, receiving the award from Sir Alex Ferguson in a virtual ceremony because of the ongoing pandemic. "Above all, I hope players continue and, indeed, increase their involvement in the game because it's a player's game; it is all about players and their welfare and for them to have as strong an influence as possible to care about the game."

Taylor at Birmingham City, 1974

MEN'S PLAYERS' PLAYER OF THE YEAR

Mohamed Salah

"When we scouted Mo, he was not the finishing monster we see now. The moment I knew it will be outstanding [was] when I knew him as a person, because he's full of desire, he never will stop developing and he's a workhorse. I know we say it a lot but he's really the first in – maybe around Millie [James Milner], maybe Millie beats him from time to time – and he's the last out. So treatment, gym work, all these kinds of things. On the pitch, if you tell Mo because of the intensity of the games, 'Mo, you go in now. Thank you very much'. 'I'm good, I'm good, get me another ten balls.' So he deserves it absolutely, and that's why he's the second-time winner of this wonderful trophy. Well deserved, Mo, by the way!"

Jürgen Klopp

Salah wheels away in celebration after scoring Liverpool's second goal against Wolverhampton Wanderers at Anfield, 2022

WOMEN'S PLAYERS' PLAYER OF THE YEAR

Sam Kerr

THE AUSTRALIAN FORWARD CONTINUED TO MAKE HER MARK ON ENGLISH FOOTBALL FOLLOWING HER 2020 ARRIVAL, PLUNDERING 20 WSL GOALS IN AS MANY GAMES

PFA: So Sam, how did it feel to win Women's Players' Player of the Year last season?
Sam Kerr: Whenever you get voted for by your peers, it's the highest honour. And to do it for the first time here in England, it was an amazing honour and one I'll remember for a long time.
PFA: Looking at the previous winners of the award, it's a special group. How does it feel to be on that list?
SK: I've followed the league for a long time, so knowing about all these players and playing against them internationally, they're all top players. To be on that list with the likes of Ji So-yun, Kim Little, Fran Kirby, Lucy Bronze, they're all legends.
PFA: A couple have done the double. Is that something you're hoping you can do? Sneak another to go level with some of the great names on there?
SK: I mean, I wouldn't shy away from it. The most important thing is that we're lifting trophies at the end of the year – I prefer the team over the individual ones – but I won't shy away from trying to do the double.
PFA: What do you make of that season, winning trophies and the Golden Boot? Was it special or just a case of doing your job?
SK: No, it was a special season. To be honest, the start of the season just seemed normal. And then after Christmas we had this fight about us that no one was going to stop us, and that's when it really changed for myself and the team. We were determined to win everything. We were down to 14 players at one point – everyone was injured, sick, pregnant – so it was just about grinding through. That mentality and drive creates something special. It was a special season for me individually, but also as a team, it's one I'll never forget.
PFA: How do you motivate yourself to go again after a successful season?
SK: The biggest motivator for me is that I hate losing. I'm just a competitor. If it's training, playing around in the locker room, just anything, I hate losing. I hate someone getting better than us or being on top of us. I think that's why last season was so special because the whole year we were second, third, second, third, and then at the very last moment it was ours for the taking.

Right | A beaming Kerr shows off her trophy, 2022

Opposite | The Blues forward celebrates Chelsea's third goal during the FA Cup final against Manchester City, 2022

"The biggest motivator for
me is that I hate losing.
I'm just a competitor"

MERIT AWARD

Roy Hodgson

Roy Hodgson's managerial career was well into its fifth decade when he decided 1,231 matches from 24 different jobs in eight countries were enough for a 74-year-old. To mark his retirement, Hodgson received the 2022 Merit Award.

The highly regarded Englishman's wanderlust began in 1976 at Swedish minnows Halmstads, and went on to feature spells at Inter Milan (twice), Copenhagen, a Europa League final with Fulham, Liverpool and West Bromwich Albion before achieving a lifelong ambition of managing England from 2012 to 2016. He also managed Switzerland, the United Arab Emirates and Finland.

"It is a real honour to receive this award, it is unexpected but that makes me all the more grateful," said Hodgson. "I will look back with great gratitude and humility for what football has given me and it's wonderful to get a trophy which proves that people believe I have given something back, I will treasure this trophy."

Yet Hodgson couldn't keep away. With Crystal Palace, the club of his Croydon heart, facing the drop in March 2023, Hodgson answered his former side's distress signal to save the Eagles from the drop. A true gentleman.

Above | Then England manager Hodgson during a World Cup qualifier against Ukraine, 2013

WOMEN'S YOUNG PLAYER OF THE YEAR

Lauren Hemp

Right | Hemp battles with Chelsea's Jess Carter at Kingsmeadow Stadium, 2022

From Ian Rush to Alan Shearer, some of the finest footballers in history have won two PFA awards for single-season form. Mark Hughes, Ryan Giggs, Steven Gerrard, Cristiano Ronaldo, Gareth Bale and Wayne Rooney all won three. When Lauren Hemp picked up her fourth PFA Women's Young Player of the Year Award, the Manchester City attacker was creating a club of just one. Herself.

Five seasons after winning her first PFA honour at Bristol City, the 22-year-old racked a career-best 21 goals in 35 appearances in all competitions, including ten (plus six assists) in a WSL term that ended with nine successive league wins as the Cityzens finished third and reached the FA Cup final. Though Hemp scored a superb equaliser at Wembley, City fell agonisingly short against Chelsea. Later that summer, though, she'd be a central cog in England's Euro 2022 triumph.

"She's frightening, I don't think she's even got a ceiling in how far she can go," 2015/16 Women's Players' Player of the Year Izzy Christiansen said. "I play against her in the league and hopefully only twice a season!"

The Englishman in action against Aston Villa during a home Premier League fixture, 2022

MEN'S YOUNG PLAYER OF THE YEAR

Phil Foden

"I'm really honoured, to be honest, especially to win it back-to-back, it shows that I've come a long way this year with the consistency of my game, and I'm really pleased to win it again. All the best players in the world have got to show consistency and keep performing at the higher level, and this year I've just tried to do that and try and help my team as much as possible – I've been really happy with my performances this year. Hopefully I can win the main award in the future, but it's all about taking small steps and improving."

MERIT AWARD

Hope Powell

Hope Powell's quest for equality began when dissuading her Jamaican mother that women's football "wasn't what West Indian girls were supposed to do" and continued for much of the next five decades.

Powell's playing career delivered three major honours and 35 goals from 66 England caps, but it was 15 years as Lionesses manager from 1998 that were truly game-changing. England's first black manager, and the first woman and the youngest person to coach a senior team, Powell was also the first woman to achieve the UEFA Pro Licence coaching standard. She championed professionalism in the women's game, was a key voice in establishing central contracts for Lionesses players from 2009 and worked with the PFA as coach educator, raising standards wherever she went.

"I have never been afraid to ask questions and challenge people," said Powell after receiving the 2022 PFA Merit Award. "I'm hoping I'll be remembered as someone who was passionate and wanted the best for women's football on a local and national level."

In short, she more than lived up to her name.

Above | Powell, Technical Advisor for England, at the U-20 World Cup, 2023

The next step

THE PFA PROVIDES ITS MEMBERS WITH THE ADVICE, SUPPORT AND EXPERTISE THEY NEED TO DEVELOP THEIR CAREER, IN THE GAME AND BEYOND, AS PAT LALLY, DIRECTOR OF EDUCATION, AND JIM HICKS, HEAD OF COACHING, DISCUSS

Pat Lally, Director of Education (top) and Jim Hicks, Head of Coaching

Opposite, clockwise from top | PFA Assistant Director of Education Oshor Williams; sports pundit Scott Minto; presenter and ex-England international Alex Scott

Name any area of work and you can pretty much guarantee that the PFA has provided a retired or retiring footballer with the support, funding and plan to smooth their transition into a career in that field. That even includes going into business taking care of our four-legged friends.

"Tony Bird, who played for Cardiff City in the 1990s, became a dog groomer thanks to our help," says PFA Director of Education Pat Lally, who also counts airline pilots, counterterrorism operatives and professional wine tasters among the PFA members the department has helped to develop a new career.

Launched in 1967, the Education department is one of the PFA's oldest. An ex-pro for Millwall, York City, Doncaster and Swansea City, Lally joined the Footballers' Further Education and Vocational Training Society, which was set up by the PFA, in 1983 on a part-time basis and played an instrumental role in setting up what became the Youth Training Scheme (YTS) for 16- to 18-year-old apprentices to undertake vocational or educational programmes alongside their football work. The PFA continues to work closely with both the Premier League and English Football League to ensure that the scheme delivered today is fit for purpose.

A player's career is exceptionally short, an average of seven to eight years, so it's vital they prepare for that transition while they're still playing," says Lally, whose team visits clubs to outline what the department has to offer. "What we provide is tailored. The presentation we give to 16- to 18-year-olds is different to that for the 19 to 23s and different again for the more senior players. They all have very distinct needs and circumstances."

The department invested £1.8 million in supporting 1,451 applications for accredited courses in 2021/22. Funding for non-degree programmes is generally around 50 per cent of the course fees up to a maximum of £2,000 a year. Those undertaking degree-level programmes receive an annual bursary of £1,250, and some bespoke programmes designed specifically for PFA members offer additional funding of up to £7,000. These include physiotherapy degrees at Salford University and York St John University, and the Professional Sports Writing and Broadcasting programme at Staffordshire University, which was taken by the likes of Scott Minto and Alex Scott.

"I'm not aware of any other organisation that provides as much support with so much flexibility," says Lally. "It shows how seriously the PFA takes a player's transition and the support that is needed at such a time. We have an obligation to provide as many opportunities as possible for our members. I used the PFA when I was a player to take courses that I thought would benefit me and that's what I advise other players to do. Don't leave it until your career's over, start the building blocks now."

PFA Head of Coaching Jim Hicks echoes those sentiments. Since the mid-1990s, his department has helped over 15,000 players undertake different coaching awards so they can stay in the game in some form. "Understanding transition, and what it's like when you're no longer a player and going into the second half of your career, is a big deal. That's why we employ former players," he says. "Clubs push players into our courses, so they're qualified before they finish their playing careers. They can then continue to employ them as coaches.

"Every scholar at a professional club between 16 and 18 will do our UEFA C Licence as part of their time in education, which we fund," he continues. "That's 700 to 800 people a year. In addition to that, anyone over 18 – male or female – who is a PFA member and wants to continue in coaching can go onto a UEFA B licence, which we heavily subsidise."

The PFA also helps with funding for any members who wish to take the UEFA A or Pro Licence, managed by the Football Association. But its work still doesn't end there. "We're much more interested in development now," says Hicks, a former Exeter City and Fulham defender who managed in the United States before joining the PFA in 2006. "If someone comes on one of our award qualifications, we maintain contact with them throughout their whole coaching journey.

"We offer a colossal amount of support. We're always getting calls, messages and texts from current or former players who want information on coaching. Support and advice might not even be about a course, it could be: 'I've got this situation, what do you think?' That's part of the holistic support we provide for members, 365 days a year.

"Employability is our cornerstone," says Hicks. "The one thing you know as a footballer is that your career will come to an end, so what we're all about is preparation. Football evolves and we try to evolve with it.

"Our influence on coaching at the professional level can't be underestimated. Our fingerprints are all over the Premier League, EFL and WSL. It's a stick of rock with 'PFA' running through the middle. We don't take them to the finishing school, but we have a significant role to play. That's pretty humbling."

"I used the PFA when I was a player to take courses and that's what I advise other players to do. Don't leave it until your career's over, start the building blocks now"

Pat Lally

a.r.u.

From strength to strength

ANGLIA RUSKIN UNIVERSITY'S SPORT AND EXERCISE COURSES ARE AMONG THE BEST IN THE UK, HELPING GRADUATES BREAK INTO CAREERS IN ELITE FIELDS

bit.ly/aru-psychology-and-sport-science

In 2000, exercise physiologist and former paralympic cyclist Dr Dan Gordon was charged with setting up a new degree course in sport and exercise science (SES) at Anglia Ruskin University (ARU) in Cambridge. In its first year, there were just five enthusiastic students and no specialist facilities. But Dan was determined to make it work.

"There was a recognition that SES was important, but we had to demonstrate that this was going to be possible," says Dan. And, indeed, it was. Fast forward 22 years and that tiny discipline now has 22 staff serving over 400 students on four different undergraduate courses, with a master's course in sport and exercise psychology launched in 2023.

ARU has become a leader in SES research and the university's state-of-the-art facilities include five exercise-science research labs and a dedicated space for its unique student-led physiological consultancy, which is open to the general public. It has been rated in the top five providers of its kind in the UK for three years running, winning the top spot in the Guardian League Table in 2021. "Our research reputation is really making people sit up and take notice at the moment," says Dr Helen Keyes, Head of the School of Psychology and Sport Science. "Our research is changing the face of sport and coaching in the UK."

But a key point of pride for Helen is that the National Student Survey reported a 100 per cent student satisfaction rating for the university's BSc Sport and Exercise Science courses. "What we're most proud of is the recognition we get from our students. I think it reflects the dedication of a very passionate team of staff, the unique learning opportunities that we provide and the sense of community that we've developed with these students."

Dan puts the success of the department down to an ethos of being "student-centred and practical skills orientated", with a focus on educational excellence. Another key to the discipline's success, says Helen, is "how strongly we link theory with practice". Real-world examples are often brought into the classroom via football, she adds, and students work with Wigan Athletic Academy and Cambridge United while they are studying. This focus on real-world application and courses

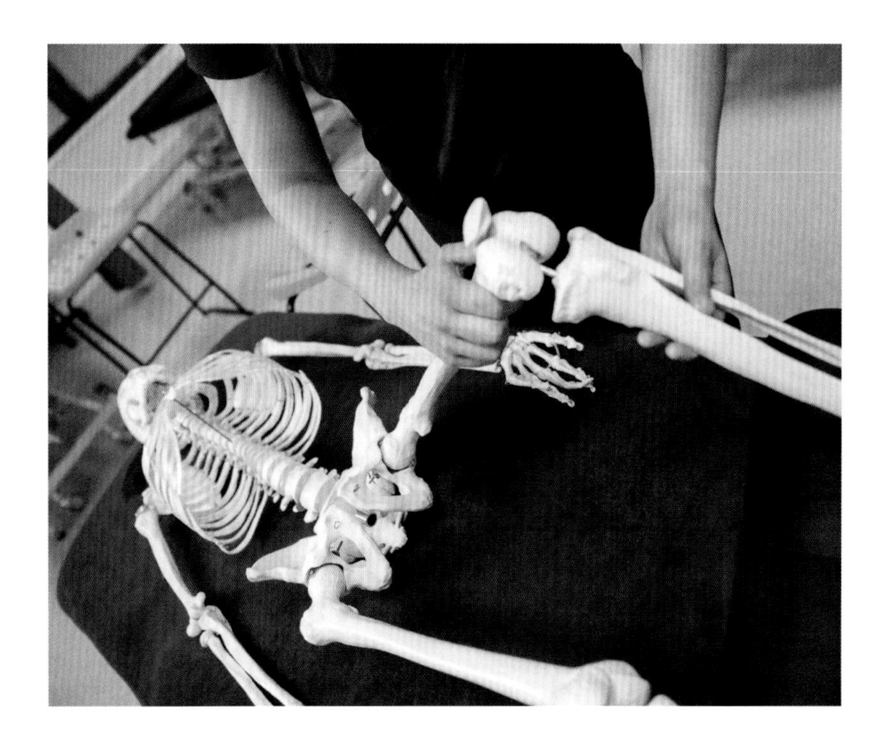

accredited by professional bodies has allowed graduates of ARU to move into top jobs in elite sport. These include posts as performance analysts for professional football teams or other sports. The head of strength and conditioning for the Sri Lankan cricket team, for example, is an ARU graduate.

And the opportunities in SES are growing, says Dan, contributing to the booming popularity of the discipline. "It's losing the stigma that used to be associated with it. For countless years, SES was seen as 'you come to university to kick a football around and you get a degree for being good at football.

"What people have learned, because of education, through the media, through schools and colleges, is that this is a really important scientific discipline, not just at a high-performance level, but all the way down to grassroots sports and the general population."

All of which is good news for ARU, as Dan and Helen seek to grow the discipline, and – to use a sporting term – go from strength to strength.

Research excellence

STUDENTS, STAFF AND ELITE SPORTS PARTNERS OF NORTHUMBRIA UNIVERSITY'S DEPARTMENT OF SPORT, EXERCISE AND REHABILITATION BENEFIT FROM BOTH HIGHLY RANKED RESEARCH AND STRONG INTERNATIONAL NETWORKS

www.northumbria.ac.uk

When Northumbria University in Newcastle was named University of the Year 2022 in the Times Higher Education awards, it was testament to a long-term strategy designed to embed quality research at the centre of everything the university does. This approach saw it become the first research-intensive modern university, recording the biggest rise in research power of any UK university, moving up 27 places to 23rd in the Research Excellence Framework 2021. "We've been driving our research forwards over the past decade to have wide-reaching impact on our society," explains Professor Nick Caplan, Head of the Department of Sport, Exercise and Rehabilitation.

The department is ranked fifth for research power in the UK for sport, conducting groundbreaking research while working alongside football clubs, the FA, UEFA, FIFA and Professional Game Match Officials (PGMOL) to support both the women's and men's games. "We look at a broad spectrum of disciplines, including physiology, nutrition, strength and conditioning, and coach education," says Caplan. "We do a lot of research understanding player responses to training and competition. We use our findings to inform practice across the game from grassroots to international players, as well as exploring the role of physical activity through football to promote health and wellbeing. Research enriches our education as our students learn from the best in the field."

Practical applications of Northumbria's research include work involving player preparation to combat the demands of congested fixtures. Studies around innovative recovery strategies have informed best practice with professional and international football teams. "Our work to understand player fatigue, and implementing recovery strategies, has informed athlete preparation at the highest level of competition. The FA has used our research to prepare players for UEFA EURO 2020, women's EURO 2022 and the recent Qatar 2022 World Cup," says the department's Professor Glyn Howatson, who describes the role the university has played in women's football, with research that gives a greater understanding of female physiology rather than simply treating women as smaller men. "The success of the Lionesses at EURO 2022 was phenomenal. They were in great condition and able to play many games in short succession. We are very proud to have played a part in that story by informing their preparation for the tournament."

Other areas of research include exploring conflict management in the game. The university works alongside PGMOL to learn from the experiences of referees, as well as with Newcastle United to understand progression of academy players into the senior squad, examining the potential of athletes to perform at elite level while gaining a qualification. The research collaboration with the NUFC women's team is to better learn how female physiology affects performance.

The university's partnership with the i2i International Soccer Academy sees students enrol on a sport or business-related degree while receiving UEFA-qualified training each day. The department's students complete work placements, enabling them to apply their learning at a top level. "We have students who will be placed in elite environments, including Newcastle United and Sunderland Athletic football clubs, where they can be involved with nutrition and performance analysis," says Caplan. "Many have gone on to work for professional clubs and the England team. A key aim is to use our links and relationships with professional sport to support our students to become highly employable graduates."

NORTHUMBRIA UNIVERSITY
BOOST
DRINKS
UNIVERSITY OF
PORTSMOUTH

Educational goals

THE FOOTBALL EXCHANGE AT LIVERPOOL JOHN MOORES UNIVERSITY BRINGS THE BENEFITS OF WORLD-CLASS SCIENTIFIC RESEARCH AND ACADEMIA TO THE PROFESSIONAL FOOTBALL INDUSTRY

www.ljmu.ac.uk

The "school of science" was a nickname once applied to Everton Football Club, but it is also appropriate for Liverpool John Moores University (LJMU) and its Football Exchange, set up in 2010 with a vision to be the home of science and football. Building on the legacy of the late Professor Tom Riley, its mission is to support football through world-class research that impacts and transforms professional practice at all levels and areas of the game. Spanning fields including nutrition, psychology, physiology, biomechanics and performance analysis, the department produces graduates and supports people already working in the game with the expertise needed to thrive in the industry.

"Working as a unit and department within the university's School of Sport and Exercise Sciences, the Football Exchange was an opportunity to put an umbrella over excellent individual work done by academics engaging with the football industry," explains Dr Martin Littlewood, Head of the Football Exchange, who has also worked as a Performance Psychologist for football clubs Bolton Wanderers, Everton, Leicester, Rangers and Aston Villa.

Liverpool John Moores University introduced the UK's first undergraduate sports science degree in 1975, and in 1998 developed a pioneering BSc in Science and Football. This has helped to attract exceptional staff to the university, such as Dr Francesca Champ, Senior Performance Psychologist for Liverpool Football Club Women's, and Dr Chris McCready, an ex-professional footballer who played for Tranmere Rovers and Crewe Alexandra and has worked with the PFA. "We have had a number of players who have started to develop a dual career," says Martin. "We offer opportunities for professional footballers to take the course part-time and have a flexible arrangement for studying. We are open to exploring further professional development opportunities. It's a route into education that complements the work of the PFA, FA and the Premier League."

Sports science is the study of the scientific principle of sport, covering areas such as physiology, psychology, nutrition, biomechanics, performance analysis, and strength and conditioning. LJMU explores this at the elite level so as to produce graduates employable in a range of roles within the sport. Football has come to embrace the innovation and research of the academic world, and the Football Exchange has been instrumental in that journey. The introduction of a Professional Doctorate in Applied Sport and Exercise Science has also seen individuals in the game engage with members of the Football Exchange to develop their practice. Graduates work in various areas of the game globally, while undergraduates and postgraduates combine classroom work with placements at clubs including Liverpool and Everton.

"We work with clubs and national associations either through consultancy research, applied PhDs or professional doctorates, and offer one of the world's only bespoke Science and Football programmes," says Martin. "LJMU has been a hotbed of football-related activity since the 1970s. Football has broadened its horizons, and we are proud of the work we have done establishing links with clubs here and overseas."

Although football and academia inhabit different worlds, there are, says Martin, similarities in development, progression and performance. "Above all, we work as a team. Our individuals operate in a variety of disciplines, but we collaborate with the goal of being the world's leading academic institution for football-related activity. What connects us is that ability to view our goal as a team and to work together to be the best in the world at what we do."

10

The talent factory

LOUGHBOROUGH COLLEGE GIVES SPORTSPEOPLE A FLEXIBLE, FIRST-CLASS EDUCATION, SUPPORTING THEM BEFORE, DURING AND AFTER THEIR SPORTS CAREER

www.loucoll.ac.uk

With an alumni hall of fame that includes superstars such as Jude Bellingham, Steph Houghton, Karen Carney and Ben Chilwell, it is no wonder that Loughborough College has been dubbed "the talent factory" by one national newspaper. The Leicestershire-based college has over 20 years' experience working with elite footballers across the men's and women's game. The college has supported more than 1,500 footballers from Level 3 up to degree level, underpinning their sporting talent with an excellent education.

"Elite sport is in our DNA," says Jo Maher, Principal and CEO. "We have a long history within football, putting education at the heart of what we do, so that we can help footballers transition through their career and ensure their education keeps pace with their career development. We firmly believe in the notion of a dual career that focuses on developing individuals and ensuring that they are qualified for a career upon retirement from playing."

The college understands the demand that top-level football places upon a player's time, so it provides a flexible approach to education while supporting players within their home clubs. It is the education provider for local men's clubs such as Birmingham City, Leicester City, Derby County and Nottingham Forest, as well providing education programmes for female players at academies such as West Ham, Spurs and Chelsea. The college is also the nominated education partner for Leicester City Women's FC Academy.

That commitment to the players' needs meant that when Jude Bellingham moved to Germany after starting his course at Birmingham City, Loughborough College provided distance-learning support to allow him to complete his course.

As well as having dozens of current and former students in the professional men's game, the college has a long and deep relationship with the women's game. By supporting players in their education as well as their professional development, it has witnessed the success of women's football first-hand. As the women's game has evolved, the college has become the FA's Women's Super League National Partner for the delivery of the Diploma in Sporting Excellence, working closely with clubs such as Manchester City, Arsenal and Chelsea. The elite Women's Super League education programme offer has doubled in

the past three years, and ten students were recently selected as part of the England women's under-17 squad for the UEFA Women's U17 Euro finals.

Jo, who is a member of the FA Council and the FA's National Game Board, models the importance of education for athletes on the college's relationship with the NFL Academy. "In the US, education is valued just as highly as elite sport, and we want to encourage that approach across all sports over here," she says. "We don't want a young player to reach 16 and get released or leave the game early because of injury to find they have no options. We want them to have a promising career, whether they are in or out of the game. We want them to be economically active as that's the morally right thing to do, and we have the expertise to provide that."

This expertise is reinforced with a £30 million investment programme, including a £13 million new sports facility to promote sporting excellence. "We run the course the professionals want in the way they want, with flexible methods of delivery," says Jo. "We can run a course in the format needed by any full-time athlete to suit their training schedule."

The school of football

THE UNIVERSITY CAMPUS OF FOOTBALL BUSINESS AND ITS GLOBAL INSTITUTE OF SPORT PRODUCE GRADUATES WHO ARE EQUIPPED WITH THE SKILLS FOR A SUCCESSFUL CAREER IN THE INDUSTRY

www.ucfb.ac.uk

Football is one of the biggest industries in the world, worth more than $25 billion in Europe and employing around 100,000 people in the UK alone. The University Campus of Football Business (UCFB) and its graduate school the Global Institute of Sport (GIS) were founded to generate the talent required to support the industry, with a student body that includes many professional footballers seeking to find a role in the sport after retirement. With campuses at stadiums around the world including Wembley, the universities share an unrivalled ability at placing graduates in positions of employment, with more than two-thirds going on to work in the sports industry.

"UCFB is our undergraduate campus for qualifications in anything you can imagine that is football related – marketing, business, journalism, finance, psychology, law and coaching," says Sharona Friedman, GIS President. "The Global Institute of Sport is our graduate school for master's degrees and continued professional development where we teach a sports directorship course, elite coaching, performance analysis, a CEO course and more. We are an end-to-end offering for people who want to work in the football industry. The only thing we don't do is teach you how to kick a ball."

The school was founded in 2011 by directors at Burnley Football Club, who wanted to develop a diverse pipeline of specialised talent for the football industry. Sharona highlights some of the unique qualities that have since made UCFB and GIS some of the leading universities for sport. Having campuses at major stadiums in London, Manchester, Melbourne, Toronto, Atlanta, New York and Miami helps secure exceptional guest speakers, including Premier League executives, leading journalists, World Cup-winning footballers and international managers, who augment the rigorous curriculum with expert insight. The universities have also developed excellent connections throughout the industry, allowing students to immerse themselves in an internship. "It's learning from theory, learning from others and learning by doing," says Sharona. "That's why we are so good at getting people jobs. We are graduating legitimately qualified talent."

Among those who have taken courses at UCFB and GIS are former professional footballers such as Joleon Lescott and Wes Morgan. Students include everyone from school leavers to founder of the Walking Football Association, John Croot. There are short courses for those who want to explore a topic before committing to a degree, and qualifications are offered through a flexible mixture of remote and classroom learning. During holiday periods, students travel to overseas campuses to learn from different sports in different countries. As student cohorts are located in different parts of the world, the university facilitates online networking between peers.

With the next World Cup taking place jointly in Canada, the US and Mexico in 2026, football is enjoying a boom in North America. To help fill the estimated 10,000 jobs that will be created, UCFB and GIS have partnered with Community Athletic Solutions, to ensure students can get a visa to work in the US and help prepare for the biggest event in world sport. This exemplifies the exceptional partnerships the institutions have built with organisations such as the Football Association (FA), the League Managers Association (LMA) and Kick It Out. "We survive on the strength of our partnerships," says Sharona. "We modelled our whole education policy on making sure that relationship was as close as possible. We speak to the industry to ask what they need and then create the right qualifications to fill the talent gap."

GIS
GLOBAL INSTITUTE of SPORT
THE DESTINATION FOR MASTER'S DEGREES AND EXECUTIVE EDUCATION IN SPORT AROUND THE WORLD
GIS
GLOBAL SPORTS SUMMIT
MIAMI GLOBAL SPORTS SUMMIT 2022

University of
Hertfordshire
Institute of Sport

Transforming lives

THE UNIVERSITY OF HERTFORDSHIRE HELPS ATHLETES EXCEL AT THEIR SPORT WHILE LEARNING, NURTURING SOME OF THE COUNTRY'S MOST DISTINGUISHED TALENTS

www.herts.ac.uk

Among the billions of people watching the Men's 2022 World Cup with close interest were staff and students at the University of Hertfordshire, many of whom felt a personal connection to the event. That came through broadcaster Alex Scott, who as a player had improved her strength and conditioning through the university's pioneering relationship with women's football, as well as through Senior Lecturer Joel Harris, a sports therapist and essential member of England Football Manager Gareth Southgate's backroom team. Both Joel and Alex exemplify the important role the university has taken in the game's continued development.

"Performance enhancement and women's football come under the umbrella of transforming lives, which is our mission statement," says Associate Professor Michael Callan from the University's Institute of Sport. "We do lots of work around performance enhancement, and what Joel is doing at a very senior level for England is an example of the kind of effort we go to. British universities are becoming more involved in competitive sport, and more universities are starting to build relationships with their local clubs, but we were pioneers. So many great women players like Alex Scott have come through our programme."

The university began working with Arsenal WFC more than a decade ago, helping players improve while continuing their education. It became the destination of choice for women players as more joined the programme. "When the England women team won the Euros the atmosphere here was incredible," says Michael. "People were in tears and felt a sense of deep pride at the historical contribution we have made to the development of the women's game. We were there in the early days when the women's game needed supporting."

Similarly, the university has introduced advanced concepts of performance enhancement at its purpose-built Institute of Sport, which opened in 2022. The centre includes state-of-the-art equipment, as well as the knowledge and expertise of staff such as Joel, with many alumni working across the professional game. "We have an environment chamber where you can take people to the altitude of Everest [base camp] or train them to prepare for exercise in extreme climates," explains Michael. "We are exploring with Watford FC some of the improvements gained by training at altitude. It's an area where we want to push the envelope."

The relationship with professional football clubs has seen the university explore ways to help academy players, not just

with their physical conditioning, but also their academic achievements. This allows all athletes to learn for a non-sporting career while excelling at sport, so they can compete at a serious level without compromising academic ambitions.

Looking ahead, Jen Jones, Head of the Institute of Sport, believes that the university will continue to nurture relationships with local clubs, while refining and pioneering new approaches to performance enhancement. The university aims to build on its relationship with the women's game, helping to develop female coaches, and is the designated lead research institution for the International Working Group (IWG) on Women & Sport 2022-26, the largest global network dedicated to advancing gender equity in sport.

"It is all a part of transforming lives," says Michael. "It's not just about the player on the pitch, it's about supporting them more holistically. This includes the exit route from the game and managing that transition. Education is fundamental to helping footballers address that part of their career and ensuring former players aren't forgotten."

Raising a smile

UK-BASED CHARITY SMILE INTERNATIONAL OPERATES THROUGHOUT ASIA, AFRICA AND EUROPE, BRINGING HOPE TO COMMUNITIES WITH ITS BROAD-RANGING FEED PROGRAMME

www.smileinternational.org

Miriam is nine years old. Every school day, she walks 5km to school in eastern Zimbabwe. When the lunch bell sounds, she walks 5km back home to collect her disabled brother and escort him to school for afternoon classes. When lessons end, there is another 5km walk home.

Every step brings Miriam closer to her dream of an education to help lift her family out of poverty. She is being sponsored through school by a charitable programme pioneered by Smile International, a UK-based Christian family organisation founded in 2000, operating in Africa, Asia and Europe.

"Miriam's story shows us education is the key to unlocking potential, enabling children to find hope and achieve their dreams," says Smile International CEO Tim Doubleday. "Smile's sponsorship means a child never has to choose between attending school and searching for food."

Food provision is the bedrock of Smile's work. But it is not all. "We work closely with in-country teams to offer a spectrum of aid in places where no other NGOs operate," says Tim. "We call it FEED (Feeding, Educating, Empowering and Developing). Without Smile, people in these areas would receive no help."

When a remote community in Uganda was plunged into starvation by crop failure and the disruptions of the global pandemic, Smile stepped in. "Our experienced local team negotiated complex government permissions to visit this remote area, consult the community and deliver life-changing aid, turning tears into smiles," explains Tim.

Smile's education programmes extend beyond school, helping some students through university to support their families and fulfil their dreams. Its empowerment programmes have included a project that supported tailors to manufacture reusable face masks during the pandemic. The tailors are now making school uniforms, further supporting education in their communities. Development programmes include provision of vital infrastructure, such as homes, community centres, toilet blocks and wells.

"It's about the full package, bringing all the elements of FEED together to provide a sense of wellbeing and hope," says Tim. "We know times are hard in the UK, but a donation here is worth a lot to people in the countries where we work. Everyone has a right to be fed, educated, empowered and developed. Everyone has a right to smile."

Northern star

LEEDS TRINITY UNIVERSITY'S INFLUENTIAL SCHOOL OF SPORT AND WELLBEING HAS NURTURED STRONG OVERSEAS LINKS AND PROFESSIONAL PARTNERSHIPS THAT OFFER STUDENTS EXCELLENT HANDS-ON EXPERIENCE

www.leedstrinity.ac.uk

Few counties in the UK have contributed more to the nation's sporting success than Yorkshire. England footballers Kalvin Phillips, John Stones, Kyle Walker and Harry Maguire all have Yorkshire roots, while cricket and rugby league remain local passions. Leeds Trinity University's School of Sport and Wellbeing exemplifies the outsized contribution Yorkshire has made in this field.

"We have some high-profile alumni who are influential and significant, including John Herdman, the coach of the Canada World Cup team," says Dr Chris Sellars, Head of School for Sport and Wellbeing. "Fiona May Iapichino, the Olympic silver medallist in long jump, is an honorary fellow, as is Professor Kevin Hylton, who has done a lot of work around racial equality, which has informed practice in a number of sports."

This focus on racial equality in sport is important to Leeds Trinity University, which places social justice at the centre of its provision. As the university has evolved, it has retained that commitment to producing students who understand the importance of being good citizens. The students benefit from the knowledge of staff such as Chris, who is a sport scientist and has worked at several professional football clubs, and Professor Mark Russell, an expert in nutrition and hydration strategies, whose research has been used by the FA.

Thanks to the relatively small size of the university, it is easier for students to access such expertise. Staff make the effort to really get to know their students, so they can guide them more closely along their chosen path. This is enhanced by the university's pioneering approach to work placements, which are built into all the university's courses. Partners include local professional football club Leeds United, as well as a range of other sporting clubs in football and other sports. Students have the opportunity to study, work or volunteer overseas, and gain hands-on experience with the latest sports technology, equipment, facilities and innovations. It is a package that combines to give students the skills and knowledge that employers are seeking.

The university plans to develop a Leeds city centre campus, as well as grow its international reach. "We are very ambitious," says Chris, "and have a strategy for growth domestically and internationally."

Fulfilling wishes

LIFESTYLE MANAGEMENT COMPANY 48 LONDON OFFERS A DISCREET, TAILORED SERVICE AND AN ATTITUDE THAT ANYTHING IS POSSIBLE

www.48london.com

Transforming a Miami home into a British Christmas grotto scene with reindeer, chilly temperatures and Father Christmas was all in a day's work for Sophie Shelton and Hope Dowlen of 48 London. In their quest to provide the ultimate concierge service, the team of two have taken on seemingly impossible challenges.

"We did a bespoke pregnancy plan for one client," says Sophie. "That involved finding the right health specialists and designing the nursery, right down to finding a behavioural specialist for the family dog to make sure it would bond with the new baby." They even had to find a "unicorn" for a photoshoot – they sourced a white horse and attached a horn to its forehead. The pair take pride in never giving "no" as an answer.

With her background in senior management roles at leading luxury retail stores such as Selfridges and Harrods, Sophie is well versed in the needs of high-net-worth clients and has a vast network of contacts. After she met Hope, who was also in a high-end lifestyle management and personal shopping role, they decided to address the gap in the market. "We thought there was a need for a boutique-style concierge company that truly had the benefit of the client at heart," says Sophie.

With wellbeing at its core, they founded 48 London in 2015. Individuals receive a bespoke service – everything from interior design and personal style, to access to the best nutritionists, trainers and health professionals. "We look for what is best for that client, and to get them the best deal," says Sophie. "We never rest on our laurels, and want clients to trust us and feel that they can ask us anything."

Their approach is founded on understanding what makes people tick, underpinned by a strong work ethic and a belief that anything is possible. In concierge and lifestyle management work, attention to detail is essential.

"We recently put together a three-month honeymoon for a client, spanning across the US and Caribbean islands with a three-week turnaround, complete with private jets and helicopters, yachts, villas, luxury hotels and immersive surprise experiences in each destination," says Sophie. "We have contacts others wouldn't expect us to have, and we are always prepared to go the extra mile."

Appendices

Acknowledgements

Thank you to all of those who have taken the time to share their stories and memories as part of this celebration of the 50th PFA Awards. Most importantly, we want to thank all current and former PFA members.

The PFA is a unique organisation with a long and proud history. A union is nothing, though, without its people. We appreciate the continued trust and support of those we work for, and we will continue to take that responsibility to our members – past, present and future – seriously.

For more information on the work of the PFA, visit www.thepfa.com

PFA commercial partners

EA Sports

Fair Result

Football Manager

Mappin & Webb

Panini

Pro Direct

Pro Secure

Stewarts

The author

Harry Harris has received 24 industry awards over the course of his long career, including two British Sports Journalist of the Year awards, a British Variety Club of Great Britain Silver Heart for his "Contribution to Sports Journalism" and two Sports Story of the Year awards. He is also the only journalist to have won the Sports Story of the Year award twice.

He has appeared as an analyst on virtually every TV news and sports programme going and has written for the *Daily Mail*, the *Daily Mirror*, the *Daily Express*, the *Daily Star*, the *Sunday Express* and the *Star on Sunday*.

One of the most prolific writers of best-selling football books, his titles include the UK and US best seller *Pele: His Life and Times*; *Gullit: The Chelsea Diary*; *All The Way Jose*; and *Wayne Rooney: The Story of Football's Wonder Kid*. He has also penned biographical works on Roman Abramovich, Jürgen Klinsmann, Sir Alex Ferguson, José Mourinho, Terry Venables, Gianfranco Zola, Paul Merson, Glenn Hoddle and George Best, to name but a few.

In addition, Harry has directed documentaries on Ossie Ardiles, Kenny Sansom, Kerry Dixon and Ron "Chopper" Harris. He is also Sports Development Director at SmartFrame Technologies, an innovative tech company that is rethinking how images are published and viewed online.

Illustrations

Cover illustration by Neil Jamieson
Picture research by Elizabeth Wood

Pages 90–1: by Marie Mangan, The National Brain Appeal (registered charity number 290173).
Pages 192–3: Somayeh, Barnet resident (p. 192); Davina (left) and Mary (right), Barnet residents (p. 193, top); Barnet Nightingales FC by John Sturrock (p.193, bottom)

Alamy
Getty Images
PFA
Shutterstock
Green Howards Museum

About the publisher

St James's House boasts a bold visual identity, one that has established us as a global leader in publishing and communications. Working across the spheres of royalty, government, and the public and private sector, we specialise in providing organisations from around the world with unparalleled access to hard-to-reach audiences and markets.

Each of our high-quality publications features intelligent and engaging editorial along with considered and contemporary design – a combination that puts us at the forefront of the publishing industry across a wide range of sectors. We provide our partners with the chance to be part of a tangible product that not only tells their story, but also gives them unique and privileged access to high-profile international events, launches and celebrations.

We are passionate about creating beautiful books, memorable events and striking publicity campaigns that provide our clients with long-lasting benefits and an enhanced global presence.

"We provide our partners with the chance to be part of a tangible product that not only tells their story, but also gives them unique and privileged access to high-profile international events"

Publishing partners index

This book is published by Regalpress Limited t/a St James's House – an imprint within the SJH Group.

Cover illustration by Neil Jamieson
Printed by Kingsbury Press on Fedrigoni Symbol Silk 130gsm. This paper has been independently certified according to the standards of the Forest Stewardship Council® (FSC)®.

ISBN: 978-1-915558-04-6

A catalogue record of this publication is available from the British Library.

St James's House
The Maple Building
39–51 Highgate Road
London
NW5 1RT

Telephone: +44 (0)20 8371 4000
Email: publishing@stjamess.org
Website: www.stjamess.org

ST JAMES'S HOUSE

50
PFA
AWARDS
2023

SJH
ST JAMES'S HOUSE

Professional
Footballers'
Association